THE PRIVATE REGULATION OF AMERICAN HEALTH CARE

THE PRIVATE REGULATION OF AMERICAN HEALTH CARE

BETTY LEYERLE

M.E. Sharpe INC.   Armonk, New York • London England

Copyright © 1994 by M.E. Sharpe, Inc.
80 Business Park Drive, Armonk, New York 10504

Library of Congress Cataloging-in-Publication Data

Leyerle, Betty.
The private regulation of American health care / Betty Leyerle.
p. cm.
Includes bibliographical references and index.
ISBN 1–56324–288–5. — ISBN 1–56324–289–3 (pbk.)
1. Medical care—United States—History.
2. Medical economics—United States.
3. Medical care—Law and legislation—United States.
I. Title.
RA395.A3L496 1994
362.1′0973—dc20
93–42516
CIP

Printed in the United States of America.
The paper used in this publication meets the minimum
requirements of American National Standard for
Information Sciences—Permanence of Paper for
Printed Library Materials, ANSIZ 39.49-1984.

BM (c) 10 9 8 7 6 5 4 3 2 1
BM (p) 10 9 8 7 6 5 4 3 2 1

This book is dedicated to the memory of my
mentor and friend, Joseph Bensman

Contents

Preface

The encroachment of bureaucratic organization into almost every area of our lives has been one of the most important developments of the twentieth century. This is not a restatement of the decades-old claim that bureaucracies are infuriating, unwieldy, and impersonal and tend to confuse their means with their goals. Bureaucracy, today, is the mechanism through which an increasingly total kind of social control can be exercised. The political and economic uses to which its mindless, mechanistic processes can be put represent a threat to democratic processes that is so extensive it is almost beyond calculation.

To complicate matters, the threat is virtually invisible to the naked eye, since it is cloaked in the ideological rhetoric of bureaucratic organization. The basic values of that ideology are "rationality," "accountability," and "technical efficiency." These three concepts have both expressed and helped to construct important social values that are based on a historically new faith in systematic, mechanistic processes. They are now so thoroughly institutionalized, so firmly entrenched in our nation's social psychology, that they are part of our taken-for-granted reality.

The new values compete with, and sometimes replace, our older faith in more communally based values, such as "trust," the "service ethic," and "individual creativity." The antithetical nature of these two sets of values cannot be overstated. The concept of "accountability," the only link between bureaucratic organization and any kind of ethical concern, is an attack on the possibility of trust itself. It is based on the assumption that people will not do what they claim to be doing unless they are watched. That idea functions very effectively to legitimate bureaucratic mechanisms for exercising surveillance and control. The idea did not precede bureaucratization, however, which began its development in the Western world long before the technical means for exercising close surveillance over people existed. Rather, the idea emerged out of the hierarchical structures and mechanistic practices of bureaucracies themselves.

During the last two decades, powerful groups have used both the ideology and the organizational structures of bureaucracies to make and to implement extremely broad social policies. As part of the process, they have constructed surveillance and control mechanisms that manipulate, divide, and help to polarize entire populations, making any kind of concerted political action impossible. This book provides a descriptive analysis of how that strategy has been used to transform the American health care system.

My analysis is indebted to the ideas of a wide range of colleagues, both past and present. Theoretically, it builds on the works of Max Weber, Karl Marx, and Michel Foucault and on Christopher Dandeker's beautifully articulated synthesis of their ideas.

Many colleagues and good friends have given their time and attention to this project, reading and responding to numerous "first" drafts. For such efforts, I owe a very special debt to my "New York contingent," Eileen Moran, Barbara Katz Rothman, and Marin Cardin. Here in Durango, Dennis Lum and Jim Fitzgerald have read and commented upon the work, while Dale Lehman and Shaila VanSickle have diverted their attention from the "high country" during daylong hikes to hear and respond to my ideas. I want to extend special thanks to my very good friend and colleague Doreen Hunter, who not only read the manuscript but has lived with the ideas expressed here almost as closely as I have during the past two years.

I thank my institution, Ft. Lewis College, for giving me a sabbatical leave during the winter 1992 trimester that I might do research and begin writing this book. In addition, a wide range of administrative colleagues gave me access to college resources that ranged from photocopying facilities to use of the library's computerized database during nonbusiness hours. For this help, I want to thank William Langworthy, Karen Spear, and Sherry Tabor.

Clearly, this book has been a collaborative effort. For that reason, I feel that everyone mentioned here shares a joint responsibility for the ideas that are expressed in the following pages.

Betty Leyerle
Durango, Colorado, 1994

THE PRIVATE REGULATION OF AMERICAN HEALTH CARE

Introduction:
Managed Competition—
The Private Regulation of
American Health Care

> All these years, [providers] have been concerned with fight-
> ing socialized medicine, and now they've been blindsided
> by capitalism.
> —*Peter Grua, Alex. Brown and Sons*[1]

For twenty-five years, the word "crisis" has been included in virtually
every discussion of the American health care delivery system. But it
was not until early 1993, when President Bill Clinton assumed office,
that most Americans began to hear for the first time that "managed
competition," sometimes called "regulated competition,"[2] was to be the
solution to our problems. A visitor from Mars, newly arrived on the
planet, might conclude that this is a new idea, the fruit of long, hard
thought by expert policy makers. In fact, it is the culmination of a set
of initiatives that were implemented piecemeal during the early 1970s
by coalitions of corporate executives who represented a wide range of
American businesses and industries, including Goodyear Tire and
Rubber, Allied Chemical, R.J. Reynolds, Continental Bank, and IBM.[3]
The only kinds of industries that were conspicuously absent from these
coalitions were those that are part of the health care delivery system
itself, such as pharmaceutical companies, hospital chains, and health
insurance carriers.

The initiatives these corporate executives launched were designed attack, simultaneously, the political, economic, and social realities that have long supported "professional dominance"[4] over health care delivery. In the political arena, for example, corporate activists supported government legislation and regulation that would limit professional autonomy and subject providers, both physicians and hospitals, to the principles of "scientific management." In the economic arena, corporate activists pressured insurance carriers to adopt new policies and create new "products" that would ration the health care services that were delivered and shift costs away from themselves onto government, small businesses, and their own employees. And, as part of an attempt to influence public attitudes and behavior, corporate activists created both "educational" and employee "wellness" programs that were intended to undermine public confidence in providers and to place responsibility for illness on the patient rather than on the health care delivery system. In the process, this strategy diverted attention away from both the social and the environmental causes of disease.

The corporate employers who launched those initiatives were striving valiantly to achieve two goals. They wanted, simultaneously, to ward off the specter of socialized medicine that hovered over the country at that time and to pare down the price they paid for their employees' health insurance benefits. The initiatives they launched, and the strategies behind them, are described in detail in my earlier work.[5] This book will trace the development of those initiatives throughout the 1980s and early 1990s and the processes through which they evolved into the system we now call managed competition.

Although the media report almost daily that managed competition is the wave of the future, many people are still unclear about exactly what it is. That is not because the concept is too complicated for ordinary citizens to understand but because the "experts" themselves, those who actually are constructing the system, define it in many different ways, depending on where their political, economic, and ideological interests lie. According to the noted health care economist Alain C. Enthoven, who is often credited with inventing the concept, "Most of what's being called managed care isn't managed care at all. It's utilization review—selecting suppliers for a price. That's a long way from organizing and managing care."[6] In Enthoven's definition, "managed care" refers to "prepaid group practices" and "multispecialty practices." It does not refer to utilization review, independent practice associations, or preferred provider insurance. (Throughout the book, I will explain and simplify this unnecessarily inflated terminology.)

However, both other experts and the media include all of these organizational structures, and many other arrangements as well, under the rubric "managed care." Charles D. Reuter, a benefits consultant with Buck Consultants, defines the term so broadly it could mean almost anything. In his usage, it refers to "business strategies to contain escalating health care costs."[7] Thus managed care means anything businesses do to contain their employees' health care costs.

Although it was corporate employers who began the process originally, businesses are not alone in promoting managed care today. Providers have responded to economic and regulatory pressures by promoting their own managed care strategies, in a vain attempt to defeat the enemy by joining it. According to a 1988 survey, consulting firms report that they increased their completed consulting projects at hospitals by 35 percent in 1987.[8] David M. Horn, writing for *Broker World,* reports that physicians, physicians' organizations, insurance carriers, employers, and brokers all promote managed competition, which he believes means simply controlling health care delivery systems through financial incentives, with the objective, again, of containing costs.[9]

Some observers identify managed care as anything that is not indemnity insurance. Others include indemnity insurance itself among managed care "products." Still others use the terms "managed care" and "health insurance" synonymously. Clearly, managed care can be almost anything one likes.

The health care journalist Maria R. Traska provides one of the most realistic descriptions of the phenomenon. According to her, managed care is a "range of products" through which "premium price is a trade-off for the control or freedom given enrollees."[10] Thus it is a set of economic incentives, of "carrots and sticks," designed to manipulate health care beneficiaries into giving up their freedom of choice while maintaining the fiction that the major advantage that managed care has over socialized medicine is precisely that it offers "choice."

Proponents of managed care often claim that keeping health care in the private sector rather than socializing it will ensure that the United States will continue to produce the most-advanced new medical technologies in the world. What usually remains unsaid is the fact that new health management experts have devised surveillance and control techniques that cut health care costs specifically by preventing the masses of consumers from getting *access* to those technologies. For example, in late 1992, some insurance companies refused to pay for the new bone marrow transplant that is being used to treat certain forms of leukemia until the medical community can prove that it is more effective than the far cheaper chemotherapy.[11] In the meantime, only very affluent patients or elite groups whose employers provide them with blue chip insurance "products" will have access to this technology.

For purposes of this analysis, then, managed care is best understood not as a specific product but as systems of private regulatory mechanisms and scientific management techniques. They offer strict controls that indemnity plans usually do not have, controls over the quality of care that is delivered, over the kinds and quantities of services that are utilized, and over the "peer" review of providers. These mechanisms operate on every level at once. They manipulate beneficiaries, patients, and providers into making "cost-efficient" medical choices; they ration health care services; and they restrict certain kinds of technological developments. These are the only features of managed care that are universal to every kind of plan. They all use bureaucratic surveillance mechanisms to control the kinds of health care benefits that people choose and the ways in which both providers and patients use medical services. Originally, in the 1970s, they regulated only publicly funded patients in hospital settings. Over the years, they have been expanded to control the care that is delivered to privately funded patients as well, and in both inpatient and outpatient settings.

It is clear that a new health care delivery system is evolving in this country, one that is simultaneously being created, defined, and legitimated. Of course, it has not sprung out of nowhere; on the contrary, it is well grounded in the control mechanisms that corporate employers began to put into place during the early 1970s. In fact, managed competition consists almost entirely of elaborations on those early corporate initiatives.

As the new system has evolved, so has a new public perception of acceptable medical reality. Some of the earliest of the corporate initiatives were controversial when they were first implemented twenty years ago. Then, as now, they were all mechanisms for rationing health care services, but that fact had to be disguised at that time. In the early 1970s, it would have been difficult to get public support for techniques that functioned in an obvious way to withhold existing, life-sustaining technologies from patients. After all, it was then less than a decade since the American public, appalled by the fact that the city of Seattle had set up a community board to decide who would get access to the limited supply of kidney dialysis machines, had prodded Congress to add kidney dialysis payments to the nation's Social Security benefits. By the time the political work had been done and the plan was actually in place, it was already 1973. That kidney dialysis legislation, along with the Medicare, Medicaid, and black lung enactments that were passed during the 1960s, reflected social developments that were revolutionary at that time. They appeared to many observers, including the representatives of corporate America, to be the first stages in the emergence of a completely socialized health care system. Almost immediately, corporate employers launched the counterrevolution that is described throughout this book.

In short, managed competition did not emerge out of any kind of "free-market" logic—because it is efficient, ensures high-quality care, or controls health care costs. It certainly did not emerge because either the public or health care providers wanted it. Rather, it is the result of well thought out political and economic strategies that were originally planned and initiated by corporate America.

Today, because media reports usually claim that the "experts" all agree that managed competition is the only way to solve our health care delivery problems, many intelligent citizens may believe that this system represents the best of a bad lot of choices. And yet many health care analysts and economists believe that only a comprehensive national health plan can simultaneously provide universal access to health care services and prevent rising health care costs from bankrupting the nation. For example, Eli Ginzberg, a professor of economics at Columbia University and a specialist in health policy, said in 1985 that "the best hope for the American health care system is that people will get so frustrated with high costs that they'll demand national health insurance—perhaps by 1990."[12] Those hopes have not been realized, of course. But, according to a 1992 *Fortune* magazine poll, 24 percent of American corporate executives had come to agree that socialized medicine might be our best hope.[13] Which group of "experts" or corporate leaders are we supposed to believe?

I will argue that managed competition will not solve our problems; in fact, it will almost certainly make them worse. The basic components of that system, the initiatives launched by American corporate leaders in the 1970s, already have been in place in the United States for more than twenty years. During that time, they have consistently failed to achieve the "reforms" their proponents claimed for them. They did not cut costs; rather, they added to them. They did not improve access to services; rather, they helped to deprive millions of people of any kind of health care insurance. They did not improve the quality of services; rather, they have resulted in the systematic denial of care to many of our most seriously ill citizens. They did not make administration simpler by eliminating government bureaucracy; rather, they have led to a system of private regulation unparalleled by anything government could possibly invent.

Despite all these failures, proponents of "free-market" initiatives continue to insist that the solution to our problem is to implement more of them. As a result, these initiatives have been expanded and elaborated upon for two decades. Every part of the health care delivery system has built upon them, until, finally, they have evolved and coalesced into the complex of entities that we call managed competition. If we institutionalize these kinds of mechanisms even further, it will not be because that is the best choice we could make but because it is the path of least resistance, because managed competition is already "grounded" in the initiatives that corporate employers launched more than twenty years ago. The choice reflects no more than their political, economic, and ideological agenda, not a wise and informed health care policy.

At a broader level of analysis, the transformation of health care delivery described here provides a dramatic example of the way radical social changes have been brought about in the United States, changes that were completely outside the control of democratic processes. Specifically, analysis of this transformation clarifies the mechanisms through which the most powerful "interested" group in the country, corporate America, dominates the process of shaping the direction such changes will take.

For clarity, and to avoid using repetitious terms, I will often refer to the corporate activists who launched the movement described here as "industry." This is the term that was used in 1978 by Willis Goldbeck of the Washington Business Group on Health, an important health care lobbying organization for corporate America. "Industry," Goldbeck said, refers to very large companies with so much power as purchasers of health insurance for huge numbers of employees that "their private decisions concerning health care benefits become public decisions affecting the economics of the entire health delivery system."[14]

To reflect current reality, in this book I use the term "industry" more broadly than did Goldbeck. It now includes the massive numbers of relatively small corporations that have begun to exercise surveillance and control over many parts of the health care delivery system. These corporations, too, have the power to make decisions that affect health care delivery for the entire country, because there are so many of them and because they control so much capital. Most important, they have helped to stimulate the emergence of our system of private regulation, which is carried out at enormous expense by thousands of new companies that do health care utilization review for corporate America.

I will begin this book by analyzing the historical and political context for the emergence of managed competition (chapter 1). The chapters that follow will list the corporate initiatives that were launched during the 1970s (chapter 2); describe the evolutionary changes and expansions they went through during the 1980s and early 1990s in the process of becoming "managed competition" (chapter 3); describe the ways in which managed care systems attempt to regulate the cost of health care services and discuss why they fail to do so (chapter 4); describe managed care attempts to control the quality of services and discuss why they fail to do so (chapter 5); and conclude with a summary of the book's major points as well as descriptions of some alternative approaches to getting our nation's health care needs met (chapter 6).

The theoretical basis for my analysis is a synthesis of the ideas of Max Weber, Karl Marx, and Michel Foucault, each of whom had a somewhat Machiavellian world view. Because the major purpose of this book is to make a policy statement, not to present an academic theoretical analysis, I do not reference those sources in the body of the book. However, interested readers who want to follow the development of my theoretical reasoning can find a detailed discussion of it in the appendix.

1
The Twenty-Year-Old Crisis

The remedies used by employers to bring down health care
costs have been "myopic."
—*John Erb, A. Foster, Higgins and Company*[1]

Virtually everyone has heard by now that the American health care system is in a state of crisis. But what, specifically, is *wrong* with it? Why is it plagued by so many problems? And why, after twenty years of tinkering, have our "experts" been unable to fix it? The list of problems is familiar: We pay more for health care than any other country in the world, and yet our citizens are not as healthy as those in other industrialized nations. Millions of Americans have no health insurance, while millions more are underinsured. Those who are medically affluent receive expensive treatments even when these treatments offer little chance of success or prolong lives filled with relentless misery, while the poor are denied far less expensive services that might actually save and enhance their lives. The health care system itself is hamstrung by private and government bureaucratic controls that hinder medical workers and confuse and infuriate the public. And, we waste huge sums of money on medically unnecessary administrative costs.

These problems seem to defy solution, since attempts to alleviate one serve only to intensify another. If we guarantee access to health care to everyone, costs will increase even more; in fact, efforts to cut costs during the last twenty years contributed in important ways to the elimination of insurance coverage for millions of Americans. If we reduce the hated bureaucratic controls, costs will probably rise even more, since they have provided the only mechanisms for cutting costs that have been at all successful, even in the short run. However, those bureaucratic mechanisms have also contributed to our health care problems in a variety of ways. They have served to reduce the quality of the health care that some Americans receive while denying it completely to others. And they are an important cause of our bloated administrative costs.

Given these realities, it is not surprising that when experts and politicians discuss the American health care delivery system they speak of "complexity" even more often than "crisis." How can the country extricate itself from this morass of double binds? The first step is to be very clear about how we got into the mess in the first place.

The complexity of our system today is not the result of either government inefficiency or physician greed, although both may be problems. It emerged as a side effect of corporate attempts to avoid socialized medicine. Originally, as noted above, a major objective of corporate strategists was to keep health care delivery in the private sector. Why did that seem so important to them in the early 1970s?

The Historical Setting

The corporate employers who became health care activists in the 1970s were motivated by many different kinds of ideological, political, and economic considerations. At that time, there was much in American social and political life to alarm them. By the late 1960s, despite our historical antipathy toward anything smacking of "socialism," the United States appeared to be moving toward some form of comprehensive national health care. Many Americans demonstrated support for such a program, both in their responses to polls and through extraordinary levels of political activism around health care issues. In response to this public enthusiasm, a wide range of proposals for a national program were put forward, both by political incumbents and by candidates for office. In 1970, Senator Edward Kennedy proposed what was at that time the most radical plan, the one that most closely resembled national health care.[2] In 1971 President Richard Nixon countered with his own proposal, a Partnership for Health between government and corporate employers;[3] this was the precursor of the scheme that gained some support, briefly, in the early 1990s, called "play or pay." It would be hard to say which of these plans was more repugnant to American business interests: an ideologically unacceptable system of socialized medicine or an unholy "partnership" that would have forced business to pay an even larger share of the nation's health care bill.

These moves toward a national health care plan were consistent with the political climate of the period. For a decade, public activism had pushed Congress to pass social legislation dealing with health and safety issues, even over passionate opposition from corporate America.[4] Within an eight-year period, Congress had enacted social legislation such as welfare reform and the Medicaid and Medicare amendments to the Social Security Act (1964), created the Environmental Protection Agency (1970), and passed the Consumer Product Safety Act (1972). It also passed workplace safety regulations, such as the Coal Mine Health and Safety Act (1969) and the Occupational Safety and Health Act (1970).

All of this legislation was, of course, ideologically repugnant to business interests. Perhaps more important, it threatened both their profits and their control over workers and the workplace. And, given the existing political climate and the legislative record of a decade, it seemed likely that Congress would override objections from corporate America and yield to public demands again, this time to pass a national health care bill.

From all over the country, corporate groups began to come forward with plans designed to de-rail that movement, insisting that we could simultaneously eliminate the specter of socialism and cut health care costs by introducing "competition" and "accountability" into health care delivery.[5] They launched a number of well-coordinated initiatives designed to achieve that goal, including lobbying for supportive government legislation and regulations. The underlying strategy was to attack every aspect of the health care delivery system at once: its structure, its political and economic arrangements, its knowledge base, and its legitimating ideology.

Rather than socializing our health care system, corporate strategists wanted to create competition within it. They believed that a competitive health care system would eliminate both government interference and the professional "cartel" of providers that had long controlled health care delivery. According to this perspective, free-market mechanisms, combined with "rational" management techniques, would not only save the country from socialism; they would decrease the cost and improve the quality of health care as well.

Like many other Americans, corporate strategists were alarmed by rising health care costs. Although rapid cost inflation had been occurring for decades, it was fueled dramatically when Medicaid and Medicare were implemented in 1965. When corporate employers were forced to pay for huge increases in their employees' health insurance rates, they blamed health care cost inflation in general, which they said resulted from two basic causes: excessive spending by government and overutilization of services by physicians.

In criticizing excessive government spending, corporate strategists were not alone. They were joined by a diverse group of professional analysts of health care delivery, most of whom charged that the real problem was that the federal government had been dominated by provider interest groups in making decisions about health care expenditures.[6] The result, they said, was not only unnecessary but uncoordinated government spending, both of which were major causes of health care cost inflation.

However, corporate strategies focused much more doggedly on the irresponsibility of physicians and patients than they did on government spending; in fact, the new government regulations that they supported themselves carried a very large price tag. Clearly, the strategy was to *use* government to eliminate physician authority, not to reform it. The most fundamental cause of skyrocketing costs, corporate strategists said, was the overutilization of services that physicians prescribed. Therefore, if we could exercise control over physicians to eliminate overutilization, our cost problems would be solved.

This opinion was not universally shared at the time. It is true that utilization of health care services increased enormously after Medicaid and Medicare programs gave access to millions of Americans who had never had it before. Yet some analysts argued even at the time that overutilization was not the major cause of cost inflation.[7] They appear to have been correct, since health care costs continued to rise for the next twenty years even though corporate strategies actually have succeeded in cutting utilization rates. Interestingly, however, some business advocates continue to make the overutilization argument.[8]

This focus on utilization rates appears to have been an attempt to achieve political objectives by "changing the subject," by shifting the national focus from value-laden questions about what kind of comprehensive national health insurance program we should have to meet our social needs to a statistical analysis of utilization rates. It was an intelligent tactic. It functioned both to undermine physician authority and to legitimate the rationing of the health care services that were guaranteed to millions of citizens under Medicaid and Medicare. But it also marked the beginning of the new application of "cost-benefit analysis" to health care delivery. This development represents a benchmark in the emergence of the new ideologies of competition and accountability that corporate strategists have used to legitimate the transformation of health care delivery. These ideologies competed directly with those that guided the American public's health care activism during the early 1970s.

At that time, a different ideology seemed to dominate the national scene. Its traces can be seen in a variety of social events: in the goals for which consumer and other political activists worked, in the medical decisions made by health care providers, and in the stories picked up by the press. A public consensus seemed to have emerged concerning several principles.

First, many Americans expressed the belief that access to health care services is a social "right." This attitude was reflected in widespread public support for comprehensive national health insurance, which included a commitment to the concept of "shared risk," an underlying principle of social "community" and of the insurance industry at that time.

Second, health care services should be delivered equally; that is, treatments should be determined by each patient's medical condition, not by his or her economic status. Not only the babies of the affluent but all babies should receive the same sets of inoculations, for example. This belief was reflected both in public support for comprehensive health care insurance and in the stubborn insistence of many physicians that they must follow the dictates of both "good medical practice" and their "service ethic" and deliver treatments based on the patient's physical requirements, not on whether he or she was publicly or privately insured.

Third, at a more theoretical level, the belief seemed to exist that medical research, which is carried out predominantly in universities and other settings that are publicly funded, should serve the public. Thus it would not be "ethical" to fund research with public money if we knew that it would yield treatments that would be delivered to elite groups while being withheld from the larger public that funded them originally because they would cost "too much." Why, then, should the public fund them? Why should it care whether or not we lead the world in the development of new, lifesaving technologies, if only the wealthy can have access to them? This seemed to have been the attitude underlying public outrage in the 1960s at the fact that, even though the lifesaving technology existed, terminally ill people could not get access to kidney dialysis.

And, fourth, there was an increasing confidence in prevention, a belief that we should attempt to prevent diseases from occurring in the first place, not only by delivering preventive health care services but by attacking their major social causes: poverty, ignorance, and pollution in both the environment and the workplace.

By the end of the 1980s, virtually all these values and assumptions had been challenged or even eliminated. For example, although it would be risky today for a politician to assert flatly that not all Americans have a right to health care services, it is perfectly safe to *qualify* that right. This is the way Gail Wilensky, deputy assistant to President George Bush, responded in 1992 when she was asked whether the president believed that every American has a basic right to decent health care: "Well the right to decent health care doesn't really explain who pays for it. . . . We want to make sure everyone has a chance to get insurance . . . but recognize that . . . insurance is going to differ for different people."[9] Thus, although the concept that people have a right to health services still exists, it is now frankly mitigated by considerations of social class. The services to which patients are entitled are to be defined by economic rather than medical criteria. Although we claim to believe that all people have a right to care, we do not agree that they have a right to *equal* care. By contrast, in Sweden, which has a socialized health care system, achieving equality of care is a major goal. Recognizing that it is precisely the poorest citizens who are most in need of health care services, Sweden makes a special effort not only to cure its citizens' ills but to provide them with preventive care. Using the excellent statistics the country's national health service is able to collect, health care specialists are able to determine the most important social causes of disease and to attack them directly.[10] This kind of epidemiological approach terrifies corporate America because statistics such as Sweden collects would identify industry itself as an important social cause of disease. It would raise unpleasant questions not only about who is responsible for the long-term and follow-up care required to treat these diseases but also about corporate liability for damages. It probably would result in increased regulation and costly cleanups as well.

The development of new medical technology raises similar problems. It is now a commonly heard complaint among health care experts that a major cause of runaway health care costs is the public's unrealistic demand for access to every high-technology service that exists. This argument is disingenuous as long as we insist on producing health care delivery as a commodity in the "free-market" sector. Advertising is a powerful industry in our economic system. It's only purpose is to shape masses of people to want everything that is available in the marketplace. Furthermore, most of us pay for this technology, since the U.S. government gives public funds to the research that is required to develop new products. If it did not, most of the technology would not exist for privileged citizens to buy.

The national move toward health care equality that began in the 1960s came to a halt largely because of the initiatives that American corporate leaders implemented in the 1970s. Those initiatives facilitated a kind of business competition that resulted in the increasing commodification of health care services in ways that will be described throughout this book. However, industry did not implement its strategy in a social vacuum. In addition to corporate employers, many others have influenced health care policy in the United States. The next section will describe some of those interested players.

The Interested Players

During the late 1960s and early 1970s, our increasingly expensive health care system became a political football. Three distinct segments of the population, all with wildly different political and ideological agendas, fiercely competed for the power to define what were our "real" problems and, thus, to determine what we were going to do about them.

First, there were huge numbers of citizen health care activists, consumer advocates, and environmentalists. These groups had simultaneously emerged from and carried out the political reforms of the 1960s; many believed that some form of socialized medicine was an idea whose time had come. Second, there was the traditional medical establishment, which included physicians, hospital administrators, and the health insurance industry. Singly or in combination, they had controlled health care policy for more than fifty years, and they did not wish to give up their dominant position. Third, there were powerful corporate leaders, their many organizations and their lobbyists, intent on derailing any national movement toward socialized medicine. During the late 1960s and early 1970s, these corporate groups began to develop a strategy for transforming health care delivery in a way that they believed would be compatible with their own interests. In the process, they expected the health care system to become more efficient, prompting costs to go down.

A major component of industry's strategy was to undermine the power of the dominant medical establishment over health care policy making. After all, it is logically impossible to revolutionize any social institution without dislocating the existing power structure. However, the relationship between medical professionals and industry is complex.

By the early 1970s, rising health care costs had already caused many critics of the system to complain that physicians were motivated by economic incentives to overutilize services. Because of the way our third-party payment system was organized, physicians could deliver services to literally everyone. What was worse, they could deliver any services they liked, and in any quantity; both their training and their license legitimated their claim that no one had the right to monitor their medical decisions. That was an increasingly archaic claim in the modern world, in which accountability, the underlying principle of scientific management, controls virtually every other kind of worker in every work setting.

Corporate employers began to say in print and at public gatherings that these respected, munificently paid, well-organized, and licensed professional workers had to be brought under managerial control. That would be no easy task.

Of course, one way to take control out of the hands of physicians would have been to socialize health care delivery, as other Western industrialized nations have done. But that choice was unacceptable to corporate employers for both ideological and practical reasons. Industry opposes socialism both in principal and because of the regulation that accompanies it. For that reason, somewhat ironically, physicians had much more in common with corporate employers than with either the public or government, since both of those entities seemed to favor a national health care system. That commonality of interests between physicians and corporate America still exists. Even today, after providers have been subjected to private regulation for more than twenty years, they now favor managed competition because it is the only "free-enterprise" game in town. They fight any suggestions to socialize health care. Since both managed care and socialized medicine are regulatory systems, each of them must simultaneously ration services and limit the patients' "choice" of providers, for reasons that will be described throughout this book. Thus, provider opposition to socialized medicine is rooted in the knowledge that their prospects for maintaining their unreasonably high pay scales are better under managed care than they would be under socialized medicine. In short, the interests of corporate employers and those of the medical elite continue to be essentially congruent.

One way to conceptualize what has been going on for the last twenty years is to see it as a struggle between these two interest groups—providers and corporate employers—for control of a health care delivery system that has remained, for all practical purposes, the same rich plum it has been for decades. Neither group wants really systemic changes; both want to keep health care delivery in the private sector. But corporate employers want to "rationalize" the system, to bring it under the control of corporate managers, while providers do not want to give up the total control they have enjoyed in the past.

However, in modern industrialized societies a health care system that is controlled by physicians presents serious ideological and practical problems. First, medical training does not equip people to determine what our national health care goals should be; those are social and moral questions. Second, medical training does not equip people to run the complex organizations that make up modern health care delivery systems. Third, and perhaps most important, when medical services are produced as commodities rather than, at least in principle, delivered as responses to a patient's medical condition, they must be marketed very differently. Producing medical services requires more managerial expertise than medical expertise. Industry attempted to eliminate all these problems by replacing the authority of physicians with that of management experts.

To achieve that goal, corporate planners exercised their economic power in a number of ways: over their own employees, over health insurance carriers, and, most important, over the federal government. Although their strategy had to be multidimensional, to immobilize every segment of opposition at once, the major tool for achieving their objectives was, from the beginning, the power and force of government.

Throughout the 1970s, corporate strategists successfully lobbied Congress to pass new government regulations and laws that were designed to undermine the power of health care providers. This legislation included the amendments to the Social Security Act that created the professional standards review organization in 1972 and the diagnosis-related group billing system in 1983, as well as the Health Maintenance Organization Act of 1973 and the National Health Planning and Resources Development Act of 1974. Among other outcomes, this legislation provides the administrative mechanisms for subjecting physicians and hospitals to the same kinds of bureaucratic surveillance and manipulation that have enabled corporate managers to control other, less high-status, workers for almost a century.[11] Very important, it also legitimated an attack on the credibility of physicians in general, by calling into question both their professional knowledge base and their ethics.

This was the beginning of a period in which, despite the ideological emphasis on competition, health care delivery was treated more like a public service agency than a part of the free-enterprise system. Within a decade, some apologists for competition would begin to disavow this roll-in-the-hay with regulation. During the 1970s, however, corporate planners were willing to use any strategy that seemed likely to work. They believed that government regulation could be used to drastically reduce the nation's health care delivery facilities, including hospitals, hospital beds, and equipment, all of which were in bloated oversupply at the time. That much was true.[12] However, they blamed the glut of facilities almost entirely on government spending and physician greed, which was a gross oversimplification; both corporate employers and the insurance industry were equally to blame for it, in ways that will be described below.

The National Health Planning and Resources Development Act of 1974 was designed to restrict both hospital construction and the purchase of expensive capital equipment. The regulation was expected to interact with market processes to pare down the size of the American health care delivery plant in stages. First, underutilized facilities would be eliminated. Then, those that were fully utilized but were "ineffi-cient" or "noncompetitive" would be forced to go bankrupt or to merge. To the surprise of no one, these were usually the facilities that were unprofitable because they served poor patients. Next, by manipulating a tight bed supply, regulatory planners could effectively ration services that were delivered in the health care facilities that remained, which would cause all utilization rates to go down nationwide. Finally, these developments would translate into lower health care costs. All these steps occurred as predicted except, of course, the last one. Health care costs continued to rise even as hospitals closed.

Except for the National Health Planning and Resources Development Act, most of the legislation that corporate strategists supported was designed to tell providers what treatments they could deliver to patients, first through peer review, then through the administrative mechanisms that are part of health maintenance organizations, and, finally, through the statistically derived mandates of the diagnosis-related group billing system.

Originally, legislation to control the direct delivery of medical services affected only patients who were publicly funded, mainly Medicare and Medicaid recipients. Throughout the 1980s, however, privately funded patients began to be regulated as well. That was possible because the corporate strategists of the early 1970s did not depend exclusively upon government legislation to achieve their goals; they also used economic incentives to force private insurance carriers to exercise control over the services that providers could deliver. For example, it was because the automotive industry demanded it that Blue Cross and Blue Shield of Michigan, in the 1970s, became the first insurance carrier to pay for second opinions before surgical procedures were performed, in an attempt to reduce "unnecessary" surgeries. At the time, this was a serious affront to physicians. By the 1980s, getting a second opinion before surgery had become an institutionalized part of many hospital admissions routines. But, even more important, by that time increasing numbers of corporate employers had begun to insist that their private insurance carriers do "utilization review," using the same kinds of statistical procedures and sometimes even the same review organizations that government used. Thus the legislation that regulated publicly funded care in the 1970s served as the foundation for regulating health care delivered in the private as well as the public sector in the 1980s and 1990s.

The objective of all these initiatives was not just to force insurance carriers to question bills from providers instead of simply paying them, as they had done in the past. Rather, it was to use insurance reimbursement policies to determine what medical treatments providers could render. The new reimbursement policies were designed to achieve two goals simultaneously: to ration the services that providers delivered to patients and to undermine the authority of physicians by creating new definitions of what constitutes "good medical practice."

In general, the process works like this: First, either government regulation or utilization review by private insurers forces providers to reduce the services they deliver to patients. In the process, new utilization data are generated, data upon which to base new definitions of "good medical practice." These definitions provide a comparative base to show that providers must have been delivering "unnecessary" services to patients all along. At that point, many services can be eliminated without arousing much political or professional opposition.

Second, the overutilization that is bound to be unmasked when this technique is used can then be explained as the result of ignorance or greed on the part of physicians. Thus the entire process undermines medical authority, debunking both the professional knowledge base and its service ethic. All of these developments then legitimate corporate initiatives to make providers "accountable," that is, to subject them to bureaucratic management techniques. Eliminating physician autonomy in this way could be expected to cut our national health care costs by making the delivery system as "rational" as a McDonald's restaurant, complete with a standardized product. The "efficiency" and "productivity" of providers would increase almost by definition if they no longer had to or could determine what services their patients received. Thus, this process was designed to eliminate "supply-side" economics in the health care system; ironically, it accelerated during the Reagan years.

It was almost certainly an unexpected consequence of this process that it resulted in the emergence of a new occupational elite in health care delivery. This elite is made up of health care statisticians, administrators, and consultants. The authority of these new experts increasingly competes with and weakens that of providers. Thus they provide an excellent contemporary example of the process Michel Foucault described, in which knowledge emerges out of the exercise of power. In this case, while the new experts created, collected, and interpreted the new utilization data that undermined physician authority, they simultaneously created a new knowledge base that supported their own claims to occupational power. Although their power to compete with the traditional experts—providers—came from their corporate and government employers, they developed their own legitimating knowledge base and, consequently, power in the process.

There are important differences between these competing occupational elites, however. Most important, the new experts work within an organizational reality different from that of traditional health care providers. They are not "free," autonomous professionals; they are bureaucratic employees of either industry or government. Thus they are not bound by the "service ethic," the ideology that has traditionally legitimated the authority of physicians. Rather, the new experts are governed by "accountability," the legitimating ideology of bureaucratic organizations.[13] By the early 1990s, all the strategies implemented by corporate activists had culminated in a health care system that is mired in obstructive, and extremely expensive, bureaucratic structures in both the public and private sectors. These structures did not emerge inevitably, out of some inherent flaw in bureaucratic organization itself or even out of government incompetence. Rather, they were created deliberately, by corporate and government leaders, to serve as mechanisms for exercising surveillance and control over physicians in an attempt to force revolutionary changes upon the health care delivery system.

Knowledge and Power

In putting together their initiatives, corporate activists demonstrated a sophisticated understanding of social processes and sociological theory. Specifically, they understood that a transformation of the health care system must include an attack on the authority of physicians, both as a tactic and as an outcome. Physicians had controlled health care policy making in the United States since the early twentieth century; their unique occupational power had to be severely undermined, if not destroyed, before any real changes could be achieved.

Corporate activists also understood that the authority of American physicians was not based on any inherent attributes of the medical profession itself. Rather, their professional power had been "socially constructed" over a long period.

That is, professional power is a result of many social processes including long-term developments such as the transfer of responsibilities for health care, education, and economic production from the home to external organizations; technological developments in health care delivery and in communication (the telephone) and transportation (the automobile) that enabled physicians to service more people than before; and changes in social conventions such as the increased reliance on hospital settings to care for the sick. Physicians also participated directly in the "social construction" of their power, both through the kinds of new knowledge on which they based their practices and through political activities such as lobbying for a license that would give them a monopoly over the right to practice medicine. Professional power continues to exist because it is now supported by many different components of the social system. These structural supports include the power of the state, economic practices and ideologies, an education system that defines and produces what is appropriate professional knowledge, and public sentiment. To be successful, corporate strategies would have to weaken all those social structural supports at once.

Historically, government has provided the most powerful and diverse supports for professional dominance. At the most obvious level, government gives physicians a monopoly over the right to deliver services to patients; unlike many other industrialized countries, the United States gives them an almost exclusive license to practice medicine. Government also has helped physicians to develop and maintain their legitimating knowledge base. For example, in 1910 the Flexner report was released. This was a study of all the different kinds of medical education that were carried out in the United States; it was funded by the Carnegie Foundation. Because the report gave its stamp of approval only to the laboratory-based, treatment-oriented medical training facilities that were favored by the white male elite, government funding has gone only to these types of institutions. It has been denied to institutions that trained lower-status practitioners to deliver treatments based on other kinds of medical knowledge that might have focused on the social causes of disease rather than providing heroic treatments for preventable diseases.[14]

Government also has supported professional dominance at a broader level, in health care policy making. For example, because providers opposed it, selling health insurance was prohibited until the 1930s, the years of the Great Depression. At that time, providers who could no longer survive economically in a completely free marketplace lobbied the government to legalize the sale of health insurance; government responded by passing enabling legislation for Blue Cross and Blue Shield. Once the selling of health insurance was legal and legitimated in principle, commercial carriers soon emerged to compete with the "Blues." During the following decades, health care insurance became an increasingly important commodity.

Finally, at an even broader, systemic level, the U.S. government poured massive sums of money into the health care sector between the 1940s and the early 1970s, first for hospital construction and, after 1964, to pay for the direct delivery of health care services through Medicare and Medicaid. Government imposed few restrictive regulations on providers, however, who made virtually all decisions about how, where, and what health care services would be delivered. Thus, health care professionals were heavily subsidized by public money while they created what John Ehrenreich and Barbara Ehrenreich have called the "American health care empire."[15] Clearly, the historical relationship between government and the medical profession has been intimate. Therefore an obvious strategy for eliminating professional dominance would be to co-opt that source of support.

Of course it was not government alone that had supported professional dominance. Corporate America had done so as well; it provided the most important source of support through the health insurance industry—by pouring capital into it through employee health benefits.

But by the early 1970s, the increasingly powerful insurance industry had become a virtual bottomless pit. It had its own agenda—to stimulate as much growth as possible in the profitable health care delivery sector. Because insurance companies were required by law to keep huge cash reserves to cover catastrophic claims, the insurance industry was an extremely powerful bank "depositor" whose executives sat on many of those banks' boards of directors. For decades, the insurance industry used its economic influence over those banks to keep money rolling into hospital construction projects,[16] just as government did. In both cases, of course, it was the American people who really supplied the capital.

Throughout this thirty-year period, corporate employers were not concerned with health care policy making but only with their own "bottom line"—with how much they had to pay for their employees' health insurance. Beginning in the 1940s, employers insisted that their insurance carriers use "experience-rating" as the basis for calculating premiums in order to minimize their own costs by making the insurance rates for their "low-risk" employees cheaper than those that were paid by other, "high-risk," populations.[17] In the process, they destroyed the system of "community-rating" that actually made it possible to share the risk of illness.

All this statistical language conceals the traditional strong-arm tactics of big business. It is not only the "risk" factor that determines what insurance rates different groups will pay; the size of the corporate employer is even more important. The fact that big business can use its muscle to buy insurance relatively cheaply provides another example of the processes through which it passes its own cost of doing business onto others. This is an important reason why small businesses find it impossible to afford insurance for their employees, many of whom are also "low risk" on insurance actuarial tables.

But industry has passed the cost of health care onto its own employees as well as to competitors. During the early 1970s, cost-sharing was not a familiar topic among corporate strategists. At that time, the common wisdom held that it was extremely difficult to withdraw benefits once they had been won. Nevertheless, corporate strategists were very optimistic about the possibility of shifting health care costs back to employees. In 1977 the Washington Business Group on Health (WBGH) made it very clear that corporate America was not dedicated to the proposition of employment-based health insurance.

> The trend toward 100 percent employer paid coverage seems to be bending, if not broken. For some companies it may be too late. But we tend to forget that only 25–26 percent of the nation's workforce is unionized and only some 40 percent of those employees have 100 percent employer paid health insurance. Therefore, the argument that it is too late "to go back" is simply not valid for most employers.[18]

Actually, at that time corporate America had even better cause for optimism than it knew; by 1992, only about 12 percent of the work force was unionized.[19] One of the most important social consequences of the deindustrialization of the United States that occurred during the 1970s was the creation of huge numbers of new, nonunionized jobs that offered no health care benefits. Within a decade, this propitious development had led to one of the best utilization control mechanisms of all time, the emergence of more than 35 million Americans with no health insurance at all. Thus, industry successfully extricated itself from paying a huge portion of our nation's soaring health care bill, even for its own employees, while vigorously opposing any kind of national health insurance program. The inevitable result has been to shift the cost of health care onto individuals, whose health insurance premiums and out-of-pocket expenses increased enormously during a twenty-year period in which their real wages declined. Or, even worse, it has been to deny access completely to those who cannot afford to pay. Another important outcome has been the emergence of an increasingly complex and competitive insurance industry, which some analysts say is the real root of our problem. Our system for administering health benefits is inefficient, duplicative, and wasteful. In the United States, more than fifteen hundred administrative units labor to accomplish this task. They include commercial and noncommercial insurance carriers; a mass of government agencies at the federal, state, and local levels; several hundred health maintenance organizations; and Blue Cross and Blue Shield. In Canada, by contrast, ten provincial governments and two territories oversee the administration of health care delivery. Each provincial government either does the administrative work itself or creates a public agency to do so; there are no profit-taking middlemen.[20]

Probably the major reason administration can be made so simple in Canada is because health care is structured on a completely different value orientation. Every Canadian resident is entitled to equal health care benefits, which are roughly equivalent to the broadest coverage one can buy in the United States.[21] The fact that everyone gets the same benefits eliminates the need for a complex administrative surveillance apparatus. I will argue that one important explanation for administrative complexity in American health care delivery is that it is simultaneously the *means* through which the insurance industry exercises its "free-market" initiatives and the *product* of that process.

This is how the process works: The insurance industry maximizes its profits by creating a multitude of customized insurance "products" that are designed to fit people's pocketbooks rather than to reflect their health status. The insurance industry markets these products to an already heterogeneous populace that becomes increasingly fragmented as a side effect of the marketing process; that is, the various social classes, occupational groups, and demographic categories that make up our citizenry are further subdivided into specialized "markets" that serve the economic interests of the insurance industry.

All this medically unnecessary customization simultaneously creates and uses a complex bureaucratic structure, not simply to do accounting functions, but to exercise surveillance over patients and providers. This surveillance is necessary to ensure that people do not "abuse" the system, presumably through such acts as having an appendectomy to which their insurance benefits do not entitle them. Highly paid administrators with an army of subordinates are "socially constructed," right along with the surveillance apparatus that they create and run, to provide this new "service," for which the American public is forced to pay.

This customization causes serious problems, both for the nation's health and for its pocketbook. It creates inadequate benefit packages for poor people, packages that often deprive them of necessary care. At the same time, it inflates the services that are delivered to the medically affluent, allowing them to use services that may be unnecessary or even ineffectual if they wish to do so, thus adding to the nation's health care bill through increased cost inflation.

In some cases, corporate strategies have led to the emergence not only of different insurance products but to a completely different kind of insurance company. For example, in the 1970s, industry stimulated the emergence of alternative insurance plans that could be used both to circumvent laws and regulations governing the insurance industry and to make structural changes in health care delivery. At that time, corporate strategists realized that, because experience-rating removes most of the actual risk, there was no reason for insurance companies to keep the huge cash reserves that simultaneously helped to inflate health care costs and gave them great economic power.

Partly to circumvent that cash reserves requirement, corporate employers demanded some radical innovations in insurance products. For example, they began to hire companies that offered administrative services only, that did not assume any risk at all. Some corporate employers began to "self-insure"; that is, they assumed the risk themselves. That was a fairly radical alternative when the Goodyear Tire and Rubber Company and John Deere and Company implemented it in the 1970s.[22]

But circumventing the cash reserve laws was not the only use to which self-insurance could be put; it could also be used to avoid the regulatory laws that protect consumers from being dumped by their insurance companies when they become ill. This practice came to national attention in 1992 following a U.S. Supreme Court decision. The case involved a Texas man who learned in 1987 that he had AIDS; the company he worked for then became self-insured. The next year, the company reduced his health insurance benefits from $1 million to $5000. It was able to do so because, being self-insured, it was not subject to the same kinds of regulations that govern regular insurance companies. When the employee sued his employer under a federal law that protects pension rights, he lost his suit. In November 1992, the U.S. Supreme Court upheld the verdict of the lower court, ruling that the employer did have the right to deprive the employee of his insurance.[23]

As a result of all these tactics, corporate America has succeeded in "deregulating" the health insurance industry in the sense that it has eliminated many regulations that protect the public. It also has played a very large role in destroying the underlying principle of insurance, the idea of "shared risk." As a result, instead of having a health care system that meets the public's needs, the American public has been fragmented into relatively weak and isolated groups that serve the needs of the market. Each group is forced to compete frantically for the best deal it can get for itself, too exhausted and demoralized by the certain prospect of yet another premium increase to spare much concern for others. Thus it is not only the insurance industry and the health care system as a whole that have become increasingly "competitive" in response to corporate initiatives supported by new government regulation; the entire population has been forced into the competition as well.

Advocates of competition claim that it will, eventually, cleanse health care delivery of "inefficiency," lowering costs in the process. When the deregulatory fever of the Reagan administration was sweeping through Washington in the mid-1980s, proponents of this view announced, prematurely as it turned out, that competition was already on its way to save us. Henceforth, the free market could be expected to work its magic, making health care delivery more efficient and effective and cutting costs in the bargain. By 1992, when it was clear that no magic had been forthcoming, proponents of competition claimed that the problem was not that competition had failed but that government interference had continued to inhibit the expansion of the market.

At that point, it became obvious to many observers that competition was not the solution; in fact, it was an important part of the problem. Although it may be true that regulation interferes with competition, it is equally true that competition sometimes makes regulation necessary. For example, in the health care sector, where competition has resulted in the bankruptcy of hospitals that service nonprofitable customers—those who are sick but lack economic resources—we must now create new regulatory processes to reinvent the services they provided, probably at far greater expense. It was because of this realization that the concept of "regulated" or "managed" competition began to gain dominance. Government had been providing support for corporate initiatives all along; now it had only to make its position overt to become part of the newly emerging, privately regulated health care system. However, it must be emphasized that this is a system of private, not public, regulation. This is not a trivial distinction. Whether the controls are in the public or private sector is a matter of real concern to the American people, who can sometimes exercise political control over elected, government regulators; they have no control at all over unelected, corporate ones.

The Role of the Public

In addition to their economic and political initiatives, corporate activists also have attempted to transform health care delivery at a more personal level, by focusing more directly on the attitudes and behavior of the American public. It is ironic that their major tool was to stress the notion of "prevention." Although corporate strategists usually have pressured physicians to utilize fewer services, they actually have accused providers of underutilizing preventive care. They argued, for example, that health maintenance organizations provided better care more cheaply than traditional providers could do, in part because they practiced preventive medicine. Corporate strategists were especially enamored of this theory during the early 1970s, while they lobbied for passage of the Health Maintenance Organization Act, which President Nixon signed into law in 1973.

Some corporations actually opened corporate health facilities to provide preventive screening services to their employees. As a national solution to cost inflation, however, this screening proved to be a self-defeating strategy for several reasons. First, after only a few years of experimentation and data collection, it became clear that preventive services were not always "cost efficient"; that is, the programs often cost more to operate than they saved in employee benefits. Second, massive screenings were likely to turn up all kinds of unsuspected health problems that would then have to be treated. Many of these would be non-life-threatening conditions that might have cleared up naturally in time or that people might have been willing to live with for much longer periods if the screening process had not intervened. Thus mass screening would create additional unnecessary utilization. And third, it was feared that many preventive screenings, such as those that were required by the new occupational and environmental safety regulations, would yield data to support claims made by many workers and consumers that corporate America actually caused most of the nation's worst health problems.

Corporate activists of the 1970s were conspicuously silent about the social causes of disease, such as poverty, workplace hazards, and environmental pollution. In their attempts to improve the health of the United States, they did not support either the poor people's movements or the environmentalists. Prevention was an acceptable topic only when it referred to people's lifestyles. Business never has addressed the kind of prevention that would be directed toward the occupational and environmental causes of disease.[24]

Thus the major focus in health care delivery continues to be on curative rather than preventive medicine. This is one more tactic for passing on the real costs of modern production to other sectors of society in the form of polluted or even poisoned air, water, and land. By passing costs on to the environment, we inevitably pass them on to people's bodies as well in the form of occupational and environmental diseases. From the perspective of business, although researching and applying medical treatments are very expensive, concentrating efforts on cures is infinitely preferable to focusing on the environmental and occupational causes of disease.

That focus would be far more effective if improving our nation's health statistics were the primary goal. One contemporary researcher, Karen Wright, has presented statistics to show that our nation's extremely expensive war against cancer has not worked; it has not improved cure rates significantly. She concludes that only prevention, not cures, can solve the problem.[25] This assessment is supported by research results showing that women with high levels of DDT in their bodies, even if they are in an otherwise low risk group, are four times more likely to get breast cancer than women with low levels.[26] A preventive approach is the one that has been successful in dealing with the AIDS epidemic so far. But attempts to change behavior are far less expensive than re-tooling industrial production and cleaning up the environment.

Prevention aimed at changing lifestyle has been a goal of corporate strategists since the 1970s, when they joined the chorus of a variety of health groups in blaming both sickness and the over-utilization of health care services on patients themselves. The problem, they said, was that too many people were hypochondriacs, or that they were overly worshipful of and emotionally dependent upon physicians, or that they lived "infantile" lifestyles, making themselves sick with their own bad habits. Once these people became ill, they forced others to pay for their treatment through health care cost inflation that is reflected in increased out-of-pocket expenses, insurance rates, and taxes as well as in higher prices for all types of consumer goods and services.

To address this particular problem, the early corporate strategists directed their efforts toward achieving one seemingly impossible goal, that of getting significant numbers of people to stop smoking and drinking alcohol, to eat right and to exercise. Psychologists and other behavioral scientists had been consistently frustrated in their attempts to accomplish this kind of behavior modification, even when they worked with willing, paying customers. Corporate strategists believed they could achieve it through economic incentives, workplace fitness programs, and public service advertising messages, all of which were among their tactics.[27] These efforts proved to be less effective than old-fashioned self-help.[28] In the long run, wellness programs, which were highly touted as cost-containment measures during the 1970s and 1980s, have not proven to be cost efficient. As one analyst explained:

> Such programs tend to cover a lot of ground, and therefore require a lot of overhead. They offer programs in anything from weight control and nutrition classes to fully-equipped exercise facilities, from smoking clinics to drug and alcohol abuse counseling. Though companies that have instituted wellness programs have reported a measurably healthier workforce and lower absenteeism, the cost often offsets any savings in health-care expenses.[29]

Of course, one problem with such programs from the corporate employers' point of view is that they highlight a very unpleasant reality; the worker's personal lifestyle is not simply a matter of personal choice, it is affected by his or her work environment. For example, according to Carl Hill of Blue Cross and Blue Shield of Delaware, the utilization rates are "atrocious" for two of his company's clients, the Chrysler Corporation and General Motors. In part, Hill says, that is owing to the nature of the industrial workplace. As he points out, "Assembly lines tend to breed health problems with drugs and alcohol." Thus, while the companies cause health problems, they also, says Hill, provide their work-stressed employees with "Cadillac benefits, largely because they're union-negotiated."[30]

A more direct "tax and regulate" approach implemented by the Reagan administration in the early 1980s has been far more effective than corporate wellness programs. A combination of higher taxes on tobacco and new regulations that prohibited smoking in many public places has paid off. By 1990, the percentage of Americans who smoked was lower than it had been in thirty-seven years. As a result of tax increases, the average cost of a pack of cigarettes was $1.74 by 1991. And regulations prohibited smoking in public places in forty-four states and the District of Columbia. These taxes and regulations probably help to account for the fact that, beginning around 1985, the percentage of tobacco users in the United States began to decrease at an annual rate of 1.1 percent. Women and blacks, who make up the largest percentage of low-income groups, were kicking the habit in especially large numbers, although these are also the groups from which the largest numbers of new smokers are recruited.[31]

By 1992, applying sanctions against smokers had become as socially acceptable as smoking itself had been during the 1950s, when 42 percent of the population smoked, mostly men. Some corporate employers have contributed to this new social reality—replacing their motivational carrots with a more punitive stick—fining employees with higher health insurance premiums for bad habits such as smoking tobacco or refusing to hire smokers in the first place.[32]

But the behavior modification programs that corporations attempted to launch during the 1970s were strategically sound even if they did not change employee behavior much at that time, for they did help to legitimate the belief that when people get sick it is their own fault. If this view is widely accepted, the public may be less likely to protest when employers withdraw some health care benefits. This view may also help explain why workers during the 1980s allowed employers to shift health care costs onto employees and patients in the form of higher deductibles and new "cost-sharing" health insurance "products" even while their own wages were going down. Still, the decreased incomes of American families during the 1970s and 1980s probably provides a more powerful explanation. During the 1970s, service sector jobs replaced those in the manufacturing sector as the country deindustrialized. Blue-collar workers experienced a permanent loss of pay, job security, and benefits as part of the process. White-collar workers joined them in the 1980s as a result of corporate takeovers, downsizing, and new administrative tactics designed to pass more of the cost of health care back to workers.

The Impact of Corporate Initiatives

Given their ambitious agenda, how successful have corporate strategists been in achieving their goals? I will argue that they have been extremely successful indeed in achieving their ideological goals but that they have failed miserably to achieve their practical ones.

Corporate strategists succeeded in implementing many of their original strategies and have added many more along the way. They have helped to create and institutionalize a complex surveillance system, not only over providers and patients, but over their own new experts as well, attempting to eliminate in advance the possibility that a new "professional" elite might be socially constructed and exercise occupational power. They have also succeeded in institutionalizing competition and accountability as dominant ideologies in health care delivery while simultaneously debunking the professional service ethic. Thus they have contributed significantly to a transformation of our health care delivery system in ways that will be described and documented throughout this book.

Politically, corporate strategists successfully warded off, at least for a time, both the move toward socialized medicine and the frightening Partnership for Health that President Nixon proposed in 1971. As part of this process, corporate strategists have also deprived both providers and the public of a voice in defining our national health care policy.

The power that corporate America enjoys over health care delivery has been reflected in the media that have served health care providers for many years now. Interestingly, that power is usually depicted in a positive way, as something that serves the public interest. For example, this statement appeared in an editorial in *Modern Healthcare* in 1979.

> Major employers, insurers and third-party payers are moving strongly against soaring health care costs and in many areas they are reducing hospital occupancy. . . . What this means is that the free markets are working. . . . This free-market competition is coming not from other health care providers but from suppliers of other goods and services. . . . Employers and insurers . . . are acting as agents for the prospective patients, giving them clout they've never had before.[33]

Seven years later, in 1986, *Hospitals* magazine announced that power in health care delivery has shifted to "those who pay" as a result of the "deregulation" of the 1980s.

> Health care providers—hospitals, physicians, health plans, and others—are being forced to adjust to a deregulated marketplace in which buyers call the tune. The topsy-turvey economics that allowed supply to dictate demand is dead. It is a profound shift in power.
> "Health care has started the process of reinventing itself," says John Elkins, executive vice-president of The Naisbit Group, Washington, DC. "The industry is going through a permanent restructuring," adds Peter Grua, an analyst with Alex. Brown and Sons, Boston.[34]

In reality, of course, since the mid-1980s, health care delivery in the United States has been increasingly saddled with a system of private regulation, the scope and intensity of which is unmatched by anything government has ever before been able to invent in a "democratic" society.

Corporate strategists have not, however, achieved their publicly stated goal of reducing health care costs. In fact, the problems they first addressed in the early 1970s have grown worse, and many new ones have emerged, often in response to the corporate initiatives themselves. While millions of people have been excluded from access to health care services during the last twenty years, health care costs have increased dramatically as we continue to pay more for much less.

The decreased access to health care services has not resulted either from flaws in traditional health care delivery or from indiscriminate and uncoordinated government spending. Rather, limited access has resulted from a number of social factors, including important economic developments during the 1970s and 1980s. During that time, most of the new jobs that were created were nonunionized, often part-time, service sector jobs that neither offered employees health insurance nor provided enough pay or job stability to enable them to buy it for themselves.

But decreased access to health care also has resulted from many of the strategies that industry has used to transform health care delivery. According to John Erb, a managing consultant at A. Foster, Higgins and Company, the remedies employers have used to bring down health care costs have been "myopic." Erb's specific example is the fact that employers in the 1980s pitted hospitals against each other, a strategy that, he says, is counterproductive in an indemnity environment.[35] In fact, corporate strategies have fostered cutthroat competition within health care delivery, both among insurance carriers and between alternative treatment units such as health maintenance organizations and their mortal rivals, preferred provider organizations (hospitals that contract directly with corporate employers to deliver health care services). This competition has had disastrous results for the public. Because of it, many insurers and service units exclude those who are not profitable customers for their commodity, including the sick, poor, unemployed, or elderly.

Interestingly, even though they have not achieved their stated goals of cutting our national health care costs and improving our services, corporate strategists continue to claim that competition and accountability are effective. This belief seems especially irrational because it is asserted by a group that showed enormous social and theoretical insight in constructing strategies to bring about social change. Thus, it seems likely that cost cutting was never their primary goal. Rather, it served as a virtuous legitimation for corporate activists to take over public policy making in an area that was new for them. I will argue that corporate strategists saw a historical transformation of health care delivery coming and co-opted it.

Apparently, corporate America has been willing to force the American public to pay almost any price to avoid socialized medicine. There is no denying the fact that the corporate strategists have also been forced to pay a high price themselves. By early 1991, health benefits consumed more than 25 percent of employers' net earnings, while the annual cost of health insurance per employee was $3,217 per worker.[36]

Perhaps that explains why a 1992 *Fortune* magazine survey indicated that 24 percent of corporate employers now favor some kind of socialized system.[37]

Summary

For thirty years, the mutually supportive policies of all these structural components—government, health care providers, insurance companies, and corporate employers—have stimulated the growth of an increasingly massive, and expensive, health care industry. Without question, it is the American people who have paid for all this unexamined and uncoordinated spending, whether it was done by government or by private industry. The people have paid for it with money, since both the government and private insurance companies derive their funds from the masses of ordinary working people. They have paid for it with the worst morbidity and mortality statistics in the industrialized world, as millions of Americans have been excluded from a system they cannot afford to use. They have paid for it with the continuing hazards of poverty and industrial pollution, which is part of the price of maintaining a health care system that offers only "cures" while studiously ignoring the social causes of disease. And they have paid for it with the intense anxiety and aggravation that now accompanies many of our encounters with the health care delivery system.

The people have also paid with a loss of political influence over their own government, a process that has occurred in many areas of life in addition to health care delivery, as William Grieder has dramatically illustrated.[38] Although it lasted for only a brief period, "people power" did succeed in moving Congress to pass important social legislation during the 1960s and early 1970s. For a time, it seemed possible that we might act collectively to create a health care system that could meet our social needs. That possibility has been subverted for more than twenty years.

When corporate America assumed political influence over health care, using government legislation and regulation to achieve its goals, it provided a classic example of the ways in which dominant groups can manipulate bureaucratic mechanisms to circumvent democratic processes and force massive and rapid social transformations upon modern societies. It is for that reason that these developments are so significant. In the midst of the "poststructuralist" era itself, these corporate and government initiatives highlight precisely the structural mechanisms through which interest groups that are powerful or wily enough to use them can plan, shape, and implement revolutionary changes in keeping with their own interests and ideologies—and all at the public's expense. At the very least, the corporate strategists can obstruct developments that are not to their liking. And they can do all that, as Max Weber would say, even in the face of opposition. In the case described here, the opposition was organized and powerful as well as diverse. It included both consumer activists and the professional associations of health care providers such as the American Medical Association (AMA) and the American Hospital Association (AHA).

Although consumer activism on a massive scale has been a relatively sporadic political phenomenon in the United States, provider interest groups such as the AMA and AHA have exercised enormous political power in Washington for decades. By the early 1970s, however, it was clear that their power was on the wane; their frantic lobbying to obstruct passage of unfriendly legislation and regulation was almost completely ineffectual. This failure was partly owing to the fact that the American public had already begun to distrust physicians and their service ethic by the late 1960s. But it was also because health care providers did not understand that they were facing a new kind of enemy. While they wasted their efforts fighting socialized medicine, which corporate initiatives had already defeated, they were "blindsided by capitalism." This was not the free-market capitalism of laissez faire ideologues, however. It was an early version of the oxymoron "managed competition"; that is, competition that is forced upon both providers and consumers through the regulatory power of the capitalist state.

None of the corporate strategies described here could have been implemented without formal, government legislation and regulation. Despite the ideological emphasis that industry continues to place on competition as a cure for everything that ails health care delivery, free-market competition has been virtually nonexistent within the system for more than twenty years, limited much more stringently by corporate surveillance and control mechanisms than it ever was by the provider cartel. With managed competition, even the pretense that we have a market-driven system finally seems to have been laid to rest—for all but the truest of believers, that is. This comment by the noted health care economist Alain Enthoven indicates that he still believes that the market is at work: "I'm not sanguine about managed care . . . [but] . . . government cannot organize and manage the system. We have to respect pluralism and try to use market forces."[39]

2
The Basic Components of Private Regulation

In spite of all the talk about deregulation being a kind of
movement that has achieved its own momentum, there
really hasn't been very much of it.
—*David M. Kinzer, School of Public Health,*
Harvard University.[1]

Although the popular wisdom holds that government spending is always accompanied by regulation, that has not been the case with health care delivery. For decades, government spent public funds copiously, without regulating either hands-on medical practice or health care policy making. One exception to this generalization was the Hospital Survey and Construction Act of 1946 (Hill-Burton), which required hospitals using public funds to expand their facilities to provide a minimum amount of charity care. During the economic boom years of the late 1940s and 1950s, with a far simpler health care technology, a relatively small population of elderly citizens, and an environment that was considerably less hazardous than it is today, that was hardly a backbreaking restriction. Nor did it interfere with the occupational monopoly physicians enjoyed over medical practice.

Far from attempting to regulate medical programs, government did not even try to coordinate them. As a result, for thirty-five years the U.S. health care system was characterized both by extremely wasteful duplications of services and by underutilized facilities.[2] Government did not interfere with providers for two important reasons. First, lobbyists for physicians and hospitals were powerful enough to exclude everyone except themselves from any kind of health care policy making. Second, no powerful social groups had seriously opposed the process that Eliot Friedson has called "professional dominance."[3] In fact a very powerful group had supported it; physician dominance has always served capitalist interests very well, both because it was a *petit bourgeois* alternative to socialized medicine and because it focuses on curing disease rather than eliminating the social realities that facilitate it. Thus, as a result of both government and corporate support, until the 1970s it was health care providers, including physicians, hospital administrators, and hospital boards, who made whatever health care policy existed.

In the late 1960s and early 1970s, in response to public activism, Congress made a few modest and ineffectual attempts to coordinate some of the construction projects and health care services that were funded with federal money. Although the American Medical Association stridently opposed all these efforts, by the early 1970s physician control was under attack from many quarters as the nation quivered on the brink of developing some kind of nationalized health care system. At that point, industry realized that the total autonomy physicians enjoyed no longer worked to serve corporate interests and set out to help undermine it.

Although it is not a simple process to wrest control from a well-entrenched, high-status occupational group, this was probably the most fortuitous time in more than fifty years to make the attempt. By the early 1970s, the AMA's power to obstruct legislation was on the wane. One after another, pieces of legislation the AMA opposed sailed through Congress. This legislation included the amendment to the Social Security Act that created the professional standards review organization (1972), the Health Maintenance Organization Act (1973), the National Health Planning and Resources Development Act (1974), and an amendment to the Social Security Act that mandated universal implementation of the diagnosis-related group billing system (DRG) (1983). Although this last piece of legislation was not passed during the 1970s, various groups and businesses were at work throughout that decade trying to create a statistical system that would exercise surveillance and control over physicians.[4] The DRG system was the result. After a three-year test period in New Jersey, the Reagan administration mandated its implementation in hospitals throughout the entire country.

Industry supported all this legislation in many different ways, lobbying for it, funding it, and, in some cases, training its own executives to work with health care regulatory agencies.[5] The objective was to manipulate government legislation, regulation, and expenditures of public money in ways that would support the goals of industry rather than those of professional interest groups.

Of course, this "regulatory strategy" had its dangers. Depending on how active competing interest groups are at any particular time, regulation may achieve very different kinds of goals. Regulatory apparatuses, like other bureaucratic mechanisms, are neutral, systematic, and mechanical in themselves; they can neither determine nor evaluate the goals of those who have the power to use them. Some details from the complex history of regulation in the United States will provide examples.

Regulation, Deregulation, and Reality

As Martin Tolchin and Susan J. Tolchin have pointed out, the primary reason that Congress created the first federal regulatory agencies in the late nineteenth century was to protect business interests.[6] Historically, that has been a major accomplishment of regulation. Sometimes, however, unusual national circumstances or extraordinary public activism has moved government to pass legislation designed to achieve societal goals. Both the New Deal legislation of the 1930s and the Great Society, environmentalist, and occupational safety legislation of the 1960s provide examples. In these cases, Congress passed regulatory legislation that was designed to serve the public's interests.[7]

During the 1960s, it did so in direct opposition to the wishes of both corporate leaders and health care professionals. Not only did Congress strengthen many existing regulatory agencies in order to promote public safety; it also established new regulatory bodies such as the Environmental Protection Agency (EPA) (1970) and the Occupational Safety and Health Administration (OSHA) (1970) and passed the Consumer Product Safety Act (1972). All this legislation was intended to protect both the general public and workers.

Very important, these new agencies were not staffed with traditional government bureaucrats who were sympathetic to business interests, in the time-honored tradition. Instead, they employed, say Tolchin and

Tolchin, former employees of public-interest groups such as Ralph Nader.[8] Clearly, even in a capitalist state, Congress can be moved to rule in the interest of the people.

Of course all of this legislation was created over the opposition of corporate leaders who, before the ink was dry, had begun their efforts to eliminate or negate it. But the roots of political opposition are often tangled. Ironically, the tactical devices that proved to be most effective in reversing the intent, if not the reality, of public service regulation during the Reagan administration were first put into place by President Jimmy Carter in 1978.

Accepting the advice of those who believed that inflation was the country's most threatening problem and that the major cause of inflation was regulation, President Carter took two steps that would provide the legitimating basis for the deregulatory strategies of the 1980s. First, he set up the Regulatory Analysis Review Group in an attempt reduce the power of Congress and to increase that of the White House over the regulatory agencies, for, as the new public service regulations had increased the power of Congress and agency bureaucrats over social policy making, they diminished the power of the White House.[9] Next, President Carter, say Tolchin and Tolchin, initiated the process of using cost-benefit analysis to achieve political goals.[10] This step was crucial.

In cost-benefit analysis, the cost of including some safety feature on a product or in a workplace is compared with the probable cost of doing without it. Then someone decides whether the costs outweigh the benefits. When one of the costs is a human life, the process can sometimes become controversial, as it did, for example, when the Ford Pinto scandal was made public and litigated.[11] In that case, the fact that the Ford corporation assigned a cash value to each life lost in a preventable burn death, compared it with the cost of replacing a faulty gas tank, and decided that it was cheaper to go with the burn deaths was highly criticized. But that fact does not prevent the widespread use of cost-benefit analysis to make decisions about all kinds of things that also have a negative impact on human lives. The "rational" nature of the process has been cited so often that we lose sight of the fact that it is a mechanical process that can only work after a *value* decision has been made. We accept uncritically the idea that the "expert" who carries out the mechanical analysis is competent to make the value judgment as well.

Cost-benefit analysis has been a controversial practice since it began to be used in an openly political way to eliminate regulatory safety features during the late 1970s, a process that intensified dramatically throughout the 1980s. As one public interest advocate has observed, "The child-labor laws would never have passed a cost-benefit test."[12] This decreased regulation had already begun to have adverse effects during the Carter years. For example, mine deaths increased by 50 percent between 1978 and 1981, after the Mine Safety and Health Administration cut the number of coal mine inspectors.[13]

Because of the precedents that were set during the Carter years, when the Reagan administration came to power in 1981 with the specific goal of disempowering the public service regulatory agencies, the managerial tools to do the job were already at hand. The goal of the Reagan administration was to return regulation to its original function, that of serving the interests of corporate America. George Bush, vice-president at the time, was made chair of a new regulatory task force. In that capacity, he invited thousands of business and civic leaders to submit their recommendations for "reforming" regulation.[14]

James C. Miller 3d, an academic economist, was also part of the Reagan transition team assigned to this job. According to Miller, when the Reagan administration came in, "We hit the ground running. . . . All the work was done in the transition period. We knew what we were doing the minute we came in. Stockman let me lose and said, 'be tough!' " In discussing the people who worked with him in this area, Miller said, "All our appointees have religion. . . . We want to make sure OSHA is no longer a four-letter word." Their ultimate goal was "to convey to the business community the President's determination to ease the burden of regulation."[15]

In 1981, the Reagan administration made this deregulatory process part of the mission of the Office of Management and Budget (OMB). Executive Order 12291 elevated the OMB into a kind of "superregulator," giving it responsibility for overseeing any regulations the agencies issued. At the same time, the order actively discouraged the agencies from developing new regulations. If, in spite of these deterrents, some agency did propose a new regulation, it was required to do a cost-benefit analysis, which would usually nip the proposal in the bud. Tolchin and Tolchin observe: "By demanding ever more information and raising one objection after another, the budget office exercises de facto control over the agencies' agendas and output. The mere fact that O.M.B. questions a proposed regulation can cause an agency to drop the proposal."[16] Cost-benefit analysis has been used not only to cut costs and to limit services but strategically, to achieve unpopular political goals, circumventing democratic processes. Thus, although the Reagan administration could not achieve its deregulatory goals by actually getting laws repealed or revised, it could do so through "administrative fiat."[17]

These developments did not proceed without opposition. Both federal courts and the Supreme Court have addressed claims that this approach to regulation is unconstitutional. However, the OMB has been quite successful in carrying out its mission. It has made, say Tolchin and Tolchin, a "wholesale reduction in regulations that protect the environment and the public's health and safety."[18]

This manipulation of bureaucratic rules and procedures to eliminate public health and safety regulation provides an interesting contrast with the stringent controls another bureaucratic agency, the Health Care Financing Administration (HCFA), imposed on hospitals during the same time period. In that case, the agency refused to exempt hospitals with excellent records from the same stringent peer review requirements it applied to those with poor records.[19] This refusal to reward merit supports the interpretation that the administrative "stick" is not simply a tool designed to achieve the manifest goal of making health care delivery more efficient or even cheaper. Rather, it is an end in itself, directed toward achieving the latent goal of establishing external surveillance and control mechanisms over health care providers.

The Reagan administration also attempted to remove the few protective regulations that had been designed to benefit the poor during the 1940s, when the federal government began spending vast sums of public money to construct health care facilities. *Modern Healthcare* reported:

> The Reagan administration wants to eliminate regulations requiring hospitals built with funds under the federal Hill-Burton program to provide minimum amounts of charity care, health industry sources say. . . . More than 4,500 hospitals have accepted federal funds under a 1946 law authored by Senators Lister C. Hill (D-Ala.) and Harold H. Burton (R-Ohio). Current rules require these hospitals to report every three years on the amount of free care they provide. . . . [They] must publi-

cize in newspapers the availability of free care and must post signs in their emergency and admitting departments saying that free care is available.[20]

Removing these onerous regulations was clearly designed to prevent poor Americans from learning about the free services to which they were legally entitled.

On the other hand, the Reagan administration supported regulation that promoted industry's agenda. For example, during the 1970s, industry had attempted to create various kinds of "alternative providers" to compete with traditional ones. These alternate settings included facilities such as freestanding surgical centers, which industry attempted to exempt from the very same peer review and certificate-of-need (CON) legislation that it lobbied government to impose on traditional providers.[21] It is one of the ironies of the Reagan administration that it implemented, through Medicare, formal government regulatory policies to actively promote these "free-market" alternatives. "Under a new regulation," reported Modern Healthcare, "Medicare will pay for almost twice as many kinds of procedures performed at freestanding ambulatory surgery centers. . . . The new list is the first expansion of the ambulatory procedures list since 1982, when Medicare first began paying for freestanding surgery center procedures."[22] Thus, while "deregulation" was a hot topic during the Reagan years, there was actually very little of it in the health care delivery sector. David M. Kinzer concluded, "In spite of all the talk about deregulation being a kind of movement that has achieved its own momentum, there really hasn't been very much of it, with the exception of the repeal of the national health planning act and the nine states that have repealed their certificate-of-need (CON) laws."[23]

Although the Reagan administration attacked regulation of health care delivery at the verbal level, it carefully preserved the components of the regulatory process that were required to enforce private, corporate surveillance and control mechanisms over health care providers. These components will be described in detail in chapter 3.

This political transformation of regulatory agencies into the servants of industry caused some of the worst scandals of the Reagan administration. For several months, six congressional committees investigated irregularities in the Environmental Protection Agency. As a result of these investigations, the administrator, Anne McGill Burford and more than twenty other appointees were ultimately forced to leave. Rita

Lavelle, who had headed the EPA's program to clean up toxic waste, was indicted on five felony charges for lying about her activities during her tenure.

As Tolchin and Tolchin have pointed out, both the politicization of the regulatory process and the scandals that have accompanied it pose threats to democratic processes. "Whether he is a Democrat or a Republican, a President with the whip hand over the regulatory agencies is likely to bend enforcement rules in the direction of his friends—toward consumer groups or toward regulated industries. President Reagan has demonstrated how quickly and easily a determined President can dominate regulatory decisions."[24] Although regulation and competition are usually seen as antithetical, that has not been the case in health care delivery. In the health care sector, the very existence of competition makes regulation necessary, for several different reasons.

First, competition forces some hospitals to close. When that happens, the ones that fail are those that work with the smallest profit margins because they serve the largest numbers of poor and elderly patients. Therefore, competition will cause our problems with access to intensify, making regulation necessary to solve them. According to Stuart Altman, an economist at Brandeis University and chair of the Prospective Payment Assessment Commission, "The public policy pendulum will likely swing toward regulation as competition forces hospital closures and exacerbates access problems."[25]

Second, as more cost-containment initiatives are put into place, the quality of care deteriorates. Thus, the fact that the diagnosis-related group billing system saves money by limiting care results in the need for more utilization review to prevent providers from saving themselves money by lowering their standards. As a result, money we formerly spent on health care services now pays for administrative surveillance. This kind of regulation is carried out in the private as well as in the public sector. Eventually, Altman believes it will be extended even further. "Regulatory pressure will come not only from federal and state governments, but also from businesses worried about the cost and quality of services they buy... . Attempts may be made to control the quality of all medical services, including outpatient and physician office practice."[26]

Altman's warning that quality control regulations might be extended to physicians' offices was prophetic. In 1989, the state of Wisconsin began a pilot study of the process of extending peer review organization (PRO) surveillance to physicians in their private offices.[27]

Third, the "competitive" mechanisms that were put into place during the 1970s and 1980s were created through government legislation and regulation in the first place; they certainly did not reflect any market reality. The continued use of government power will be required both to maintain these mechanisms and to create new ones. In short, it is competition that is the problem, not regulation. As Tolchin and Tolchin point out, regulations provide the public with its "major protection against the excesses of technology whose rapid advances threaten man's genes, his air and water, his life itself . . . [from] the excesses of an industrial society."[28]

Of course, many critics of U.S. health care delivery believe that government regulation is the system's major problem, that it has resulted in an administrative nightmare. But the bureaucratic controls of corporate America, as well as those of government, are responsible for the excessive paperwork that characterizes the health care system. Thus, even if we could eliminate government regulation, the surveillance systems that have been built into the insurance and utilization review industries would remain, along with their attendant paperwork.

Thus the question is not whether regulatory controls *should* exist; the questions are: Who will control them? And in whose interest? Although it is unclear whether *anyone's* interests actually have been served by the developments of the last twenty years, it is clear that industry has exercised enormous control over both the regulatory and the deregulatory process.

Although corporate America has often been accused of lacking foresight and of engaging in a reckless pursuit of short-term gains in making its own investment decisions, industry's approach to transforming health care delivery has displayed a sophisticated understanding of sociological insights and theories, with an eye on the long haul. As told to Joseph Califano, secretary of health, education and welfare, "Planning must be viewed as a long term, evolutionary process."[29]

The following section will describe the history of the four legislative enactments that served to carry this "evolution" forward. Rather than discussing them in chronological order, I will present them in the way that best shows how they interact and affect one another.

Formal Legislative Control Mechanisms

The National Health Planning and Resources Development Act

The National Health Planning and Resources Development Act of 1974 was the most comprehensive regulatory legislation that industry supported.[30] The act established 212 local health systems agencies (HSAs) authorized both to make health care policy and to enforce it by granting or withholding certificates of need (CONs). The rationale behind this plan was that hospitals duplicated services and purchased expensive equipment in order to compete with each other. Once they had the facilities or equipment, they used it unnecessarily in order to pay for it. The HSAs were supposed to determine whether their own geographic areas were adequately served by hospital facilities and capital equipment. If they were, hospitals would not be allowed to start up, expand, or purchase equipment. Those that did so without having a CON would lose government funding.

Corporate activists understood the contradictions inherent in their support for this regulation. Nevertheless, as they told Secretary Califano, industry supported the 1974 act in general.

> While a vote would not be unanimous, business can be characterized as being very supportive of the planning process. Through the Health Systems Agencies and the other public bodies established by P.L. 93–641, the major employer/purchaser is finding new access to direct involvement in the health delivery system. This, in turn, is stimulating an increased degree of corporate commitment to become truly informed consumers. . . . Health planning, as defined by P.L. 93–641 and its regulations, will not work equally well in all communities, and will experience some failures. But, it is viewed by the major employer-purchasers as a big step in the right direction. And those who would oppose this planning legislation in a vain search for yesterday should keep in mind that *the alternative is not less regulation but more stringent controls.*[31]

This warning has proven to be prophetic. Currently, although some formal regulation has been eliminated, surveillance and control mechanisms have become both more universal and more "stringent."

Industry itself made a considerable commitment to the HSAs. It helped to fund them, trained some of its own corporate executives to serve on them, and then gave these highly paid workers time off from their jobs to serve on the agencies in their geographic areas. It was the government, industry complained, that was not sufficiently supportive of its own regulatory requirements; government "underfunded" the agency.

> Corporate support for the HSAs can be a vital factor in their fiscal solvency and management capacity. This is especially significant while the HSAs remain underfunded by the government. . . . The government must fund the HSAs at a reasonable level if they can ever be expected to perform their designated tasks.[32]

At the operational level, industry heartily supported using tight and extensive CON policies to limit the expansion of health care facilities.

> The certificate of need procedure should include all medical and health facilities (home health, ambulatory care, corporate extended care clinics, leased space, site and facilities acquisition, etc.). . . . Large capital expenditures for equipment should also be subject to certification, no matter where they are located. . . . All federal, state and local government hospital beds and health facilities should be included in the formulas used by HSAs to determine need.[33]

However, industry supported this regulation only in order to restrict traditional providers. From the beginning, it expressed concern that subjecting investors in private hospitals to the CON process would interfere with the expansion of these desirable, "efficient" facilities: "However, we are concerned this orientation may place inequitable burdens upon the investor-owned hospitals without proper regard for the efficiencies they may represent."[34]

That concern was justified. Certificate-of-need laws presented real obstacles to the growth of the huge for-profit chains. In 1986, the Illinois Health Facilities Planning Board denied a CON to the Humana Corporation to build a $48 million, 224-bed, teaching hospital in North Chicago. The health systems agency decided the area did not need the hospital because adequate facilities already existed in Chicago and Milwaukee. In short, Modern Healthcare reported, "The board denied the CON application because Humana and the medical school couldn't demonstrate a need for additional hospital beds in the Chicago area."[35]

Thus the HSAs provide a good example of the unintended, although not unforeseen, consequences of government regulation. They were established to control one set of providers—those engaged in traditional, fee-for-service medical practice—but, from the beginning, they interfered with attempts by corporate strategists to facilitate the emergence of nontraditional, competitive providers, especially HMOs. In the early days of corporate intervention, however, before other less cumbersome control mechanisms emerged, these regulations were extremely useful in decreasing the size of the U.S. health care systems' capital plant. Some statistics are instructive.

In 1970, there were 7,678 hospitals in the United States; they served a total population of just over 205 million. In 1988, there were 6,927 hospitals; the population was almost 249 million. Thus the number of hospitals had decreased by 10 percent while the population had grown by 21.5 percent. During the same period, the demographic makeup of the population changed enormously, in directions that increased our need for health care services.

First, Americans over sixty-five years of age increased from almost 10 percent of the population in 1970 to almost 12.5 percent in 1989. Second, Americans who live at or below the poverty line increased from 12.6 percent of the population in 1970 to 32.5 percent in 1987. These statistics are even grimmer if we look at the increase in the percentage of Americans who are poor but whose family incomes are only 25 percent above the official poverty line. In 1970, 17.6 percent of Americans lived below 125 percent of the poverty line; in 1987, 43.5 percent resided there.[36]

As a result of all these changes, by the mid-1980s, the National Health Planning and Resources Development Act of 1974 actually performed not only an obsolete but a dangerous function. For ten years, the health system agencies had put so much pressure on hospitals that many had been forced to merge or close, usually, those that were the least "cost-efficient" because they served disproportionate numbers of uninsured or underinsured poor patients. At that point, the CON process reached a point of diminishing returns. It had already eliminated many of the facilities that served the poor; now it could only prevent the development of those that served well-insured elites. But these include the elite facilities that use new, high-technology medical procedures, the kind that President George Bush often told us we can have only with a private, not a public, health care system. Thus the nation was being asked to help maintain a ruinously expensive health care system that fails to meet the most basic needs of massive numbers of people in order to finance a social product—scientific, high-technology medicine—that is too expensive to use on the population as a whole.

By 1988, the Federal Trade Commission was testifying in numerous court cases that the CON laws were anticompetitive. *Modern Healthcare* reported: "FTC studies have indicated that CON laws increase health care costs. That's the opposite effect [from that] for which health planning laws were created—to minimize consumers' health care costs by trimming excess health care services."[37]

But there was another even more important reason that formal planning had become unnecessary as well as ideologically repugnant. Many of the surveillance and control mechanisms it embodied had become "panoptic"; that is, they had been diffused into administrative cost-accounting mechanisms.[38] The diagnosis-related group billing system, which became effective nationwide in 1983, served most of the original functions of the HSAs. As John S. Hoff, an attorney for the National Council of Community Hospitals says, under the DRG system, health planning "is basically old hat. . . . With limited utilization and [with] competition in the marketplace, hospitals are going to give any capital purchase a second look."[39]

In 1981 the health planning act was repealed; several states also began to repeal their own certificate-of-need laws. Competition, not regulation, was expected to exercise control over unnecessary construction and capital purchases in the future. But competition was not to be directed toward meeting the demands of a free market in any ordinary sense. That outcome would be a recipe for disaster, given the public's "insatiable" desire for health care services. Rather, competition was designed to reduce the effective *demand* for services, to control utilization. As David Kinzer says, that was the underlying goal of all the legislation that industry has supported.

> Utilization control was what Professional Standards Review Organizations (PSROs) were created to do, and what peer review organizations (PROs) are attempting to do now . . . [through] mandatory concurrent review, discharge planning, preadmission certification, and second surgical opinions. Limiting the panel of participating physicians in a managed care enterprise only to "conservative" performers is a relatively

new strategy that has gained a large following, especially in the private sector. The entire HMO movement is, at its heart, a utilization control strategy.[40]

Until the 1970s, the trend was toward increasing access to health care services, toward defining health care as a right. Since then, that trend has been reversed as part of the "cost-control crusade." Kinzer continues:

> There are now multiple efforts in demand reduction, none of which have had enough time to show intended results. Co-pays, co-insurance, and deductibles are on this list, along with cafeteria plan options that give purchasers the chance (and the risk) of not buying coverages (psychiatry, for example) they do not think they will need. Wellness programs are another as yet unproven attempt to limit demand. In fact, *probably the most effective and direct approach to limiting demand is to reduce the number of people with adequate health insurance coverage or entitlements under government health programs. The Reagan administration has tried to do this but without much success.*[41]

Government may not have been able to withdraw all services guaranteed by Medicare and Medicaid, but those services have been decreased through peer review, the DRGs, and hospital closings. And the fact that more than 35 million Americans are without health care insurance, while millions more are underinsured, suggests that the Reagan administration enjoyed more success than Kinzer's statement indicates.

The health planning act regulated the size of the nation's health care plant. The other legislation that industry supported during the 1970s was designed to operate at a completely different level, to intervene in the face-to-face interaction that occurred between patients and providers. The first legislation to achieve this goal institutionalized "peer review," over the passionate opposition of American physicians.

The Professional Standards Review Organization

Peer review was implemented in 1972 by the amendment to the Social Security Act that created the professional standards review organization (PSRO). The PSRO itself was a massive bureaucratic structure.

The original plan was to establish 203 PSROs in designated areas around the country; by 1979, there were 190 in operation.

The PSRO was created to exercise direct surveillance over the way physicians diagnose illness and treat patients and to evaluate provider performance on the basis of the charts physicians keep for their patients. Peer reviewers examine these patient records to determine whether the treatments and diagnostic procedures that were proscribed by the physician were necessary and whether they were delivered in an appropriate setting; the objective here was to increase the use of outpatient services to reduce the more expensive hospitalization of patients. Using the term "peer" to describe those who carry out the review process was a vain attempt to placate doctors who were accustomed to exercising autonomy in their work; the reviewers were usually lower-level personnel, such as nurses.

Proponents of peer review believed that, once reviewers had collected patient diagnostic and treatment data from the medical records, physicians who overutilized services would be visible and could be sanctioned and controlled. This was the early stage of the process during which providers lost their power to control patient data; today, such data empower competing groups of new experts to define what is the very best, the most scientific medical practice. In the process, physicians have lost status as well as political power; some analysts say they are now seen as little more than "skilled technicians."

> The former mystique of health care delivery continues to erode. As an art, the practice of medicine requires judgment and choosing. As a science, it requires application of known protocols and standard treatments. The physician is becoming more of a highly skilled technician and accordingly exercises less independent judgment. Health care delivery is becoming less of an art and more of a science. . . . This transformation is . . . making consumer loyalty more difficult to earn.[42]

This analysis by Donald F. Beck and Jack Dempsey is a description of how the rationalization process works in contemporary society. Here physicians have lost power because their "knowledge" is inadequate; it is an art. For that reason, the ways that physicians practice medicine are increasingly subordinated to decisions made by another group of experts, those who are more "scientific."

Industry supported peer review legislation from its inception and continued to support it even though, by 1977, studies indicated that the PSRO was not cost efficient; it did not recover the cost of its own operation. As Willis Goldbeck told Secretary Califano a few months after a Department of Health, Education and Welfare (HEW) status report disclosed this fact: "Employers are increasingly aware of the value of the professional standards review concept. The PSRO program has not been as effective as had been anticipated, but the concept is valid. In the next year, more employers will be seeking an extension of the PSRO review to private sector patients."[43] This statement reflects one of industry's major goals: to extend peer review to the private sector. It has certainly achieved that goal, through processes that have been both mandated and funded by government.

In 1982 Congress repealed the law that created the PRSO in response to the Reagan administration's recommendation that federal funding should be phased out. That has not yet happened; federal policy still mandates peer review and federal money still pays for it. Actually, the PSRO was "privatized," not eliminated, in 1982; it was transformed into the peer review organization (PRO), a "leaner and meaner" structure made up of organizations that bid for government contracts to review the records of publicly funded patients. Perhaps more important, the principles and practices of peer review also have been incorporated into a whole new private industry that emerged during the 1980s, an industry that does commercial utilization review. These developments will be described in detail in chapter 3.

Proponents of the PSRO said it would cut costs by preventing individual physicians from delivering unnecessary services. However, the PSROs, along with other new organizational entities that emerged during the 1970s, such as the original diagnosis-related group billing system, were designed not only to reduce utilization but also to create and institutionalize new definitions of "necessary" services and "good" medical care, as well as the principle that physicians should be governed by accountability rather than the service ethic. In the language of Michel Foucault, the process of redefining medical knowledge and reality is both the tool for exercising power and the major legitimating mechanism for expert authority. For that reason, the right to define medical knowledge had long been monopolized jealously by health care educators and practitioners. Thus to launch an attack on existing expert knowledge and simultaneously to create another, competing knowledge base were crucial components of industry's strategy. One structural mechanism that seemed likely to achieve both goals consisted of the "alternative" health care delivery form that was most favored by industry during the 1970s and early 1980s. It seemed to combine all that was best in health care delivery; it consisted of free-market, capitalist enterprises whose employee-physicians could be subordinated to administrative controls. It contained built-in rationing mechanisms and practiced a kind of preventive medicine that was compatible with corporate ideologies. It was the health maintenance organization system that was so despised by traditional providers.

The Health Maintenance Organization Act

Congress passed the Health Maintenance Organization Act in 1973 in response to intense corporate lobbying.[44] Through this legislation, government attempted to support the emergence of huge numbers of health maintenance organizations (HMOs), just as it had supported the dominance of traditional providers in the past. Corporate strategists found HMOs very attractive because they seemed to make government regulation unnecessary. They were competitive, privately owned businesses that contained administrative surveillance and control mechanisms within their own organizational structures. These were precisely the reasons they had been so *un*attractive to physicians. In the hands of bureaucratic administrators and cost-efficiency experts, rather than physicians, these control mechanisms could simultaneously impose and legitimate the subordination of highly trained experts to the same principles of scientific management that had controlled other workers in industrialized countries for almost a hundred years. Eventually, industry believed that the HMOs would eliminate the private, fee-for-service medical practices that helped to support the autonomy and power of traditional physicians.

Paul M. Ellwood, M.D., who is credited with originating the "health maintenance strategy," is president of InterStudy, a Minneapolis-based organization that conducts human services policy research; he has also been active in getting those policies implemented in Minnesota. Originally Ellwood envisioned a massive organization of about one thousand HMOs around the country, organized like large corporations and each serving several million people.[45] The "strategy" was to create so many HMOs that they would put competitive pressure on traditional providers, forcing them either to become competitive themselves or to leave the field.

During the early 1970s, corporate strategists lobbied furiously for passage of friendly legislation that would facilitate the development of HMOs. Although industry succeeded in obtaining strong federal support for the concept, it was unable to prevent HMOs from being subjected to the same regulatory processes that were applied to traditional medical practitioners. Thus HMOs were hampered by the health planning act that passed in 1974 with support from industry, and, even though they were actively promoted by both government and industry, they did not spring up all over the country during the decade that followed.

President Nixon first announced the HMO strategy in 1971; his goal was to create 450 HMOs by 1973 and 1,700 by 1976—even more than Ellwood had originally envisioned. These HMOs would be available to 90 percent of the population and would enroll 40 million or more people.

The reality fell far short of the vision. By 1976 there were only 175 plans serving just over 6 million people. In 1980, when President Reagan took office, there were still only 236 in the country, serving just over 9 million people.

HMOs got a boost in 1981 when the health planning act was repealed, and several state governments began to eliminate their certificate-of-need requirements. All those regulations had seriously interfered with the development of HMOs. When the regulations were eliminated, new HMOs began to proliferate; by the end of 1985 there were 393, serving almost 19 million people. The number of HMOs had increased by 66.5 percent in just five years; their memberships had more than doubled. One year later, in 1986, there were 595 HMOs, an increase of over 51 percent. By 1987, however, the rate of increase declined dramatically. That year, there were 662 HMOs in the United States, an increase of only 10.3 percent. The number of enrolled members continued to increase, although slowly; in 1987, the 662 HMOs in operation served 28 million members. By 1990 the actual numbers of HMOs had decreased, although those that were left were larger and continued to serve more members; at that time, there were 575 HMOs, serving just over 33 million Americans. Thus, by the time the dust had settled, between 1980 and 1990, the number of HMOs had increased by about 147 percent and their combined memberships had increased by over 370 percent.[46]

This was a period of cutthroat competition, not only for HMOs but for hospitals as well. Its impact was extremely destructive, as Kinzer summarized:.

> Now we are starting to hear expressions of concern that these actions have triggered competitive medical "arms races." The most publicized example has been what has happened in Houston, Texas, a state that repealed its CON law in 1985. Since then, the city has had what one critic described as a "construction frenzy" (O'Donnell 1987), with nine new hospitals being built, including five psychiatric facilities (Lutz 1987). This building occurred at a time when hospital occupancy in the city was running an average 60.7 percent.[47]

Thus, although decreased regulation did allow many new competitors to enter the marketplace, the result was neither a permanent nor an irreversible increase in the numbers of HMOs in operation. Rather, it was a frenzy of competition that culminated in bankruptcy for many of the new companies. Nor did the competition eliminate facilities that were underutilized; rather, it resulted in more of them. According to John Erb, a management consultant at A. Foster, Higgins and Company, corporate employers were largely responsible for this proliferation, stimulating the competition with their "myopic" cost-cutting strategies.[48]

Once the numbers of HMOs began to decrease, the profits of those that survived did begin to rise. These profits were not the fruits of their superior competitiveness and efficiency, however; the companies collected them the old-fashioned way—by raising rates. According to InterStudy, HMO premiums increased by an average of 16.8 percent in 1990. Of the firms surveyed, InterStudy "found that 93 percent of HMOs cited premium increases—rather than improved cost controls or other factors—as the leading reason for increased profitability in 1989 versus 1988."[49]

Both industry and government had become somewhat disenchanted with HMOs as the solution to health care cost inflation by 1990. Some of the very corporations that had originally promoted them as competitive "alternatives" to traditional care have begun to look elsewhere.[50] Not only have the HMOs raised their premiums; it does not appear that their competitive presence has had the desired impact on national health care costs. In particular, the new, more competitively oriented HMOs do not operate in the same "cost-efficient" ways as did the older ones, according to a 1990 Health Care Financing Administration (HCFA) report. Kathryn M. Langwell summarizes HCFA's findings.

> Even though there is some evidence that managed care, particularly HMOs, may have an impact on utilization of services and the overall level of costs, most of this evidence is based on data from older, well-established HMOs that were operating in the 1970s and earlier. . . . The effectiveness of managed care in constraining the rise in health care costs has not been demonstrated when provided to a large proportion of the population through diverse organizational arrangements that include a variety of utilization management strategies.[51]

In short, the data do not support claims that the HMO strategy works in the ways its original proponents claimed it would. HCFA apparently believes that the explanation lies in the new HMOs' not making use of the administrative surveillance and control mechanisms that made HMOs so attractive to industry and government in the first place. For example, *Modern Healthcare* reports the HCFA has charged that the Medicare HMO the Humana Corporation that it operates   in Florida has been "involved in an array of illegal and shoddy practices." Among other charges, HCFA said that "Humana failed to spend enough money on administrative expenses to ensure the plan operated effectively."[52] Despite such failures, attempts to demonstrate that the HMO strategy really works have not been deterred. Apparently, when the data do not support the "theory," the tactic is to collect more, and more selective, data until they yield the desired result.

Obligingly, two studies in particular have indicated that HMO savings do have a "spillover effect" on national health care costs.[53] After analyzing data from the years 1984 to 1987, one researcher, W. Pete Welch, wrote in a report published by the Urban Institute that "in communities where HMOs have at least 25 percent of the market, fee-for-service expenditures would drop 3 percent to 9.7 percent over time."[54] This is a testable hypothesis, since there are now about a dozen metropolitan areas around the country in which HMOs enroll 20 percent or more of the population.[55] Another researcher, James C. Robinson of the School of Public Health at the University of California at Berkeley, reached the same conclusion. Using data from 283 hospitals in California for the period 1983 to 1988, he concluded that

"HMOs indirectly influenced hospitals by stimulating price competition among all insurers that were able to contract directly with medical facilities. In other words, non-HMO insurers pressured hospitals to act as though their patients belonged to HMOs."[56]

Skeptics might draw conclusions different from those drawn by these researchers. First, since both used data from a period of unprecedented, cutthroat competition that apparently was neither desirable nor sustainable, these generalizations are not likely to hold in more ordinary situations. Second, even if the HMOs did have some impact, it was not large enough to support arguments that the HMO strategy really will solve our health care cost inflation problems. In his study, Robinson acknowledges that in California "costs per admission still rose by 74.5 percent, to an average of $6,386 in 1988 from $3,653 in 1982."[57]

By the late 1980s, many corporate and government analysts believed that HMOs themselves would have to be subjected to external surveillance and control mechanisms if they were to play an effective role. Even those who worked within the HMOs came to agree with this assessment, a development that will be discussed in chapter 3. Although HMOs have not lived up to their promise, at least part of that failure might be attributed to some government planning and regulatory legislation that hit the wrong target.

Although corporate strategists were enamored of HMOs, they did not wait passively for the HMO strategy to transform health care delivery. Instead, they supported another mechanism that would control the services that physicians and hospitals delivered to patients—the diagnosis-related group billing system.

The Diagnosis-Related Group Billing System

The last, and most important, legislative control mechanism to be discussed here is the diagnosis-related group billing system (DRG). Invented at Yale University in 1976 and tested for three years in New Jersey, between 1980 and 1983, the DRG system actually tells physicians and hospitals what medical treatments can be delivered to patients on the basis of their diagnoses. It does so through the mechanisms of a rational accounting system. Based on statistical averages of the services that are delivered to a patient in any given diagnostic category, the DRGs spell out exactly what services, and how many of them, Medicare and Medicaid will pay for. If more services are delivered than the DRG formula specifies for that diagnosis, the provider has to absorb the loss.

The Yale version of the DRGs that was tested in New Jersey during the early 1980s had created 383 categories of patients based on their diagnoses, age, and sex. However, the HFCA version that was mandated for use throughout the country uses 468 categories in its DRG system. There were other important differences as well. The New Jersey system took severity of illness into account to some degree; the federal system did not. This fact has made it possible to create a system that systematically withholds services from the very patients who are most seriously ill. Because they are likely to overstay their DRG proscriptions, some hospitals now attempt to avoid the sickest patients, preferring instead to sell their products to healthier, more profitable consumers.[58] While hospitals are not reimbursed for more services than those that are specified in advance for a given diagnostic category, if they deliver *fewer* than the specified services they can keep the difference. Thus the system simultaneously punishes providers for overutilization and rewards them for underutilization, a bias that did not become a topic for debate until the mid-1980s, when an early advocate of corporate activism, Richard Egdahl, labeled the result of the bias "undercare." Kinzer reported:

> While their [peer review organizations'] prime reason for being is to save money by cracking down on hospitals that allegedly overutilize under Medicare, they are also told to be on the lookout for what Dr. Richard Egdahl (1986) has labeled "undercare." They are charged with investigating complaints of this nature and complaints about substandard care and are empowered to levy fines on hospitals and doctors they find guilty.[59]

This new function of peer review, to simultaneously prevent over- *and* underutilization, reflects a growing emphasis on "outcomes" research that began to emerge as a new topic during the 1980s. In theory, DRGs were supposed to prevent providers from delivering unnecessary services to patients; thus they should have cut health care costs. But their proponents claimed the DRGs would also improve the *quality* of care by eliminating dangerous, unnecessary services. Instead, the DRG system has been under attack for a decade for reducing the quality of care. This problem is discussed in detail in chapter 3.

From the beginning, the DRG accounting system served an essential function for peer reviewers. In its early stages, peer review suffered from the fact that no universally accepted standards of medical practice existed that could serve as a comparative base for evaluating medical decision making. The DRGs solved that problem; they function simultaneously to study, standardize, and ration the services that Medicaid and Medicare patients receive when they are hospitalized. Thus, DRGs directly shape the services that physicians utilize, regardless of what their medical schools might have told them was "good medical practice."

As a routine part of its operation, the DRG system would collect data upon which, simultaneously, to set empirically based standards and to legitimate itself. This legitimacy could be claimed either on the grounds that the system promoted "good medical care" or that it promoted "cost efficiency," whichever definition of "reality" the newly emerging data happened to support. Thus the data would provide the basis for new definitions of medical "knowledge," definitions that combined information about the efficacy of treatments with new standards of "cost efficiency." This process, like the construction of all new knowledge, would be self-legitimating. When providers actually succeeded in reducing utilization rates during a given year, which they eventually would have to do or face bankruptcy, that fact would demonstrate that they *could* change practice patterns, thus supporting claims that overutilization had existed in the first place and legitimating an even more extensive withdrawal of services during the coming year. The overall reduction of services that enforcement of the DRGs produced then would provide new statistical averages, new "norms of practice." Through this process, these statistical norms have become ever more prevalent, institutionalized, and legitimate.

The DRG system was not found to reduce costs significantly during the three years it was tested in New Jersey; nevertheless, the system was implemented throughout the country in 1983, when President Reagan signed into law the DRG amendment to the Social Security Act. Although this strategy has not cut costs appreciably, it has been extremely effective in changing practice patterns. On the basis of the new norms the system generates, the DRG proscriptions are recalculated every year and the payments for each diagnostic category are lowered even further. The more desperately providers attempt to avoid bankruptcy by reducing services in compliance with the DRGs' standards, the more they drive down the payments for each diagnostic category. Thus, in the very best double-bind fashion, the DRG system simultaneously mandates hospital "efficiency" and punishes it. It is for these reasons that the DRG system has been termed a "counterrevolution" in health care delivery financing; it could not have been better designed to undo the public-oriented services that were established during the 1960s and early 1970s.[60]

These developments were staunchly supported by industry, which wanted DRGs applied to privately as well as publicly funded patients. For example, industry groups such as the Arizona Coalition for Cost-Effective Quality Health Care, founded by the four largest employers in the state, lobbied for legislation requiring hospitals to use a uniform billing system based on DRGs by February 1, 1984.[61]

Of course, when the DRGs were first implemented, no data existed to support its proponents' claims that it would improve the quality of care, that it actually reflected the "best" medical treatment. In the long run, advocates of the DRGs might have hoped that the system itself, in its routine operation, would yield data to justify those claims. Of course, it would take several years to accumulate such data, during which time use of the system would have been institutionalized.

Now that the system has been in operation for a decade, it is clear that the data do not support claims that it improves the quality of care; in fact, they indicate that it has had the opposite effect, that the quality of care has deteriorated under the DRGs. That state of affairs is bound to continue as long as cost cutting remains the nation's most urgent priority in health care planning. As a result, although researchers continue to search for data to support their claims that the system improves the quality of care, new regulatory mechanisms are now being put into place in an attempt to offset the negative impact of the DRG system itself, to prevent underutilization. In the meantime, proponents of the system continue to justify it on the basis that it is cost efficient.

Although the concept "cost efficiency" is common and well institutionalized today, it was a newly emerging idea and value during the late 1970s, when President Carter adopted it to regain presidential control over the regulatory agencies. I first began to notice the term in widespread use among health care analysts, and to find "cost-benefit analysis" listed in the indexes of the books I used as sources, in material from the 1980s.[62] This development reflects a fair level of success on the part of corporate planners, since, ideologically, cost-benefit analysis is much more compatible with the values and goals of expert accountants than with those of physicians.

In principle, the DRG system standardizes and controls both the services providers can deliver and the prices they can charge; neither services nor prices can respond to the demands of the direct consumers, those who actually use health care insurance and services. Thus, although DRGs are enforced through different social processes, they function like regulatory mechanisms. Whereas formal regulatory processes work through bureaucratic organizations, the DRGs work through routine accounting procedures. Both forms of regulation are antithetical with "free-market" mechanisms, and yet both are now used to limit the demand and utilization of health care services, in the private as well as the public sector. Although it serves that function, the DRG system is touted as a competitive alternative to regulation.

Of course, the continuing increase in the share of our gross national product (GNP) that is eaten away by health care costs makes it clear that the DRGs have not cut costs any more than they have improved the quality of care. Keeping in mind that in Canada the national health care system uses, on average, 7 percent of the country's GNP,[63] the comparable statistic for the United States is instructive. In 1970, five years after Medicare and Medicaid were implemented, health care costs consumed 7.3 percent of our GNP. By 1979, it was 8.6 percent, an increase of 1.3 percent in ten years. By 1989, it was 11.6 percent, an increase of 2.5 percent during the "deregulatory" Reagan and Bush years.[64] Clearly, the phenomenon "iatrogenesis" does not occur only in the practice of physical medicine; the professional practice of rational accounting can also create fiscal malfunctions.

That said, it must be acknowledged that the DRG system has decreased utilization rates for patients whose services are controlled by them. Thus, in one sense, at least, DRGs have been more effective than other techniques in achieving that goal. For that reason, corporate America mandates their use for patients who are privately, as well as publicly, funded. Today, private insurance companies, at the insistence of their corporate customers, employ utilization review firms, most of which implement something very much like DRGs for privately funded patients. This kind of utilization review requires all the same kinds of data collection and cost-benefit analysis as do government bureaucracies. Thus, the *real* health care regulatory apparatus has been extended far beyond formal government programs, into the private sector, where there is no danger that the public will have any voice at all in making public health policy.

As a regulatory mechanism, the DRG system was truly revolutionary. First, it accomplished through accounting techniques alone many of the regulatory realities of the health planning act, the health systems agency, and the professional standards review organization combined. Second, it was far more "efficient" than HMOs in standardizing and regulating physician practices. And third, it is superior to the original form of peer review in that it regulates medical practices *before* they occur, not after the fact.

Interestingly, in violation of the popular wisdom, the government appears to be a more cost-effective regulator than the private sector. The DRG system that is federally mandated and funded for Medicare and Medicaid patients has actually reduced both the utilization of services and health care costs of these beneficiaries. Unfortunately, it has done so mainly by reducing services, which is what makes the more recent quality assurance regulations necessary. Although proponents of the system continue to claim that it reflects the best medical practice, its critics argue that it has only enforced the goal of rationing health care mechanistically and that it does so on the basis of cost accounting, not on the basis of disease entities. Because the rationing is achieved through administrative mechanisms, the services that are delivered to Medicare and Medicaid patients have been reduced or eliminated without the necessity of getting congressional approval for making the cuts.

In theory, the DRGs should have eliminated the need for HMOs. Although both of these organizational forms work simultaneously to control providers and to ration services, HMOs are far less efficient than DRGs, since they require massive duplications of functions and still permit wide variations in the ways physicians practice medicine around the country. They cannot completely "standardize" practice because individual HMOs create and enforce their own goals, based on diverse professional norms and values regarding patient care. The DRGs mechanistically create new, universal, standardized, statistical norms of practice, with the primary goals of reducing utilization and costs—and with no necessity for looking at a living, breathing patient. But the system itself is not to blame; like all bureaucratic mechanisms, it is "value-neutral." Thus it serves the ideological and economic interests of anyone who has the power to use it.

Why, then, did DRGs not eliminate the need for HMOs? Because the DRG system is an accounting process, not a delivery setting; it must be applied within some actual organizational structure in which real people struggle for control. And the struggle, of course, is ongoing. Both physicians and other health care delivery workers continue to resist the bureaucratic control mechanisms for reasons ranging from naked self-interest to a passionate concern for their patients. For that reason, it is probably harder to apply the DRG system in traditional settings than in HMOs, which have already institutionalized some rationing mechanisms to control utilization.

All the "panoptic" surveillance and control mechanisms described in this chapter should be much cheaper to use than formal regulation, if Foucault was right. However, they certainly have not led to reduced health care costs for the United States as a whole. In fact, they may have significantly increased them, precisely because industry has succeeded in implementing them universally. Kinzer states the problem succinctly.

> It may be that our pluralistic health care system is now so complex that any and all regulatory strategies will ultimately fail to achieve their cost-control objectives. In fact, acceptance of a health care financing and delivery system as complex as we now have as a given in our regulatory equation is probably a mistake. Efforts to regulate such a system must be complex also and, over the long term, expense generating. In fact, there is substantial evidence to support the point that the relatively high expense of the American system, as contrasted with the systems of most other developed countries, is more due to its overall complexity than to the alleged waste and inefficiency of health care providers or any of its other components.[65]

And there is no doubt that all this complex surveillance apparatus carries a very expensive price tag. In 1987, the Canadian health economist Robert G. Evans observed that the overhead costs of prepayment and administration, which jumped from $14.5 billion in 1983 to $26.2 billion in 1985, were six times higher, as a proportion of GNP, in the United States than in Canada.[66] Thus, the DRGs have created an enormous administrative apparatus whose primary purpose is to exercise surveillance and control, not to fulfill accounting functions.

The principle involved here is similar to the one that corporate strategists discovered during the 1970s. Based on data collected from corporate health programs,[67] they learned that practicing "preventive medicine" would not be as cost efficient as they had supposed, because screening massive numbers of people, even at a very small cost per head, is often more costly than treating the relatively few cases of disease that are uncovered. An even more appropriate analogy would be to compare these surveillance and control mechanisms to the force that imperial nations must exercise to keep their colonies in their places. At some point, the costs outrun any possible gains.

Although the "regulatory strategy" has not succeeded in cutting health care costs, it has been very effective politically. It transferred control from providers to administrators; simultaneously, it shifted health care dollars from patient care to administrative services. Thus, it has met a goal articulated by Clark Havighurst, an early advocate of competition in health care; it creates a system that "makes a profit for somebody besides physicians."[68]

Summary

During the 1970s, industry lobbied for passage of government legislation and regulations that were designed to support the emergence of a new kind of health care system, one that was organized and controlled by managerial experts rather than by traditional physicians in private practice. The components of the new system worked in a variety of mechanical ways to exercise surveillance and control over both patients and providers in order to ration the services that are delivered.

Although some of these mechanisms did, in fact, reduce utilization rates, they did not lower health care costs. On the contrary, they have added to them in important ways, increasing our health care costs at the same time that they have decreased the services that patients receive.

Throughout the 1980s, these mechanisms have served as the foundation upon which even more complex, mechanistic control structures have been built. The next chapter will describe that "evolutionary" process.

3
The Evolution of
Private Regulation

"I've got cost data coming out of my ears," but I still don't
know whether a hospital "made the patient better, did nothing, made him worse or killed him."
—*Merill C. Horine, Hershey Foods Corporation*[1]

If Sequoia's experience is typical—and there's no reason
to suspect it is not—health-care regulatory costs nationwide measure in the billions of dollars.
—*Sidney Marchasin, Sequoia Hospital*[2]

When corporate strategists first attempted to refocus the entire national
debate about health care delivery, changing it from a debate about
comprehensive national health insurance to one about cost cutting,
they directed their transformation strategies primarily toward health
care providers. They pounded home the argument that it was not pathology but physician-prescribed "overutilization" of health care services that caused the acceleration in our nation's health care costs. By
overutilizing services, they argued, physicians actually created disease,
first in the process of diagnosing some condition as pathological and
then through iatrogenesis: physicians actually created new pathologies
with their medical treatments. This argument has been described in
detail by Ivan Illich.[3]

As the ancient admonition first to "do no harm" makes clear,
awareness of iatrogenesis is as old as the medical profession. Feminists

documented its reality empirically during the 1960s by presenting a variety of evidence to support their claims that traditional physicians practiced sexist medicine, that they performed unnecessary surgeries on and prescribed harmful drugs for women.[4]

During the 1970s, industry generalized these feminist arguments to other groups for which no comparable evidence of overutilization or iatrogenesis existed. This tactic served to undermine public confidence in physicians in order to divert attention from questions about whether access to services was adequate and what the social causes of disease were.

Few spoof writers could have rivaled corporate interest groups for their ingenuity in exploiting this particular idea. For example, during the 1960s, representatives of the coal-mining industry lobbied hard but unsuccessfully to prevent Congress from passing the Coal Mine Health and Safety Act of 1969, which required coal mine owners to screen their employees for black lung disease. Among other arguments, industry representatives said the owners feared that coal miners would become the victims of iatrogenesis if they had that much contact with physicians.[5]

But iatrogenesis was not the major target of corporate strategists. Rather, they argued that overutilization of hospital inpatient services, especially by Medicare and Medicaid patients, was the cause of rapid health care cost inflation. Government spending for health care services gave providers a blank check, just as it had done in the past by funding hospital building and capital purchases; thus eliminating government spending and provider overutilization would control costs. Industry supported various new strategies for achieving that goal, including the legislative enactments described in chapter 2.

These pieces of legislation were aimed at different levels of health care delivery, from the broadest, structural level to the most minute, face-to-face interactions between patients and providers. Each had a different goal. The National Health Planning and Resources Development Act reduced utilization rates indirectly. It pared down the size of the nation's health care "plant" by closing hospitals, decreasing the numbers of hospital beds, and reducing the amount of high-tech equipment to which physicians had access. The Health Maintenance Organization Act was designed to facilitate the emergence of alternative delivery settings that would put so much competitive pressure on traditional providers that they would be forced to deliver services more "efficiently" or lose money. The professional standards review organization and the diagnosis-related group billing system were qualitatively different kinds of control mechanisms. They aimed at placing individual providers under total and constant surveillance to force them to accept new definitions of medical knowledge and change the ways they practiced medicine. These two organizational units interacted with each other in dialectical ways, each supporting and adapting to the other.

Although the DRGs made some functions of the old PSRO organizational apparatus obsolete, they did not eliminate the need for physician surveillance in general. On the contrary, they increased both the possibility and the need for surveillance. They increased the possibility of surveillance by setting universal standards, without which meaningful review is impossible. They increased the need for surveillance by requiring providers to comply with the standards. In the language of theorists of deviant behavior, they created rule violators as part of the process of creating new rules. As a result, the system had to be policed with even more zeal.

The implementation of the DRG system made possible some dramatic simplification of the peer review system. By the 1980s, the old PSRO system had lost favor for a number of reasons. First, it had grown to be an extremely complicated bureaucratic apparatus; it would have been pared down even if it had been retained in its original form. Second, the PSRO was obviously a regulatory apparatus, and the deregulatory fever of the Reagan years had arrived. Third, actual experience with peer review had eroded the confidence of many corporate activists that regulation would lower health care costs. Fourth, medical "reality" had changed. Peer review had been implemented in 1972, before any official statistical standards existed, which meant that reviewers varied widely in their judgments about what was "good medical practice." Once the DRG system was implemented, peer reviewers could simply target providers who failed to follow statistical norms in a mechanical, assembly-line process.

Separating the formal enforcement apparatus of peer review from the standards-setting DRGs effected a division of mental and physical labor characteristic of advanced industrial societies.[6] It enabled corporate bureaucrats, rather than medical professionals, to define and shape medical reality. Through this division of labor, surveillance and control functions were embedded in two different administrative apparatuses—peer review and the DRGs. Together, they embodied the principles of scientific management and accounting techniques that control workers in factories and offices throughout the United States.

At this point, a different kind of peer review was required to enforce professional compliance with the DRGs. In 1982, with a stroke of the pen, President Reagan brought about the required transformation. He partially "privatized" peer review in the sense that he replaced the formal government bureaucracy with a simpler, more centralized, network of private organizations, the peer review organization (PRO). HCFA's DRG system was retained, however, and the review process was still mandated by the government for publicly funded patients.

Whether or not peer review could actually result in lower utilization rates, industry understood that it was a sound strategy. First, regardless of what services were actually delivered to Medicare and Medicaid patients, with stringent peer review the government would pay for fewer of them. Actually, industry might have believed that providers would continue to deliver services to patients if they were "really" necessary, even if they were not reimbursed; if so, that would indicate that corporate strategists had some lingering confidence in the service ethic. Or, as seems more likely, corporate strategists might actually have believed in the principles of scientific management that their strategies reflected; they expected the DRG formulas to produce results similar to those of speedups and unit rate reductions in factories and offices. First, the DRGs would increase worker productivity (they would lower the unit cost of production) through economic rewards and punishments. Later, they would reduce the unit rate of pay as part of the annual recalculation of DRG reimbursement formulas.

Economic theory suggests that decreased government spending for health care should reduce health care cost inflation. But industry hoped to do more than limit services delivered to publicly funded patients. Corporate strategists were also in the process of implementing surveillance and control mechanisms that would ration services delivered to privately funded patients, especially their own employees. They believed this combination of public and private controls would transform the entire health care delivery system, making it more rational and cost efficient.

When Congress created the PSRO in 1972, industry could use its economic power to establish peer review in the private sector by pressuring its own insurance carriers to use it. By the end of the 1970s, 25 percent of PSROs had such private contracts.[7] From the beginning, then, government and industry have used not only the same strategies but even the same *organizations* to exercise surveillance and control, organizations that were created and maintained with public funds through the enforcement power of the state.

When the new PRO system was created, physicians may have been overly optimistic about the new, private form of peer review. Because the original PRO provisions stated that professional medical societies were to be given first shot at these government contracts, it appeared for a time that physicians might end up reviewing themselves, although they would have to establish a funding base in order to do so.[8] As things have turned out, medical societies are not likely to have these contracts. In fact, many of the PROs are actually the same organizations that serviced the old PSRO system. In Florida, for example, the PRO contract went to the Professional Foundation for Health Care, which formerly had served as a PSRO.[9]

By 1985, three years after President Reagan privatized the system, the Florida PRO maintained three offices and employed 125 reviewers, most of them nurses. This is a fairly small number of workers, considering the size of the job to be done, but keep in mind that PROs review only statistical samples, not entire populations. The Health Care Financing Administration sets the percentage of cases that must be reviewed, which changes with each contract period. For example, during the first two years the PROs were in operation, they reviewed about 50 percent of Medicare cases. By 1989, they were reviewing about 20 percent.[10] Thus the new system came to review an even smaller caseload than did the original PSRO because the process had been mechanized. The DRGs now serve many of the surveillance and control functions that originally had to be carried out by the peer review system itself.

Although the percentage of cases that PROs review has decreased, the importance of peer review has not. Medical utilization review (UR) is now an industry in its own right, maintaining surveillance over millions of privately insured patients every year.

The Increased Scope of Review

The kinds of undesirable medical procedures that peer reviewers are charged with finding and eliminating have expanded over time. For example, the first PSROs were supposed to look for cases in which care was unreasonable, unnecessary, or done inappropriately, in a hospital, when it could have been done on an outpatient bases. Later, treatments were included that were "outside the broad band of acceptable medical practice" such as using more than the average numbers of penicillin injections.[11]

During the 1980s, when the quality of the care that was delivered under the DRG system was becoming an important topic, PROs increasingly were empowered to define, look for, and sanction the delivery of "substandard" care. Presumably, such care results when providers attempt to make a profit in precisely the way they were told to do, by delivering fewer services than those allowed by the DRGs. As a result, recently PROs have assumed responsibility for "educating" both the public and physicians. They must provide "educational outreach" programs for the public. As one analyst has explained:

> The PROs' new work scope also requires them to join with health care providers in developing a public education campaign aimed at ensuring that Medicare beneficiaries receive accurate information about the PRO program. This outreach program would be geared toward educating beneficiaries about the purposes of PRO review and *to inform them of their Medicare rights.*[12]

This explanation suggests that PROs are functioning as patients' advocates as well as educators. They train the public to understand that they have a "right" to all the services the DRGs allow for their diagnosis. Thus the PROs, which forced providers to deliver fewer services, now try to teach patients how to make them deliver more. In the process, they encourage Medicare recipients to see their relationships with providers as adversarial, an early goal of corporate strategists.

PROs also must educate physicians, thereby duplicating functions of the medical school in addition to defining scientific standards of practice. The Texas PRO, for example, runs a "mini-residency" program.

> The Texas Medical Foundation will launch a "mini-residency" program at Texas Tech Health Sciences Center for physicians whose Medicare treatment patterns show problems. . . . Unlike continuing medical education, the course assesses what physicians know before and after they complete the residency program. . . . Physicians will leave their practices for one-week courses at Texas Tech's family practice department.

Pre- and post-course tests will be given, and PROs will monitor the physicians' performance after they return to their medical practices. . . . *More outreach programs directed at hospitals, physicians and beneficiaries are critical if review groups want to overcome rocky relations and maintain contracts with the federal government, HCFA's Mr. Morford said.*[13]

This statement provides examples of some of the sanctioning processes that are used to control not only providers but the PROs themselves. Making physicians go to school is one way of sanctioning them for not meeting the standards of care set by PROs. But the necessity of threatening PROs with losing their contracts indicates that they have resisted this expansion of their functions. In fact, many PROs complain bitterly that they are victims of "scope-work creep"; that is, HCFA has expanded their workload without increasing their funding. This is a basic principle of scientific management for increasing "productivity." It also makes it possible to implement politically motivated policies that could not survive democratic processes, such as getting congressional approval for cutting services that are guaranteed by federal legislation.

Although PROs dislike this expansion of their unpaid functions, they constantly attempt to expand the scope of their paid responsibilities. For example, PROs pressed long and hard for the right to review health maintenance organizations. One report explained: "The Office of Management and Budget is studying a plan under which . . . Medicare peer review organizations would evaluate health maintenance organizations under contract to Medicare. . . . *The plan would be the first comprehensive effort to review the quality of ambulatory care.*"[14] This expansion of functions represents a significant increase of authority in several directions at once. PROs would review many Medicare patients now missed—those serviced by HMOs—thus increasing the sheer volume of their work. They would review ambulatory services for the first time, rather than being restricted to the relatively limited and declining number of cases of inpatient care. And they would do reviews in "alternative" settings, in HMOs. This is a particularly interesting development. In the early 1970s, industry attempted to use HMOs to undermine traditional fee-for-service practice. At that time, industry favored HMOs precisely because they contained their own rational, administrative surveillance and rationing mechanisms and did not require external regulation, which would have been an expensive duplication of functions.

It is not surprising that this proposal to expand PRO functions was put forward by Thomas G. Dehn, M.D., president of the American Medical Peer Review Association (AMPRA), the trade association for PROs. It *is* somewhat surprising, however, that the task force for which Dehn is the spokesperson also includes the American Medical Care and Review Association (AMCRA), which represents independent practice associations, a type of HMO, and the Group Health Association of America (GHAA), which represents group- and staff-model HMOs.[15] Apparently, HMOs do not perceive review by PROs to be against their own interests.

These attempts to expand PRO functions have met with opposition from high places. Officially, the Reagan administration objected to this review on the grounds that it would cost too much. However, Andrew Webber, AMPRA executive vice-president, has another explanation for the administration's resistance; ideological opposition to peer review as an unnecessary intrusion into health care. "Their concern is that any mushrooming of reviews would make it difficult to reduce or eliminate the PRO program later on, which is what they really want to do," said Webber.[16]

Another explanation might be that neither public nor private peer review has been cost effective. This "intrusion" argument is shaky. Although the Reagan administration aimed at eliminating some government regulation, its concern to avoid intruding on the health care business did not cause it to oppose surveillance processes carried out by private utilization review firms in the interest of enhancing competitive practices. The other argument Webber makes—that the administration feared it would not be able to eliminate the program later—is more realistic. Everyone involved in restructuring the health care delivery system is acutely aware of how hard it is to eliminate or delegitimate interest groups that have entrenched themselves in existing power structures. Even the incentives of very powerful presidential administrations can be reversed when a new administration, with a different political agenda, comes to office.

Even with such powerful opposition, however, the PROs won this particular struggle; they are now empowered to review HMOs[17] and hospital outpatient care as well. A private peer review firm even monitors the quality of care provided in the U.S. military services.[18] The next step probably will be to expand peer review to physicians in their private offices, an undertaking of monumental scope that is now in its first stages.

In December 1989, the Wisconsin PRO began a two-year, $2.7 million pilot study designed to "find a way to measure the effectiveness of care that physicians provide in their offices."[19] Thus in response to a request from Congress in 1987 and funds from HCFA, the PROs have expanded their functions even further. Now they are charged with nothing less than demonstrating statistically whether Western medicine actually works.

This kind of review poses special problems, since the data that are required must come from physicians who, apparently, not only continue to practice medicine as an art but keep records that are undecipherable. One analyst explains:

> Quality judgments based on office records will pose some unique problems for PROs, because physician notations about medical treatments are as individual—or undecipherable—as the person who orders them. There are about 500,000 practicing physicians in the United States, said the American Medical Assn., Chicago. . . . To scale down the massive task, [the group] will review 43,000 Medicare physician office records.[20]

In situations such as this, one can probably expect to see some classic demonstrations of the "social construction of reality." That is, reviewers will be forced to construct categories under which to subsume these "individual" and "undecipherable" treatments, thus imposing some order on them.

The purpose of the Wisconsin study is supposed to be to add information to "outcomes research," which became a hot topic in health care surveillance circles during the late 1980s. Such data, finally, might legitimate the complete standardization of health care services, eliminating a great deal of beneficial hand holding as well as ritualistic rattle shaking in the process. Providers, of course, are likely to see it as just another cost-containment measure. *Modern Healthcare* reports: "Despite the program's emphasis on medical outcomes, PROs recognize that some physicians will view their latest review endeavor as another Medicare cost-containment scheme. 'Anything that PROs do will be seen as having some insidious cost implication,' Mr. Simmons [CEO of the Wisconsin PRO] said."[21]

The emergence of outcomes research suggests something much more insidious than cost consciousness, however. Considering that the process could simultaneously create new power and new knowledge to legitimate the surveillance experts themselves, it seems likely that they would favor such an undertaking whether or not it resulted in reduced costs in the long run.

In short, there is a conflict between the new experts who actually carry out peer review and those who hire them. Government's role in promoting peer review and, thus, in facilitating the emergence of a new group of experts, has been supportive and crucial over the long run but it has varied with political administrations. The challenge is to use a new group of experts to overthrow the old ones without creating a Frankenstein monster in the process. At least some providers believe that "scope-work creep" has been a deliberate strategy of the Reagan administration to "kill the PRO program by strangling PROs with additional duties." [22]

Although HCFA denies this charge, it is consistent with the kinds of strategies and tactics that corporate and government planners have used for twenty years in their attempts to replace fee-for-service physicians with those who are less autonomous. Now the same tactic might serve to keep the new experts in hand. In any event, in 1986 President Reagan was looking for ways to extricate government from involvement with the PROs by completely privatizing the system.[23] His dissatisfaction was not based simply on his antipathy for government regulation, however; the quality of health care had become a very thorny issue. At that time, critics of the DRG system complained that it had led to substandard care for Medicare patients, including both inadequate treatment and premature dismissals from hospitals. Ironically, the PROs were now charged with monitoring the quality of care in order to prevent the abuses that resulted from their own cost-cutting mechanisms. One analyst reported:

> A top-secret memorandum circulating within the Reagan administration contains serious reservations about the ability of Medicare's peer review organizations to identify cases of poor-quality care. The November 25 memorandum contradicts earlier assertions by administration officials that quality of care hasn't declined since the start of prospective pricing in 1983. The memorandum was sent to C. McClain Haddow, acting chief of the Health Care Financing Administration, by

Health and Human Services Inspector General Richard P. Kusserow. "Based on our preliminary findings, we are deeply troubled at the ineffectiveness of the existing procedures used by PROs to review cases of substandard care. . . . We believe that it is imperative that HCFA take strong action to place more emphasis on *PRO responsibilities for analyzing raw data* and taking corrective action where there are patterns of poor care" [he said].[24]

The PROs were being put in the same situation as were the old PSROs: they were being held responsible for collecting and analyzing raw data and setting the standards that would define the quality of care. Thus they increasingly incorporated some of the functions of the DRGs, simultaneously duplicating service and recombining mental and physical labor.

All observers seem to agree that there are major flaws in the PRO system. Not only does this kind of peer review strangle hospitals with administrative tasks; it also costs them millions of dollars in paperwork and personnel costs.[25] Clearly, exercising this kind of surveillance is very expensive, but the surveillance system itself does not seem to be in jeopardy. By 1990, the peer review units and the new "professionals" who run them were well institutionalized.

New Categories of Workers and Experts

Originally, the actual work of peer review was done by lower-level personnel, usually nurses, who made their judgments after examining the charts physicians kept for their patients. Nurses continue to do the actual work of review, assisted by clerical workers who enter data and copy and transport massive numbers of records. These new clerical and administrative job categories have expanded rapidly, as huge numbers of people are required to handle the increasing categories of things that must be added to the official records. This is the process through which surveillance becomes panoptic; it is spread out, dispersed, and fragmented. Like a factory assembly line, where no worker can recognize a product as his or her own, surveillance is divided into many different tasks. The heart of this process is to redefine and recreate the patient chart, transforming it from a working tool that simultaneously protects the authority of providers to a surveillance mechanism for bureaucratic managers.

Many new, high-status, and very highly paid occupations have emerged out of this process, along with groups of experts to fill them. Entirely new professions have been created, legitimated by the knowledge base created from the data that government and corporations require providers to collect. At the top of this group are the highly paid health care consultants and managers who sell their services to government, corporate consumers, and providers. These consultants provide their clients with techniques for outwitting the strategies of experts in the other groups. For example, one kind of advice that consultants have given hospitals is to avoid bankruptcy by managing their "case mix" effectively; that is, hospitals must attempt to recruit high-profit (relatively healthy) DRG patients and avoid low-profit (sicker) ones.[26]

Some of the new occupational groups work within the hospitals themselves. For example, when the government created the National Practitioner Data Bank to conduct outcomes research, it made "risk management" an occupational "rising star." Gary Kraus, attorney and director of quality assurance and risk management for the American Association of Nurse Anesthetists, has observed that government regulations "are going to propel this discipline into a full-fledged profession. It's going to be good for risk managers in terms of their individual practice," he explains, "but it's going to be more demanding on health care facilities."[27]

Once these new professions are created, their occupational incumbents are in a position to use the system to "professionalize" themselves even further. Ellen Barton, president of the American Society of Healthcare Risk Managers (ASHRM) in 1990, provides a textbook description of this professionalization process. As reported in *Hospitals*:

> Risk managers suffer from the lack of a consistent image.... This is partly because "risk managers have *a wide variety of backgrounds*." ... Some come from the legal field, others have a clinical background, and still others come from hospital administrative or insurance work. In addition, there is *no generally recognized certification* for health care risk managers.... ASHRM has been working with the Insurance Institute of America ... which developed the Associates in Risk Management program—*to create a curriculum for a more advanced designation*, similar to a CPA, for risk managers. This is needed *to*

standardize risk managers' qualifications, says Barton. A top priority of ASHRM has been *to develop model job descriptions* so that every risk-management job shares certain areas of responsibility. For instance, Barton says, ASHRM recommends that all risk managers play a role in risk-management financing decisions, such as purchasing insurance. "This begs the question, *does the person have the training to make this decision?*" Barton says. Creating a more advanced certification would answer this question. Another way that ASHRM is promoting professionalism is through *the creation of a code of ethics.* . . . Risk managers can give valuable insight on hospital ethics committee concerns.[28]

The process has worked like this: Public and private regulation created a need for a new category of workers. A diverse, untrained group of employees, utilizing a wide variety of disparate techniques, were empowered by the government to exercise authority over highly trained, high-status professionals. As part of that process, the untrained group became a new occupational elite. The group emerged, standardized its practices, developed a body of knowledge, and created a code of ethics. This is much like the processes through which medicine itself became a profession, and most other occupations as well. Interestingly, the inefficient "service ethic" that industry has attempted to exorcise from physician practice through accountability measures is now resurfacing within the new surveillance professions.

These new professionals are now in hot competition for control of the new data and processes that literally created them.

Risk managers disagree over what role they should play in the operation of the data bank. Some say a risk manager should be the hospital's primary person; others say risk managers should be secondary to medical staff in their involvement. "In larger institutions, we're seeing a lot of jockeying for power over this control," says Kraus. Vying for control are medical staff and quality assurance administrators, along with risk managers. The risk manager is the most logical choice in most institutions, Kraus asserts, [because] "the risk manager is usually the only one who tracks costs and outcomes of litigation."[29]

Once they are established, these new occupational groups can influence further developments in the transformation of health care delivery. For example, expansions of peer review functions described throughout this chapter were usually initiated upon the advice of one of the new groups of experts: health care consultants. It certainly is in their interest to continue to expand the surveillance system even further. Reflecting that fact, some health care consultants are recommending that their clients extend the review process to areas not covered by existing government programs, such as mental health and substance abuse programs and even "case management." This last category would not evaluate provider performance at all; instead, it would be a management function, aimed at coordinating the treatment received by employees insured through their jobs who have access to multiple health care providers.[30]

So, from being a system designed simply to police compliance with DRGs, utilization reviewers in both the private and public sectors have assumed impressive new functions. They create medical knowledge, dispense it to the public, educate physicians, and enforce "good medical practice." Now they claim to be competent to police the treatment of the most intractable of human disorders—behavioral problems—while simultaneously functioning as management coordination experts. Their position represents a formidable combination of occupational functions and power.

What qualifies utilization reviewers as professional experts who are competent to replace or advise research units, medical schools, medical societies, ethics committees, and other management personnel? That is an interesting question. A writer for the business-oriented *Journal of Compensation and Benefits* answers it like this: "There is no body of overseeing credentials in the utilization review industry, but a number of firms have developed the capability to audit the services of utilization review vendors."[31] It is interesting to reflect on the fact that industry originally legitimated its initiatives to transform health care delivery on the grounds that physicians were not accountable to anyone; did not really know enough about health, illness, or treatment to justify the autonomy they enjoyed; and made their decisions on the basis of their own economic self-interest rather than the welfare of their patients.

Despite the obvious problems of trying to use peer review organizations to collect data, construct medical knowledge, educate the public and physicians, and police providers in thousands of hospitals and hundreds of thousands of private offices, the system continues to expand. Circles of surveillance have continued to widen, not just within government bureaucracies but in private review organizations as well. *Modern Healthcare* reports:

In testimony before the Institute of Medicine on June 6 [1988], provider groups expressed frustration over inflexible standards used by private utilization review groups to control hospital admissions and physician services. The rapid growth of review groups has caused an "administrative nightmare" for hospitals, said Bruce McPherson, vice president of the American Hospital Assn., Chicago. "Many hospitals must respond to requests from as many as 50 different review organizations." Utilization review is "inappropriately used" by many review groups, he noted, which has prompted the AHA and other hospital groups "to seek national standards for private review organizations."[32]

Thus health care providers, under siege, are attempting to use the same strategies and even the same language that have been used against them, demanding that PROs be held "accountable" for using "appropriate" services and following universally accepted "standards" governing peer review functions and processes. Providers also have accused PROs of fraud and abuse. Two lawsuits in Georgia, for example, accuse the Aetna Casualty and Surety Company and State Farm Mutual Automobile Insurance of conspiring with an independent utilization review firm to deprive patients of services to which they are legally entitled. Documents filed in the Aetna case indicate the existence of a "conspiracy" going back to the early 1980s. The *Wall Street Journal* reported:

> The plan apparently set overall dollar amounts that local offices wanted their adjusters to save on medical claims. For instance, one performance report for an Aetna adjuster asked the employee to "contribute $17,000 per quarter"— apparently indicating she should weed out that much from claims under the plan. The next year, the same adjuster was asked to "save $100,000."[33]

Of course, these developments mean that a whole new set of professional standards will have to be created in order for PROs to comply with them, along with new surveillance and sanctioning mechanisms to enforce that compliance.

Surveillance and Sanctioning Power

To enforce compliance with their standards and rules, PROs have the power to use disciplinary actions against hospitals and physicians;

those powers have also increased with time. From the beginning, PROs could fine offending physicians; later they were empowered to bar them from treating Medicare patients at all. Later, as noted above, they could require physicians to undergo a "reeducation" process.

The extent to which sanctions are actually implemented, however, varies with political and economic circumstances. Nationwide, the use of sanctions against providers increased significantly within a short time period. In 1986, the *New York Times* reported that within the "last few months" PROs around the country had "started disciplinary proceedings against more than 1,100 doctors and hospitals . . . charging them with providing unnecessary or poor medical treatment." Although the *Times* said there had been a dramatic increase in such cases over previous years, PRO officials "say many cases may be dropped or resolved without formal action."[34]

The PROs can use another method for enforcing their standards: they can stir up adverse public opinion, in the most far-flung dispersal of surveillance that I have observed so far. First in a few states, then nationwide, PROs began to give the public access to raw data collected to evaluate the performance records of hospitals. As reported in 1988:

> The most familiar case in point was the 1986 release of hospital death rates by HCFA, using data that hadn't even been verified by the hospitals. That agency felt it had to yield to the tremendous pressure from the public and patient advocacy groups. With more care and caveats, HCFA released the information again in 1987, in spite of a general consensus among health care professionals that these numbers had no clear relevance to quality performance. As Dennis O'Leary, M.D., the president of the Joint Commission on Accreditation of Health care Organizations (JCAHO) put it, "The release of these data, which have no quality, is a negative distraction with little redeeming value."[35]

The publication of data such as these has required legal clarification, since it violates some of the traditional patient confidentiality rules that still exist, rules that providers tried very hard to maintain throughout the 1970s and early 1980s.[36] The confidentiality principle has not been upheld in court challenges, however, when hospitals have tried to prevent these statistics from being published. For example, in

January 1987, the West Virginia Supreme Court ruled that any peer review records that were used as a basis for disciplining physicians were public records and therefore open to public scrutiny. In doing so, claimed one analyst, "the state supreme court voided part of a law that made disclosure of peer review data held by the board illegal."[37]

In this case, the court granted the newspaper access only to peer review records that the board had used to arrive at a particular formal disciplinary action. It did not grant access to data describing a hospital's performance in general. But fear of public disapproval in such cases could still be a powerful sanctioning tool. As a result of this decision, Gil DeLaura, general counsel to the PRO, said he thought physicians might be more willing to listen to advice from the PRO committee because they feared peer review records going public at the board level. A few months later, the California PRO released raw, unanalyzed data that were even more comprehensive and specific. *Modern Healthcare* reported:

> California's peer review organization has released hospital-specific death rates for Medicare beneficiaries for most common diagnoses. Last month, California Medical Review, San Francisco, released death rates for each of the state's 543 hospitals. It also released statewide and regional averages. CMRI is the only PRO that has made this type of quality information available to the public, said Andrew Webber, executive vice president of the American Medical Peer Review Assn.... Reports on each hospital are available for $10.[38]

Here is another example of the process Foucault described. The exercise of power, which involves collecting data to ensure compliance with standards set in large part by the surveillance agency itself, and the creation of new kinds of "public knowledge" occur simultaneously and are, in fact, all part of the same process.

Of course, collecting and disseminating this "quality" information for the public is also expensive. It is not peculiar to California, either. According to Mark Epstein, executive director of the National Association of Health Data Organizations in Washington, thirty-five states now have laws that require public agencies to "collect and disseminate health care cost and quality information."[39] Because these requirements are new, it is impossible to assess how much they will cost, but they involve hospitals in a considerable investment. For example, in 1986 Pennsylvania passed a law requiring hospitals with more than one hundred beds to buy and use a computer software system called MedisGroups. It analyzes the hospital's performance, classifying its admissions by length of stay, severity of illness, charges for services, and both actual and expected mortality and morbidity rates. Pennsylvania legislators believe that public disclosure of such information, which began last year, will eventually reduce health care inflation as a result of "purchasers" having better information on which to base decisions. According to Donna Wegner, acting deputy secretary for quality assurance at Pennsylvania's Department of Health in Harrisburg, it is employers who want this data, although data about the quality of care that hospitals provide is higher on their agenda than cost. Wegner is a member of the state's cost-containment council, which was formed as part of the law's passage.[40]

Wegner's assessment is supported by the comments of Merill C. Horine, special programs director for human resources at Hershey Foods Corporation in Hershey, Pennsylvania. "I've got cost data coming out of my ears," he said, but what I don't know is whether a hospital "made the patient better, did nothing, made him worse or killed him."[41] Thus the quality-control function that these kinds of data actually can serve remains unclear. In a "free-market" health care system, most civilians probably will continue to evaluate the quality of the medical decisions a specific provider makes on the basis of how much he charges, just as we evaluate the quality of most other products. The only other alternative may be to go to medical school ourselves.

Nevertheless, in addition to releasing unanalyzed data to the public, the rules that govern PRO procedures can function to generate public disapproval in very direct ways. For example, since 1986 PROs have been empowered to deny Medicare payment for services rendered if they determine that the quality of care was substandard, but they must write a letter to the patient explaining why they withheld the payment.[42] This requirement is particularly threatening to providers, who fear it will increase malpractice suits. As Michael Rust, vice-president for finance at the Florida Hospital Association in Orlando, says, "If a patient receives a letter saying the care didn't meet industry standards, chances are the patient will call a lawyer."[43]

These rules could also cause problems for the PROs themselves by actually making it harder to sanction providers for delivering substandard care. As the likelihood of lawsuits increases, physician reviewers may be less willing to expose their peers by citing them for poor quality care. For the same reason, it might even be impossible to find enough physicians to do the reviews. In the worse case scenario, PROs might be sued by providers who are hit with malpractice suits as a result of PRO actions. According to Thomas Morford, director of the HCFA's Health Standards and Quality Bureau:

> Other provisions in the proposed rules may strain hospital–physician relations because they make hospitals financially responsible for poor physician care. Under the rules, a hospital wouldn't get paid if the treating physician provided substandard care. . . . However, some observers say the financial liability for physician errors *may be a small price to pay for increased leverage over physicians.*[44]

In extreme cases, physicians could be barred from treating Medicare patients. When PROs were actually given the power to sanction physicians for "gross and flagrant quality problems," outraged providers took their grievance to the courts.[45] But it was Congress that drastically curtailed the power of PROs to sanction physicians. In 1987 it passed a provision that required PROs to *prove* that the physician was " 'unwilling and unable' to change his behavior."[46] While it is fairly easy to demonstrate a lack of compliance with statistical standards, it is virtually impossible to prove the existence of a psychological state. As a result, there was a sharp decline in PRO recommendations for sanctions and fines against physicians. *Modern Healthcare* reported: "Information compiled by Public Citizen Health Research Group, using American Medical Assn. data, indicates PROs recommended seven sanctions midway through 1989, compared with 14 in 1988, 33 in 1987 and 49 in 1986. No fines—another disciplinary tool—have been levied in the past two years."[47]

According to Health and Human Services (HHS) Inspector General Richard Kusserow, this reduction in sanctions indicates that the congressional action has had a " 'chilling effect' on PROs' ability to discipline physicians, which has permanently crippled the program."[48] HHS originally hired Kusserow, a former Federal Bureau of Investigation (FBI) agent, in 1983 to launch what was, at the time, a new antifraud drive.[49] He provides a first-rate example of the new surveillance experts.

Controlling the New Surveillance Experts

It is not only providers and patients who are the targets of surveillance; PROs themselves are subjected to it, following all the best principles of scientific management. Observers of the regulatory process have often pointed out that regulators usually come to serve the interests of the organizations or industries they are charged with regulating. Government, of course, is intimately familiar with this process. HCFA has tried to ward it off in the case of peer review by keeping the PROs under surveillance, sanctioning them when their performance is insufficiently punitive. The most powerful sanction against a PRO is the threat of losing its government contract. In fact, this is not an uncommon occurrence; by 1989, ten PRO contracts had changed hands,[50] a fairly high number since there are only fifty-four of them. To win contract renewals, PROs must maintain a certain level of productivity, which is defined both by the percentage of cases they review and the number of sanctions they hand out to providers. For example, in 1985 the Pennsylvania PRO was threatened with loss of its contract because it reviewed only 7,755 Medicare cases between October 1984 and January 1985; HCFA expected it to review at least 42,000 records during that time.[51] This difference in productivity expectations is startling. In 1989 the Empire State Medical Scientific and Educational Foundation in New York lost its contract, at least in part because it sanctioned only three physicians during a four-year period.[52]

How many sanctions are enough? To answer that question, management must fall back on statistical averages of performance for PROs just as it does for providers. But this process raises a disturbing reality; just as there are individual variations in how physicians practice medicine, there are also large variations in the numbers of sanctions delivered by PROs in different states. A 1989 survey by the Health Standards and Quality Bureau showed that one PRO, out of thirteen surveyed, had done one-tenth of the reviews but turned in more than half of the "serious" violations, those with the potential to do actual harm to the patient. According to AMPRA's William Moncrief, M.D., there should not be that much difference. In fact, "If the program is implemented the same, we should find the same percentage of variations [from quality standards] across the country."[53]

Gregg Simmons, chief executive officer of Wisconsin's PRO, says these variations are "troublesome" because they cause "political problems." He attributes them to the fact that "some PROs don't take the quality assurance aspect [of their job] as seriously as others."[54] Variations in the rates at which PROs sanction providers is a matter of great concern for HCFA, whose officials assume that it actually reflects differences in the "quality" of the work done by the PROs themselves, not real differences in the hospitals they review. Thus, HCFA defines "quality" as conformance with statistical standards, whether it is physicians or peer reviewers who are being evaluated.

Providers interpret the statistics very differently. They claim the DRG system is insufficiently sensitive to the severity of patients' illnesses, which providers say is actually what accounts for most variations in treatment norms. As a result, PROs are also insensitive to the differences between hospitals. They are forced, as one analyst explains, to "apply the same levels of review for high-quality hospitals and physicians as for those with quality problems."[55] For years, hospitals have tried to get HCFA to decrease review requirements for hospitals that have long records of high-quality care in order to ease their paperwork burdens, thereby rewarding compliance with standards. HCFA has been unwilling to do so.[56]

Thus PROs are in an extremely difficult position. They are not allowed to recognize differences that actually exist between hospitals but are forced to see differences in terms of statistical averages. The fact that there are wide variations in the numbers of sanctions PROs hand out may indicate that their ability to see hospitals in those terms is, as yet, imperfect.

Aside from real variations in the quality of care delivered in different hospitals, another important reason for the differences in PROs' sanctioning rates is that physicians continue to make very different kinds of professional judgments. Despite all the data collection that has been done over the last twenty years and the emergence of statistically based reimbursement patterns, actual practices in medicine have not yet been standardized. The tool experts claim will do this job, "outcomes research," is in its infancy in terms of telling either physicians or reviewers what is "good medical practice." *Modern Healthcare* reports:

> More uniformity in PRO judgments may not be possible until effectiveness research catches up with the quality calls reviewers need to make, said Alice Gosfield, a Philadelphia attorney who has represented hospi-

tals and practitioners in dealing with peer review since 1972. Until PROs have better experience with outcomes, some quality judgments "will continue to be elusive," she said.[57]

Thus, even after years of data collection, PROs are in the same situation as were the early PSROs. They must enforce treatment proscriptions without any real evidence that they reflect "good medical practices."

And HCFA, in turn, must attempt to enforce quality control among the PROs themselves. To do that, an agent is needed to collect and analyze data describing PRO performance. For that purpose, HCFA established yet another level of surveillance, the "super-PRO." *Modern Healthcare* reports: "SysteMetrics Inc., Santa Barbara, CA has been awarded a 14-month, $2 million contract to evaluate peer review organizations. . . . The firm already has contacted some of the 54 PROs with Medicare contracts to begin collecting the information it will need to function as a 'Super-PRO.' "[58] The super-PRO creates the same kinds of problems for PROs that PROs create for providers; it increases both their workload and their costs of doing business. Paul Osborne, executive vice-president of the Kentucky Peer Review Organization, explains that the typical PRO "must bounce back and forth between hospitals and the SuperPRO" to assemble the records needed by the super-PRO. "We've had two staff members and a secretary working full time on the SuperPRO for the past four months." Moreover, PROs are expected to pay hospitals for records that the super-PRO requires.[59]

Finally, one more layer of surveillance must be added to make this description complete. The General Accounting Office (GAO), the investigative unit for Congress, also exercises surveillance over health care spending. It uses data collected by the super-PRO to watch both the PROs *and* HCFA, to ensure that they are achieving maximum savings. *Modern Healthcare* observes:

> Hospitals may be providing more inappropriate medical care than Medicare peer review organizations are uncovering, a new General Accounting Office report said. Between 1986 and 1988, PROs denied 2.1 percent of Medicare admissions on the grounds that hospitalization was unnecessary. But random case samples examined by the "super PRO," a separate reviewer that contracts with the Healthcare Financing Admin-

istration to check the work of the PROs, questioned the appropriateness of 12 percent of admissions, the GAO said. . . . To reduce the level of inappropriate hospitalization, the GAO recommended that PROs be required to conduct *more prior reviews* of Medicare cases. It also said HCFA should consider getting *"advisory"* review decisions, a practice used in the private sector, that warns physicians of a payer's intent not to cover a service.[60]

The Costs of Review

Of course, all this scrutiny is expensive, both for HCFA and for those being reviewed. HCFA had a budget of $300 million a year for the program in 1990, up from $150 million in 1984.[61] Estimates of how much review costs hospitals vary, depending on which interest group does the calculation. For example, HCFA says meeting the requirements of Medicare peer review cost hospitals about $4.3 million in 1985; the American Hospital Association says it costs more than $75 million a year.[62]

Which figure is closer to "reality"? Sidney Marchasin, an internist and vice-president of the board of directors of Sequoia Hospital in the San Francisco Bay area, describes the cost of regulation in his hospital with a thoroughness that deserves quoting at length.

> The average number of inpatients today is the same as it was in 1966. The staff is about 175 percent the size it was then. Some of the rise is because the number of outpatients has grown. Some of it is because patients need more intense care than they did then—the hospitalized are sicker because government regulations prohibit admitting many patients at the point they used to enter the hospital. Much of it, though, is due to new requirements of government. To comply with the string of regulations and government directives requires a staff of 140 full-time employees. . . . The federal government insists that medical care be continually assessed and audited for quality and appropriateness. At Sequoia, four full-time employees and one part-timer spend all their time reviewing patient records. Nine or 10 employees appraise the appropriateness of hospitalization. The Federal Peer Review Act mandates that all hospital work paid for by the government be reviewed by an independent agency under contract to the Health Care Financing Administration. Providing duplicate hospital records, lab reports, X-ray data and billing information to outside "peer review agencies" is an

enormous task requiring 20 additional staffers. As for Medicare funds, to get those the hospital must undergo a third audit, by the Joint Commission on Accreditation of Health Care Organizations. Each auditing agency issues directives, generating multiple forms that must be filled out by nurses, hospital pharmacists, record-room personnel and doctors. To lighten the paperwork load for practicing physicians, the hospital has added four people to its medical staff office. The government forms require formatting by three data processors. Paper work also eats away at nurses' time. If Sequoia's experience is typical—and there's no reason to suspect it is not—health-care regulatory costs nationwide measure in the billions of dollars.[63]

It is certainly true that the process has created an enormous cost burden for hospitals. The fact that PROs have used bureaucratic procedures, called "transmittals," to shift their own costs to hospitals has added to the burden. In order to cut their costs, while still meeting HCFA's requirements that they review 20 percent of hospital inpatient cases, PROs have required hospitals to copy and transport patient records to their offices so they can do reviews inhouse. In 1985, the American Hospital Association sued Health and Human Services, "claiming the department violated the Administrative Procedures Act by issuing PRO transmittals and directives informally rather than through the public rulemaking process."[64]

In 1986 the use of transmittals resulted in another court case in Wisconsin, where seventeen hospitals joined ranks to sue the Wisconsin PRO and HHS as well, although the Reagan administration denied that the federal district court had jurisdiction to try the lawsuit.[65] In this case, the hospitals charged that the HHS regulation requiring them to provide photocopies of medical records "violates the law governing Medicare's prospective pricing system."[66] The hospitals charged that, in passing these costs on to the hospitals, HHS was in fact passing them on to non-Medicare patients, which is illegal. *Hospitals* reported:

> HHS violated a ban on shifting Medicare administrative costs to non-Medicare patients. This cost shifting occurs because "providers are forced to incur costs in complying with the PRO's request for photocopies that will ultimately be borne by non-Medicare patients through the mechanism of higher charges for medical services rendered," the complaint said.[67]

Andrew Webber, executive vice-president of the American Medical Peer Review Association, which represents PROs, acknowledges that the hospitals have a "legitimate" complaint. He believes the lawsuit "reflects the frustration of the hospital industry and the fact that PROs themselves are under the gun financially."[68] This appears to be an accurate assessment. However, the Wisconsin PRO's cost-shifting maneuver "could cost the state's hospitals as much as $1 million a year in extra photocopying, labor and shipping costs."[69] In October 1986 the U.S. District Court in Madison nullified the PRO's requirement that hospitals provide free copies of medical records. The ruling was expected to result in a flood of lawsuits in many other states, since these rules are supposed to be applied nationwide.[70]

All these regulatory requirements add to the cost of health care each year, although they have not been adequately analyzed in discussions about health care reform. They are disguised, hidden behind the euphemism "administrative costs," and attributed to some inherent flaw in bureaucratic organization rather than to deliberate political policy. Meanwhile, the costs are constantly and silently shifted and dispersed throughout the system.

Of course, cost shifting has always been an inherent feature of "free-market mechanisms" and other phantasmagoria dear to the hearts of corporate strategists. Currently, it is practiced in extremely creative ways by many different groups. Industry itself, for at least fifty years, has used the practice most effectively, and in ways that have been the most destructive to our national health care delivery system. For example, industry has reduced its own health insurance costs by insisting that insurance companies use experience-rating. By shifting costs, industry has avoided paying its full share of real health care costs, which includes the maintenance of the health care delivery apparatus. More important, the strategy has destroyed the underlying rationale of insurance itself—shared risk. Part of the problem the country faces today is the task of reinventing it. Of course corporate strategists do not agree with this view, since shared risk is antithetical to the competitive ideology. Rather than sharing risk, the objective is to provide a multiclass system in which people get the health services they are able to pay for, not the services that are related to their physical conditions. Cost shifting is now a fact of life in every area of health care delivery, although, ultimately, all costs are pushed back on the general public.

Clearly, copying and transporting patient records created an enormous expense for hospitals. The economic realities of the process are instructive. Presumably, it would be less expensive, overall, for reviewers to travel to hospitals and review the massive numbers of records involved than for the hospital to duplicate and transport them. Certainly, the real costs involved could not have been reduced significantly; they have only been shifted around. Thus, when "management" pressures PROs to do "more for less," the result may very well be an increase in overall costs, even though the PRO itself may appear to have improved its "productivity." The DRG system provides a more complicated example of the same principle of control that is involved with transmittals. It effectively rations services without changing the laws that guarantee health care services to Medicare patients.

The peer review program is well entrenched and institutionalized; even court rulings favorable to providers would not eliminate it. But the courts could issue orders forcing HCFA to comply with the Administrative Procedures Act in the future, following formal procedures for changing organizational practices. If so, providers would, for the first time, have the opportunity to make their own comments about the goals and objectives of peer review. That, of course, would mean that the entire surveillance and control apparatus would be unable to maintain any pretense that it is effective. It could still be extremely difficult to dismantle, just as the control apparatus of traditional providers has been. In the meantime, these kinds of legal contests to settle power struggles between contenders can also be included in the price we pay for health care in America.

The Effectiveness of Review

Has peer review achieved any positive goals? It certainly has resulted in a loss of status and power by physicians, although they continue to enjoy more of both than do most workers. And, following the logic of corporate and government strategists, there is some evidence that it has reduced the utilization of inpatient services. In 1984, 11.5 million people over age sixty-five were admitted to hospitals; in 1988, 11 million were, a decrease of half a million admissions. But outpatient services increased enormously during the same period. In 1984, patients over age sixty-five utilized 232 million outpatient visits; in 1988, they utilized 295 million, an increase of 62 million visits.[71] Thus a large portion of the costs was merely shifted from one treatment modality to another. In addition, the patients who *were* admitted to hospitals were sicker in 1988 than they were in 1984; thus their care could be expected to cost more. If it did not, given health care cost inflation, one suspects that could only have been because the DRG system forced providers to deliver inadequate levels of care.

It is not clear that these shifts in utilization modes and reduced services actually have lowered the cost of services for Medicare patients. For example, the number of disallowed Medicare claims increased from 3 percent to 10.6 percent in New York after the PRO took over, a finding that *could* force hospitals to return $80 million to the public coffers,[72] however, these hospitals have challenged the adverse rulings. Some hospitals have taken their PROs to court and won their cases on the grounds that the adverse decisions were based on incomplete medical records that the hospitals submitted when they were still in the process of learning exactly what was required.[73]

In this particular case the process may never pay off, since the missing material actually can be supplied and the courts' decisions can then be reversed. Since the PROs have caused providers to keep much more detailed records, this technique for cutting costs would not work a second time, because even if the records indicate that the hospitals had committed real violations in the past, the sanctions will have accomplished their goal—getting providers to change the services they deliver. In that case, surveillance will have been successfully dispersed, controls will have been institutionalized and internalized, and the expensive surveillance system should no longer be required. At that point, another transformation movement would have to be mounted to get rid of the structures and occupations created by the first transformation. It seems unlikely that this problem will arise, however, since the ideology of accountability literally mandates the continued existence of a surveillance system.

According to both academic studies and the "infomedia," peer review has not been effective in cutting health care costs. HCFA reports that, since the DRG system was implemented in 1984, "the overall audit impact was small, typically only a fraction of 1 percent."[74] The media directed toward providers tell the same story about the utilization review that is carried out for privately funded patients. It has not turned out to be "the 'silver bullet' that employers are seeking to shoot down fast-rising health care costs."[75]

But, aside from its failure to cut costs, review has also had a serious negative side effect. It has lowered the quality of the health care that is delivered to many Americans.

Quality and Regulation

For several years now, evidence has accumulated that quality of care is a growing problem in our health care delivery system. Media reports reflect this reality and indicate that the next move is to use government to try to ensure quality as well as to control costs. For example, the Institute of Medicine, a branch of the National Academy of Sciences, issued a report in 1990 calling on Congress to overhaul the PRO program to emphasize quality assurance instead of cost containment. The report also calls on Congress to double the annual PRO budget, which was $300 million at that time. The PROs should be renamed; henceforth, they should be called "quality review organizations, or QROs. They would use outcomes data to make judgments about providers' performance."[76]

Contemporary peer reviewers also want to utilize their own kind of expertise to improve medical practice; they would establish "algorithms and decision trees" for providers to follow. Writers for *Business and Health* urge the following:

> Physicians and utilization review (UR) professionals must work together to solve the health care crisis. A rule book should be developed indicating when certain procedures, tests, or drugs should be given. [The goal of a good UR] should also be the rationalization of health care. Medical decisions should be based upon what has worked statistically. . . . The UR rule book should contain medically acceptable algorithms and decision trees.[77]

Many providers, then, believe that cost cutting has lowered the clinical quality of care. What impact, if any, does government regulation itself have? Apparently, the impact is negative. During the late 1980s, studies began to surface linking high levels of regulation with a low quality of care. For example, Stephen Shortell and Edward Hughes published a study in the *New England Journal of Medicine* that correlated HMO market penetration and stringent state regulations with higher inpatient mortality rates.[78] One commentator observed:

The study suggests that quality may be suffering in the name of cost containment. "It's a new awakening in the health policy establishment, that maybe we've gone too far in controlling costs," Hughes says. . . . But eliminating regulation is not the answer, Shortell says. "We expect the main effect of the study will be to call greater attention to the need to monitor patient outcome."[79]

In addition to the managerial controls of HMOs, the kinds of regulation to which Shortell and Hughes referred were certificate-of-need programs and utilization review rates that are required of peer review organizations. Where CON laws were highly stringent, the mortality rate was 106 percent of the expected rate; where they were not, the rate was 90 percent. Where utilization rate reviews were highly stringent, mortality was 104 percent of the predicted rate; where they were not, mortality was 98 percent.[80] Of course, these regulations were only doing what they were designed to do—decreasing health care services utilization. They were not created to improve the quality of care, although their advocates claimed, without evidence, that they would do just that. Now Shortell and Hughes, among others, are calling for a kind of regulation that will ensure a high standard of clinical outcomes. Of course, if that call is answered, we will have to create and legitimate another technique for rationing health care services.

Summary

Although almost everyone is aware that "administrative costs" make up a huge percentage of what we pay for health care delivery, few analysts have attributed those costs to the bloated, self-reproducing, complex, and alienating surveillance systems that make up the most important part of what administrative systems do in America, whether they belong to government or to capitalist enterprises.

When government dissolved the original PSRO system, it did not eliminate the cost of peer review. All this regulation, both formal and informal, costs a lot of money because, whether it is public or private, it requires extraordinarily extensive surveillance on rapidly reproducing levels. Every time a new surveillance apparatus is established, a new one has to emerge to watch *it*.

Foucault points out that, because surveillance is so expensive, it cannot survive unless its functions are diffused into many informal social practices. In that way, although the intensity of surveillance actually is increased, its costs are decreased. This model does not describe events that have occurred in the transformation of American health care delivery. Both surveillance and its costs continue to increase; they continue to be part of the cost of health care services in this country.

How well have these control mechanisms worked to achieve industry's other goals, those unrelated to cost control? In terms of the sheer *mechanics* involved, strategists were correct in assuming that peer review, particularly when it is coupled with the DRG billing process, would lead to both lower professional status and lower hospital utilization rates. Why did not these outcomes result in lower health care costs, as predicted?

Several factors probably account for that failure. First, peer review itself is an extremely expensive process, both to implement and to maintain. During the last decade, it has come to be even more costly because, throughout the 1980s, it led to the emergence of whole new industries, along with expensive professional "experts" to staff them. In addition, the areas over which peer review must exercise surveillance have expanded continuously. At this point, rather than overutilizing health care services, we are overutilizing administrative surveillance.

Second, hospital utilization has decreased only very slightly, while outpatient utilization has increased significantly.

Third, the control mechanisms were focused on the wrong problem in the first place. As a 1977 HEW status report to Congress pointed out, overutilization is only a secondary cause of health care inflation.[81]

A fourth, and probably more important, explanation for the increase in health care costs may be that the commodification of health care services inevitably creates cost inflation that we all must pay for. Under this kind of commodification, creating and marketing the "sexiest" products to the most affluent "consumers" may inevitably result in a proliferation of products that are extremely profitable to drug and medical equipment manufacturers but that do nothing to improve our health statistics. But that is a topic for a different discussion.

The primary goal of peer review was to take control of the system itself, not simply control of their own work, out of the hands of physicians. Clearly, corporate strategists understood the power of surveillance to accomplish that goal. The restructured system would be run by efficient managers who would not have incentives to deliver unnecessary services, as physicians do; for that reason, health care costs would go down. This analysis did not account for the tendency of bureaucrats, whether they work in the public or the private sector, to create increasing functions and power for themselves. Nor did it include the high cost of extensive administrative surveillance that, actually, is designed to accomplish broad, societal goals; its function is far more complex than controlling one specific institution.

Some contemporary analysts argue, from a great deal of data, that overutilization is no more the cause of our health care cost "crisis" today than it was in the 1970s; some even argue there is no cost crisis.[82] Others seem to believe in the validity of part of the scenario that was established by industry in the 1970s, although not all of it. For example, Donald F. Beck and Jack Dempsey, noting that people continue to use medical services even when they are made to pay more for them through co-insurance and deductibles, believe that this behavior will change in the future. They believe that introducing "scientific rationality" into medical practice, rather than allowing physicians to continue practicing it as an "art," will cause physicians to lose even more status. This loss of status will lead to decreased utilization and, finally, less willingness by patients to pay for care. However, they do not believe scientific rationality will lead to lower health care costs. Health care will be even more expensive to deliver as a science than as an art; there will just be "far fewer mistakes."[83] Thus, in their view, the transformation of health care is desirable not to cut costs but to improve the quality of care.

As surveillance over providers yielded increasing amounts of data during the 1970s, regulators quickly thought of new ways to use them. In fact, they demanded more and different kinds of information than even the DRG system originally had required hospitals to collect. Today, hospitals must invest in expensive computer systems, and the personnel required to use them, in order to comply with demands for information, not just from government bureaucrats but from private regulators as well.

All these data have been used both to control professional workers and to create a new knowledge base that continues to legitimate corporate strategies. Simultaneously, it justifies bureaucratic surveillance and redefines the DRG proscriptions as an ongoing process, spelling out what goods and services providers can deliver. Thus providers under DRG surveillance collect data that function to legitimate and intensify the surveillance while simultaneously creating a new body of medical knowledge controlled by a different group of experts.

This is a classic example of the process Foucault describes, in which the exercise of power generates new knowledge that serves the interests of those who exercise the power. Therefore, it is not surprising that all these developments have been accompanied by power struggles among various groups including not only the original players—industry, government, and providers—but all the new occupational experts that have emerged as part of the ongoing process.

The new bureaucratic organizations and management techniques that have been discussed so far are components of the "new" system of private regulation that now dominates discussions of health care reform. The next chapter will describe contemporary attempts of the new experts to "manage" the cost of health care in America.

4
Managing Health Care Costs

> Quality is overrated. . . . People by and large are not buy-
> ing quality. People are buying price.
> —*Joel I. Shalowitz, Northwestern University*[1]

It is clear that there has been a real revolution in health care power arrangements during the last twenty years. Despite all the talk about the power of providers as an "interest group," physicians have been unable to stop the historical transformation that their profession is undergoing. As *Modern Healthcare* has said, "Managed care systems will grow as the health care industry consolidates and as power shifts from providers to the purchasers of care."[2] Of course, the term "purchasers" means corporate employers and, to a lesser extent, government bureaucracies—not the American public.

All these management plans will continue to cause increases in both administrative functions and health care costs, since a major function of managed care is to expand utilization review to services delivered to every kind of patient in every delivery setting, either in or out of hospital. Like indemnity insurance before them, managed care systems contribute to health care costs as part of the ongoing process of shifting these costs around. However, unlike the old indemnity system, which shifted costs from big business to small business, from consumer group to consumer group, and from business to government, managed care is increasingly used to shift the costs of health care away from corporate America and government altogether, back onto workers

themselves. That goal is clearly stated in some media descriptions of what managed competition is designed to do. For example, Alex. Brown and Sons, a Baltimore-based brokerage firm, predicts that "HMOs, preferred provider arrangements and strong utilization review programs will complement employers' efforts to shift more of the burden of health care costs to their workers."[3] For corporate employers, this is very good news.

Clearly, the social control mechanisms contained in managed care strategies transcend either purely managerial or medical functions; they work to maintain corporate control over the entire health care institution and to enforce new kinds of health care policy making, especially policies that determine who should pay for health care services. Thus corporate America aspires to control the system without having to pay for it. Corporations control the details of health care management in some fascinating ways; often, their principles and policies are indistinguishable from those of governments. The managed care plan that aerospace giant Martin Marietta began offering its employees in 1989 provides an instructive example.

Martin Marietta's plan requires employees who keep their traditional indemnity insurance coverage to pay a deductible that is 0.5 percent of their wage. In addition, they pay 20 percent of their medical costs, up to a limit of 5 percent of their salary. After they reach that point, the company pays all additional expenses. The company's chief executive officer, Norman Augustine, says, "This way those who can afford to pay more, pay more. . . . Coverage for catastrophic illness should be superb; as to sniffles and scratches, employees are on their own."[4] Thus during the 1980s, a period when the federal government adopted increasingly conservative policies, including a tax "reform" that favored the wealthiest Americans, Martin Marietta developed a managed care program that is based on some of the same principles as the progressive, graduated income tax.

Management strategists aim their cost-containment measures at a wide range of targets, including "insurance" beneficiaries, patients actually receiving care, and providers; all these groups are manipulated into trading their control and freedom over health care choices for economic benefits, at least in the short run. Specifically, workers who choose the cost-cutting plans management desires get lower premium prices, at least for as long as they do not get sick; providers who work within those plans get more patients, although at a lower price per head. Thus these "free-market" mechanisms function to institutionalize a level of private control that competition ideologues have insisted the American public would not accept from a national health care service. And they are doing so in complete freedom from bothersome, democratic processes.

The managed care systems some experts envision are massive in scope. For example, some observers envision national oversight programs through which unrelated, even competing, HMOs can be organized and controlled. The Xerox Corporation and the Kaiser Permanente HMO in Oakland, California, have been working together to develop such a national managed care program. As a result of such activities, many observers expect that a number of "strong, regional managed-care systems" will have emerged by the turn of the century.[5] This model is reminiscent of the network of massive HMOs that Paul M. Ellwood envisioned in the early 1970s.

Government, at both state and federal levels, also uses managed care systems in an attempt to cut costs through "behavior modification" strategies. For example, the National Governors' Association staff says that "managed care strategies are designed to promote the cost-effective use of health services by modifying the behavior of both providers and patients."[6]

Providers have responded to pressures from business and government by promoting their own managed care strategies. In particular, hospitals are now using far more consulting services. According to a 1988 survey, consulting firms increased their completed consulting projects at hospitals by 35 percent in 1987.[7] This is the same process that occurred in the 1970s, when physicians began fighting the incursion of HMOs into their traditional practices by joining independent practice association HMOs.

That process worked like this: shortly after the Health Maintenance Organization Act was passed in 1973, supporters of HMOs realized that these "alternative" treatment modalities had a serious economic drawback; they were extremely expensive to start up.[8] Independent practice associations (IPAs) were invented then, precisely because they provided a way to eliminate high start-up costs. In the IPA-model HMOs, physicians used their already existing facilities and equipment to serve both their regular patients and their new HMO members. Of course, this process shifts health care costs away from the corporate employers who buy the HMO coverage for their employees, allowing those purchasers to ride piggyback on the physical plant that is paid for by non-HMO patients. Thus, health care providers gave private subsidies to employers, allowing them to shift part of their real HMO costs onto others. This process is similar to those through which traditional indemnity insurance shifts costs away from the largest corporate customers—experience-rating, special "volume" rates, and, most recently, the practice of "discounting." Thus, from the very beginning these new IPAs also manipulated providers into subsidizing the very "alternative practices" that reduced their own power and autonomy.[9]

The transformation of health care organization that began twenty years ago is still far from complete; some experts believe it will continue for another decade. For example, James Lee, a consultant for the technology and management firm Arthur D. Little, says that managed health care itself "is undergoing a massive transformation. We can expect this roller coaster ride to continue, perhaps for the rest of the century."[10]

Very specifically, what do these managed care systems consist of? For one thing, they offer a wide range of choices, at least for health care "elites." Peter Fox, vice president of Lewin and Associates, describes the broader set of "product lines" that is "evolving" within the HMO industry. Typically, these products include three kinds of coverage that beneficiaries can choose from: managed indemnity insurance plans; HMO membership; and preferred provider organization (PPO) coverage.[11] This simple practice, offering a range of "choices," is called by various complicated names, including "point-of-service," "triple-option," "multiple-option," "self-referral option," or "open-ended" products. The jargon expands in direct proportion to the new expert occupations the system spawns, making the process appear to be far more technical than it is. For clarity, I will refer to these products as multiple-option plans.

Under one roof, these plans offer beneficiaries access to a variety of products, including indemnity insurance, fee-for-service medical practices, and HMO eligibility. The plans began to develop as it became increasingly clear that the market for "traditional" HMOs was limited. Presumably, the experts believed that was precisely because they did not offer choices, since choice is what they added to the pot to make it more attractive.

Apparently, these alternative structures have never been very popular; if they were, more people would have enrolled in them willingly, without being subjected to such extensive, and expensive, manipulation. Finally, managed care systems have been forced to offer the same options as do traditional providers to enable HMOs and all their hybrids to survive economically.

Ironically, the options offered by managed care systems are probably one result of the war that corporate America launched against socialized medicine in the 1970s. At that time, industry collaborated with provider interest groups to make "choice" a major selling point to divert the public from dreams of health care services that were universal and free. Throughout the 1980s, both the Reagan and Bush administrations continued to praise these "free-market" alternatives, contrasting them with the specter of "rationing." Now, having made such a point of it, health care managers must deliver what they promised: choices. At least they must appear to do so; in reality, those choices must remain more illusory than real. If managed care plans are to survive economically, they must create incentives that will prevent all but the most affluent of patients from actually exercising choice.

The National Governors' Association staff has described this reality clearly. The staff supports the multiple-option plans that do offer beneficiaries a variety choices, but at very different prices. These plans are designed to "encourage" enrollees to obtain care through "provider networks," the form of health care delivery that the managers want beneficiaries to choose because they ration patient access to services in the most stringent way, just as the old, traditional HMOs were supposed to do. According to the staff, "The stronger the incentive for individuals to access the network, the more effective the managed plan will be in containing costs."[12] Those new, economic, incentives substitute to some extent for the rationing mechanisms that are built into the organizational structure of HMOs. They help perpetuate the idea that people "choose" the level of coverage they "want," concealing the reality that they could not afford to choose anything else.

Thus, even though they are touted as the wave of the future, even with all their sophisticated managerial manipulation, and even with powerful support from corporate America and government, managed care might not survive economically. According to the experts, making a profit out of health care benefits, while simultaneously cutting costs, is virtually impossible. For example, Gerald McManis, president of McManis Associates, believes that health care management firms are not likely to make a profit unless they also market other financial services and products. He says, "It's a fallacy that you can make a profit out of group health coverage alone."[13] This is a fascinating assessment. It says, in effect, that managed care companies must shift the deficits that their health care plans are bound to produce onto one of their other products, one that actually is profitable, just as IPA-HMOs shift the costs of their HMO patients to non-HMO members. The question is, What would motivate managed care firms to offer health care products under those conditions?

The major flaw in the new multiple-option plans is, of course, that they reintroduce precisely the element of uncertainty, of risk, that makes it impossible for HMOs to make accurate, and low, cost estimates. As a result, the new plans have actually begun to reinvent the structures and, therefore, the problems characteristic of the old, traditional health care system.

For example, insurance regulators in 1991 began to recommend that the multiple-option plans be required to "put up larger cash reserves to offset any possible financial losses that would result in insolvency."[14] Although the regulators debated whether to add the deposit requirement to the HMO act that already existed, they chose not to do so "because that would imply that they approved of the point-of-service concept."[15] Apparently, these regulators understood that through the policies they made to govern insurance reserve funds, they could create a resurgence of indemnity insurance within managed care systems themselves.

In any event, they have already reestablished one of the disadvantages of indemnity insurance that the early HMOs eliminated; it has become necessary for HMOs to keep large cash reserves on hand, just as indemnity insurance carriers must do.

According to Seth H. Shaw, a health care analyst at Prudential-Bache Securities in New York, by the late 1980s HMOs had begun to adopt other characteristics of indemnity insurance as well. For example, HMO rate hikes were 17 percent in 1989, which almost matched increases in indemnity premiums. As a result, Shaw predicted, corporate consumers may become so discouraged by spiraling health care costs that they actually press lawmakers to pass a national health insurance plan.[16] By 1991, a *Fortune* magazine poll of 197 chief executive officers indicated that 24 percent of them did favor such a plan.[17]

HMOs are adopting the practices of indemnity insurers as well as their prices; for example, HMO capitation fees are increasingly based on experience-rating. As a result, today HMOs must collect extensive, and expensive, data to convince employers that there is an experiential basis for the rates they charge. According to Joel I. Shalowitz, director of hospital and health services administration at Northwestern University, employers "want experience-rated premiums. They want to pay for what they are getting."[18] Thus just as corporate employers destroyed the practice of shared risk in the traditional insurance industry, they have done so in HMOs as well.

Clearly, the "new" product lines sold by managed care plans include many components of the old, traditional, indemnity-driven medical practices that HMOs were promoted to replace in the 1970s. For twenty years HMOs helped to weaken traditional choices such as indemnity insurance and fee-for-service practice. Now, managed care companies are selling those choices back to us as new product lines. The major difference between the old and the new products is that the new one is controlled not by providers but by the experts who represent corporate and government employers.

Like HMOs, the insurance industry has changed enormously in response to economic and political pressures. In the 1970s, in response to corporate demands and manipulation, it began to perform more purely administrative and fewer risk-sharing functions. In the 1980s, the industry began to offer a much broader range of product lines; it even began to sell HMO coverage. Thus HMOs offer indemnity insurance, while indemnity insurance carriers offer HMOs. And, like HMOs, indemnity insurance carriers did these things in response to pressure from corporate employers.

Ironically, as costs continued to escalate, more and more employers began to go around *both* insurance carriers and HMOs; now employers often deal directly with providers, cutting out the middleman altogether. This process became very common during the 1980s, as corporate employers contracted directly with hospitals and medical groups to deliver preferred provider organization (PPO) services to their own employees.

By 1992, the practice of "consumers" dealing directly with providers was becoming increasingly institutionalized. These consumers are, of course, corporate employers, not patients. By 1992, the Buyers Health Care Cooperative, which formed in 1988, had grown to include four hundred employers with 380,000 employees. The cooperative uses a computer software system to analyze hospital charges; on the basis of that analysis, it contracts directly with hospitals to cover its members.[19]

This process is giving some power back to providers, although in a crucially altered form. Experts in "strategic planning" now predict that it is providers who will be best situated to create new innovations in managed care during the 1990s. Jim Souders, divisional vice-president of managed care services at SunHealth Alliance in North Carolina says, "You're going to continue to see large employers and providers look at ways to get closer together—and cut out the middleman."[20] According to Robert Blendon, who chairs the Department of Health Policy and Management at the Harvard School of Public Health, "Ultimately, people are going to look for capitated arrangements between employers and groups of hospitals—modified HMOs. . . . But we're not near that yet."[21]

One reason for this elimination of the middleman is the enormous administrative cost associated with managed care, of which even managed care advocates are well aware. *Trustee* reports:

> Large administrative costs negate much of the savings that HMOs and PPOs generate through aggressive contracting and medical cost controls, experts say. "Managed care requires a big administrative staff at the plan, plus it requires hospitals to add a number of managers," Blendon says. "There's been a big increase in administrative costs at these plans."[22]

Thus Diane Milikan, senior manager at Ernst and Young in Chicago, says, "I think that more direct relationships between employers and providers are going to be the wave of the future. . . . They'll minimize that administrative cost."[23]

In this latest scenario, providers will have a "new role," since both corporate employers and the federal government are driving the new "push toward provider-based managed care."[24] One result will probably be that some of the close links that existed between hospital administrators and physicians before industry launched its initiatives in the 1970s will be reestablished. The experts now say that hospitals are going to have to rethink their relationships with physicians. For example, Blendon says:

> Negotiating with plans is going to require physicians and hospitals to sit on the same side of the table. . . . Many CEOs are uncomfortable with

this role. But managed care agreements require limited referrals, short-ening the patient stay, and packaging the doctor's fee in with the overall charge. This requires hospitals to reach some arrangements with their medical community.[25]

Of course, before the transformation of health care began in the 1970s, physicians and hospital administrators always sat at the same table—the better for physicians to tell administrators what to do. The new partnership will be quite different. Putting physicians back in the loop does not mean returning their traditional dominance over the way health care delivery is organized.

In this latest scenario, the social roles of insurers and providers have been reversed to some extent. Now it is the insurance carrier, not the provider, who is portrayed as the culprit primarily responsi-ble for runaway costs. Thus, although the insurance industry did most of what it did in order to cooperate with its large corporate clients, its future has become very uncertain since, as it turns out, its corporate clients were wrong in assuming that its initiatives would control costs.

Now, as a result of all these developments, some providers that survived the competitive wars of the 1980s have begun to rebuild mutually supportive bridges. Presumably, they finally have learned from experience what corporate strategists knew from the beginning—the power of providers is more likely to be ensured through some level of cooperation among themselves than it is in a "war of all against all."

Of course, this development is likely to lead to the invention of some new technique for controlling providers. Otherwise, in the end, we will be back where we started in the 1970s—with a completely provider-dominated system, and all the problems that entails.

What Managed Care Manages

Even as the managed care industry has grown to monolithic proportions, health care costs have continued to rise. Clearly, the plans have not been able to solve our cost problems any more than the patchwork of initiatives from which the system has evolved. In fact, the financial health of the managed care delivery systems themselves has been ex-tremely problematic, a situation which makes their continued promotion by corporate and government leaders all the more interesting. In 1987, the health care journalist Paul Kenkel reported that the plans continued to grow even though they were achieving "poor operating results." "Many managed care companies had a difficult time making money . . . although enrollment and gross revenues for most health maintenance organizations, preferred provider networks and other alternative health care delivery systems continued to rise."[26]

Here, by managed care Kenkel means HMOs. One reason HMOs lost money was because of the intense competition that occurred during the 1980s, which was discussed in chapter 3. But another reason was because of "unexpectedly high medical expenses." For example, for one HMO, the "medical loss ratio," which is the percentage of the premium collected that actually is used to pay medical expenses, soared from 80 percent in 1986 to almost 93 percent in 1988. The norm is 87 percent for independent practice association–model HMOs such as U.S. Healthcare and Maxicare, according to the Group Health Association.[27]

Another reason the HMOs performed so poorly was because their capitation payments were too low to cover the real risk associated with medical care. For example, by 1988, some provider groups began to restructure or to cancel risk contracts with health maintenance organizations

> because they say they no longer can afford to *subsidize* those organizations. . . . The Northwestern venture, which functions as an independent practice association, acts as the middleman to channel HMO patients to physicians, who continue to treat non-HMO patients. . . . Under the pacts with HMOs, the IPA ended up financing the HMOs, [Pamela M. Waymack, Executive Director of Northwestern Healthcare] said, and "more business just meant bigger losses."[28]

As a result, some IPAs began to abnegate the terms of their contracts. For example, in 1988, about two thousand Colorado physicians who provide care to the 178,000 enrollees of Comprecare forced the HMO to raise its capitation payment 16 percent at midyear.[29] Thus, the IPAs that were created during the 1970s specifically to shift costs away from corporate employers were, by the late 1980s, no longer financially able to provide that subsidy.

These processes certainly explain, in part, why many HMOs lost money throughout the last half of the 1980s even though they continued to increase both their revenues and the number of their enrollees. The key to financial solvency is not simply an increased share of the market; to make a profit, one must also charge a rate that more than covers real costs.

Many analysts now say that, in order to survive, HMOs will have to reduce their costs by controlling utilization of ambulatory care. A report from InterStudy in 1989 indicates that, while HMOs reduced the lengths of their enrollees' hospital stays, they were unable to prevent them from utilizing outpatient services.[30] If this were the only factor involved—which of course it is not—it would seem to indicate that many outpatient visits are more expensive than relatively few inpatient services, especially if these hospital treatments are delivered before the patient becomes extremely sick.

Managing People

By the mid-1980s, corporate America had embraced managed care and utilization review programs as their favorite techniques for controlling health care costs for their own employees. According to the Health Research Institute (HRI), these programs actually had replaced corporate attempts to shift costs to employees.[31] This assessment is suspect, since managed care systems such as IPAs also shift costs. Nevertheless, according to HRI's director, William E. Hembree, by 1986 employers had concluded that shifting costs to their own employees had limited potential because employees actually fall into three very different categories. First, there are workers who never use health care services. Therefore, attempts to shift costs to them, even through a "million-dollar deductible," will have no effect, except to make them mad. Hembree does not mention that another technique for shifting costs to workers—making them pay a larger part of the insurance premium—does affect this group, as it forces all workers to pay more, whether they use services or not. The second category of employees is probably the largest of the three. It consists of those who do use their plans, but not very often. Hembree acknowledges the fact that cost shifting does affect this group. However, since these employees do not use many services, especially the more expensive ones, they do not account for the nation's major health care expenditures. Thus shifting costs to them also makes them mad but it does not solve the health care cost problem. The third category is the crucial one; it consists of employees who have serious health problems. Although this group accounts for the largest medical bills, cost shifting has relatively little effect on them, Hembree says, because they are "too emotionally involved" to be concerned about comparative shopping for health care. "Deductibles don't matter as much—longevity becomes the issue," he observes.[32]

Thus, according to Hembree, employers now realize that cost shifting to employees is not an effective cost containment method because it only works for the second group, which does not cause the "largest drain on the medical plan." Consequently, employers are finding other alternatives for containing health care costs.[33] Those alternatives include all the surveillance and control mechanisms that have been discussed throughout this book.

The implications of Hembree's account are both obvious and horrifying. It is the group with "serious" problems, the group that ignores deductibles because it is worried about staying alive, whose use of health care services has to be cut by "other alternatives." Thus one of the characteristics of our present health care system—the fact that it systematically withholds treatments from the sickest patients, forcing providers to deliver services to them based on statistical norms rather than on their actual health status—is not an accident, a pathology, or an unintended consequence of contemporary health care policy. It is a clearly stated objective of cost-cutting strategists.

It should be underlined here that long before 1986 corporate employers, like the rest of us, were aware that it is the sickest patients who cost the most money to treat. In May 1980 the *New York Times* reported that two studies by researchers in Boston showed that "a mere 13 percent of the patients used as many medical and hospital services as the remaining 87 percent." The *Times* went on to observe that, if that statistic reflects a national pattern, "then only 1.3 percent of the population consumes more than half the hospital resources."[34] This research studied utilization patterns in the 1970s. By the time the studies reached the mainstream media, it was already obvious that the objective of corporate strategies was to eliminate not only overutilization of "unnecessary" services but some crucially required care as well. This was the real beginning of the overt imposition of rationing in medical practice, and it was directed precisely at the nation's sickest citizens.

Managing Costs

Proponents of managed care continue to claim that these plans control costs more effectively than do other kinds of insurance. For example, in 1988 Kenneth S. Abramowitz, health care analyst at Sanford C. Bernstein and Company, a New York investment firm, predicted that "the average HMO's hospital reimbursement rate will be about 40 percent less than that of a typical indemnity plan by 1992."[35]

Richard H. Egdahl, M.D., director of the Health Policy Institute at Boston University, appears to disagree. He said in 1990 that, although managed care can result in some short-term savings, he did not believe those savings would solve our health care cost problems in the long run, for two reasons.[36] The first reason is "corporate culture." Every chief executive officer wants to save money for his or her own corporation, but very few want to get involved in the whole managed care process. This assessment is common among management experts, who say that employers are interested only in health benefits for their own employees and in strategies that shift their own costs onto someone else.[37] These CEOs are not interested in making the kinds of social structural changes that would be required actually to cut health care costs.

The second reason Egdahl cites is the fact that many different forces are driving health care cost inflation, forces that will not be affected by administrative cost control mechanisms. One important factor is that medical technology is continuously being upgraded in ways that prolong life. Although this technology may delay the onset of chronic illness, it cannot, of course, eliminate it. Treatments for those chronic illnesses go on for the remainder of the patients' lives, often for many years. As a result, Egdahl says, the "single biggest factor [in] increasing costs [is] care for elderly people with medical problems."[38] That population has been growing rapidly as a result of technological developments. It will skyrocket when the baby-boomers begin to turn sixty-five.

For these reasons, Egdahl does not believe managed care will cut health care costs in the long run, whether it is in the form of utilization review, outcomes research, statistical norms of practice, patient satisfaction surveys, or wellness programs. What does Egdahl think might work? He says, "The only way we'll ultimately get a long-term answer . . . is to create some sort of presidential commission" that might initiate significant changes in health care in the United States.[39] Thus, he believes federal government intervention will be required to change the system itself.

Egdahl's current assessment is particularly interesting in light of the leadership role he has played since the 1970s. At that time, his Health Policy Institute in Boston was a central locus of the corporate movement to transform American health care delivery; many of the basic components of managed care were born or nurtured in that setting.[40] The orienting ideology of that movement was the assumption that market mechanisms would transform the system. Most corporate strategists minimized, or even ridiculed, the role that government played, even as they lobbied for passage of legislation friendly to their own initiatives.

Even Paul M. Ellwood, M.D., the father of the "health maintenance strategy," now says that HMOs and managed care groups have exhausted their ability to cut costs. In fact, he says that techniques for cutting costs now have become "so generic and effective" that many types of organizations know how to use them.[41] If that is true, one must wonder why health care costs have continued to rise astronomically throughout the 1980s and early 1990s, with no end in sight.

Since the late 1980s, Ellwood has been predicting that eight to ten "supermeds"—huge companies such as the Humana Corporation—will eventually dominate prepaid care. He believes that they will solve our cost problems; the reason they have not done so as yet, he says, is because their ascendancy has been delayed.[42]

By 1989, Ellwood was also espousing a new theory, called "outcomes management." According to this theory, the supermeds could compile huge databases that show everything that happens to patients after they receive treatment. Periodically, these patients would provide information to update their records by answering survey questionnaires. The computer would compare their experiences to those of "similar patients who received treatment for like ailments" to inform providers about the impact of the treatments they deliver. Ellwood explains:

> This information would be fed into the data base to develop a huge clinical library that physicians could tap when making medical decisions. The result would be a collection of objective criteria that would help providers, payers and purchasers define the relationship between medical intervention and health outcomes.[43]

Using this model, the new basis for knowledge in Western medicine would be statistical norms based on patient survey responses, used comparatively with data from completely different kinds of sources. In that case, we can probably expect a barrage of "public education" messages designed to help the public interpret their own experiences.

Presumably, Egdahl would not agree with Ellwood's assessment that outcomes management will cut costs, since he has said that outcomes research, while it might improve our medical knowledge, will not solve our cost problems. Other analysts believe it will actually increase costs.

One theory that is espoused by proponents of managed care is that it will cut costs by working at the systemic level; that is, it will force nonmanaged care systems to "use many of the cost-saving techniques typically used in managed care."[44] This, of course, is exactly the claim that was made for HMOs during the 1970s; as we have already seen, that promise has not been fulfilled.

Managing Managers

Good managed care requires more than controlling providers and patients. The costs of managing managed care must themselves be calculated into the equation. According to Charles D. Reuter of Buck Consultants,

> Management review often neglects an assessment of the resources and capabilities of its administrator, fees charged by the administrator in relation to the services actually rendered, and the way the administrator's performance actually tracks against desired performance levels. . . . Management of long-term costs can be attained only through initial and ongoing evaluation of the administrator's performance.[45]

How does Reuter believe employers can ensure that they receive good service from their administrators? "One viable approach is to put the administrator at risk financially for its performance," he says.[46] This statement provides an interesting example of the way the concept "shared risk" has changed during the past two decades. During the 1970s, one corporate initiative that was designed to reduce utilization by providers was to put providers "at risk," to cause them to lose money if they delivered "excessive" services. That was an important goal of HMOs and, later, of the DRG system. Then, throughout the 1980s, passing costs on to employees through deductibles and joint premiums emerged as a way of putting patients at risk when they used services. Now, Reuter believes managers, too, should be put at risk.

This is a fascinating characteristic of the processes that corporate America has launched. During the last twenty years, industry's initiatives have eliminated the kinds of insurance that allowed the public to share *its* risk. At the same time, those initiatives have produced a system through which corporate employers and managed care providers can share their own financial risk. Thus, increasingly, real risk sharing is the prerogative only of very powerful interest groups, who use it against the public.

Provider Responses to Managerial Controls

All these developments are leading to changes in the ways that the old, traditional health care system interest groups interact with each other, including physicians, hospitals, and insurance carriers. Many of the initiatives that industry launched during the 1970s were designed to weaken those relationships. At that time, corporate strategists said that overutilization resulted from the fact that physicians dominated hospitals. That was why they supported both the bureaucratic regulatory organization of health systems agencies and new kinds of hospital boards that were set up to exclude physicians from hospital decision making. At the same time, the new systems gave the representatives of corporate America seats on those boards, as voting members. It was to achieve that goal that new meanings of the term health care "consumer" were created, legislatively, during the 1970s, when, for the first time, corporations were legally defined as consumers.[47]

Corporate strategists also attempted to end what they believed were "overly friendly" relationships between insurance carriers and all providers, including both physicians and hospitals. Thus a major objective of the corporate strategies that were implemented in the 1970s was to manipulate physicians, hospital administrators, and insurance carriers into adopting adversarial positions, in a familiar "divide-and-conquer" strategy. For example, corporate employers wanted administrators to make hospital purchasing decisions on the basis of cost efficiency rather than permitting each physician to select the brand of appliances, drugs, or supplies he or she favored. Later, other control initiatives pushed administrators to attempt to manage direct patient treatments as well. All these actions contributed to a new animosity between administrators and physicians.

By the early 1980s, many physicians had come to accept, if not embrace, HMOs. For a time it seemed that "traditional" and "alternative" providers might accommodate each other. By the late 1980s, however, the provider press reported that competition had driven a wedge between physicians and HMOs. *Modern Healthcare* reported:

> Some once-promising alliances between physicians and health mainte-nance organizations are ending up in bitter court battles. In three sepa-rate cases, physicians and HMOs are fighting it out in the courts. The allegations range from anti-trust to libel. Analysts expect more lawsuits involving physicians and HMOs because of increasing competition in the health care industry.[48]

This development was predictable. The purpose of starting HMOs was to exercise managerial control over providers, not to form "alliances" with them.

Historically, of course, mutually supportive cooperation has always been an important foundation for the power enjoyed by all three of the groups at the core of our health care system—physicians, hospital administrators, and insurance carriers. Corporate America has under-stood that fact from the beginning. During the 1980s, even providers came to understand it. For example, writing for *Modern Healthcare* in 1990, Phillip E. Hoggard, executive vice-president of a physician search and consulting firm, says that hospitals and physicians "need to be allies, not adversaries." According to Hoggard, because of intense cost-containment efforts "initiated in the 1980s [sic] . . . hospitals began competing not only with other hospitals but also with their med-ical staffs. Competition broke out among staff physicians trying to increase or maintain their share of patients." Because hospitals and physicians were not equipped to handle this kind of competition, in some cases it "actually increased costs and excess capacity rather than having the desired effect of reducing costs."[49]

New alliances between traditional and alternative providers became necessary for one very important reason; even when HMOs actually did succeed in cutting costs, they were punished, not rewarded. According to consultant Peter Fox of Lewin and Associates, HMOs have been so successful in persuading corporate employers that they would save money that employers were pushing for increasingly large shares of those savings. On the "supply side," Fox says, physicians were likely to make more demands in the future, so that "HMOs will feel pressure from both sides."[50]

One of the major competitive tactics among HMOs has been to provide large, corporate purchasers with discounts. By 1986, some HMOs and employers as well were beginning to realize that this was not a good strategy in the long run. Bill Weinberg, a consultant for preferred provider organizations and other alternate delivery systems for the Blue Cross and Blue Shield Association in Chicago, explains why. "At first, everyone wanted discounts. Then we began to look at that. Discounts weren't the real issue; the real issue was price. Now, we recognize that the total cost of buying services is a combination of the price per unit and the number of units consumed."[51]

According to Paul Ginsberg, a benefits analyst with the Rand Corporation in Washington, D.C., "The HMO Act has actually given HMOs some protection from the market power of employers."[52] As a result, Ginsberg says, many employers would like to get rid of the HMO Act because, if the dual choice option did not exist, HMOs would be forced to price their premiums lower to keep their corporate clients.[53]

Although free-market ideologues have claimed that competition among plans would eliminate only those that were inefficient, the size of the plan is probably a more important factor than efficiency. According to Seth H. Shaw of Prudential-Bache, the only way many HMOs will be able to survive will be to merge with some well-heeled competitor or with an insurance company.[54]

For a variety of reasons, all these developments are leading to a decrease in the cutthroat competition that has characterized HMOs for the last few years. First, as competing firms have merged, the number of plans has decreased, leaving the largest ones in the most powerful positions. The decrease in plans is reflected in the fact that employers are offering their employees fewer HMOs. *Modern Healthcare* reports, "In 1988 firms with at least 5,000 employees offered an average of 19 HMOs, compared with 24 in 1987."[55]

Second, the surviving plans themselves may adopt strategies to reduce internecine competition.

Again, according to *Modern Healthcare,* "Health Insurance Plan of

Greater New York . . . already may be exercising the survival strategy of the future for independent managed-care plans. That strategy is for such plans in the same area to team up to take on the big competitors and avoid knocking each other out of the market."[56] Thus providers are attempting to eliminate the threat that competition poses to all of them by cooperating with each other.

Although the mid- and late 1980s was a rocky period for many HMOs, others grew and flourished. The Harvard Community Health Plan (HCHP) in Boston provides an illustration of the social processes through which HMO growth was first impeded, then facilitated, by government regulation. Originally, the HCHP was

> financed by loans from Harvard Medical School and by grants from the Commonwealth Fund, Rockefeller Foundation, and Ford Foundation. . . . The first center opened in Boston in 1969, five years before the HMO Act provided for federal funding. The plan had marketing problems from the beginning because state legislative requirements forced it to market itself through Blue Cross and Blue Shield, which performed poorly. . . . In 1977 a new state HMO-enabling act made it possible for the plan to drop its Blue Cross affiliation and contract directly with subscriber groups. Also in 1977 the plan obtained federal qualification and began to expand, doing its own advertising and marketing.[57]

A report by the health care journalist Mark Baldwin indicates that the HCHP's growth during the 1980s was supported by an entire network of powerful groups, including the prestigious, 720-bed Brigham and Women's Hospital, which is associated with Harvard Medical School, and the regulatory apparatus of the Massachusetts state government.[58] In April 1985 HCHP signed an agreement with Brigham and Women's Hospital under which HCHP would send most of its adult patients in need of hospital care to that hospital, which could result in a "windfall of up to $110 million" for Brigham and Women's Hospital over the next five years.[59] By taking this action, HCHP would be diverting patients away both from its own hospital and from other hospitals in the area. But, in return, Brigham and Women's Hospital would give HCHP a discounted rate for patients and ensure that HCHP would have enough hospital beds available to enable it to continue growing. This consideration was important because HCHP's enrollment almost doubled between 1981 and 1984.

That growth was facilitated by regulations enacted by the Massachusetts state government. According to Mark Coven, Massachusetts assistant secretary for health and welfare in the Office of Human Services, "The whole regulatory environment in Massachusetts encouraged HMOs to expand." [60] First, state regulations permitted HMOs to negotiate discounts with hospitals, while they required all other third-party payers to pay the same rates for all patients. Second, the state exempts HMOs from the certificate-of-need procedures that restrict other providers from building or acquiring new facilities.[61]

As a result of this felicitous environment, the HMO movement in Boston has been both moderately successful and extremely competitive; by 1985, the four largest plans in the area—HCHP, Bay State, Multigroup, and Tufts—had enrolled 400,000 members. I say the movement in Boston was "moderately successful" because HMOs there had about the same level of market penetration as did HMOs in the rest of the state, where HMOs enrolled about 800,000 members, about 14 percent of the state's population. By contrast, HMO penetration in the Minneapolis–St. Paul area in 1985 was approximately 40 percent. Compared with the rest of the country, however, Massachusetts was doing quite well. According to InterStudy, by June 1984 only about 6 percent of the country's population was enrolled in an HMO.[62]

By February 1986 experts were predicting that HMOs would enjoy about one more year of large enrollment increases, at rates of about 25 percent. After that, they said, the industry would be in for hard times. For example, analyst Roger Gordon of Dean Witter Reynolds in New York City "predicted that by 1990, there will be 700 to 750 HMOs in operation, with a total of 40 million enrollees. The growth of national chains will be slower and of lesser significance, he says, than the growth of regional HMOs."[63] As it turned out, Gordon was overly optimistic about HMO growth rates; by 1990, there were 575 HMOs in the United States, serving just over 33 million Americans.[64]

More important, employers no longer believed that HMOs could control health care costs. According to a survey carried out by A. Foster Higgins and Company, a national health benefits consultant, although 60 percent of employers believed that preferred provider organizations control costs, only one-third of them believed that HMOs did so. At the same time, a survey conducted by Confederation Life indicated that HMOs were "losing ground to utilization review and PPOs."[65] A major reason was the increase in HMO premiums. Employers responding to the Confederation Life survey reported that HMO premiums went up 16.5 percent, from $1,991 to $2,319 per employee, between 1988 and 1989. Other research results told the same story. CareAmerica Health Plans reported that HMO premiums increased 16.7 percent in 1989 and were expected to increase another 12 percent by 1992. At that point, reported *Life Association News,* "Some industry leaders say the cost increase of HMOs is at a higher rate than the overall rate increase of the health-care system."[66]

In spite of these rate increases, however, HMOs continued to lose money. American International Healthcare in Rockville, Maryland, reported that the HMO industry lost more than $2 billion between 1986 and 1989.[67] HMOs were failing to live up to other kinds of expectations as well. Because they function to ration health care services, proponents of HMOs have claimed that they would be particularly effective in cutting costs for publicly funded, Medicare and Medicaid patients. Certainly, if access to patient populations were a guarantee of success, it would seem that a marriage between HMOs and publicly funded patients was made in heaven. That has not been the case. Like other providers, many HMOs have been unable to serve these patients, given the "inadequate federal reimbursements" allocated to the care of older, sicker patients, says *Modern Healthcare.* "HCFA pays Medicare risk contractors 95 percent of their average adjusted per-capita costs. . . . Because of insufficient reimbursement, two dozen HMOs dropped their risk contracts with the Health Care Financing Administration last year and 36 plans said they would not renew contracts for 1989."[68]

In mid-1990, Gail Wilensky, then head of HCFA, told the House Ways and Means Health Subcommittee that higher Medicare rates would be necessary to reverse this trend, to "maintain and encourage greater involvement of managed-care programs in Medicare."[69] At that time, just over 3 percent of Medicare's 31 million beneficiaries were enrolled in ninety-seven HMOs around the country. The panel argued with Wilensky's assessment on the grounds that "one provider group shouldn't be singled out for special reimbursement . . . with no evidence that HMOs either save money or provide high-quality care."[70]

Ultimately, the rate increase was not allowed. Instead, the Medicare pay increase in 1991 was set for 1.4 percent, well below the medical inflation rate, which was more than 7 percent that year. The result, according to Thomas R. Hussey, director of Medicare for Kaiser Foundation Health Plans of the Northwest, Portland, Oregon, was that "Medicare is forcing more of the costs back onto the beneficiaries."[71]

HMOs are no more eager to take Medicaid patients than they are to take Medicare patients. Although experts say that state and federal governments save money when HMOs do take these patients, they "have been money-losers and headaches for providers and HMOs, mainly because the record-keeping costs generated by eligibility requirements is an expensive component of care."[72] Thus, the surveillance process continues to add significantly to health care costs.

Of course, since the 1970s, analysts have argued that the major reason HMOs were able to deliver services more cheaply than the traditional health care system was because their enrollees consisted disproportionately of young, working people with families, the healthiest group in the nation. Rationing the services that are delivered to healthy people is relatively easy to do. Once government agencies pressed HMOs to serve a real cross-section of the population, which includes older, poorer, sicker patients, their primary advantage disappeared. At that point, HMOs began to experience difficulties with their bottom lines. They responded by becoming increasingly like the traditional practitioners and indemnity insurance plans they were intended to replace.

Rationing Health Care

In the late 1980s, experts began to predict that rationing would be required to solve our health care cost problems. In 1990, an editorial in the *Economist* stated that, because health care costs took a 12 percent bite out of the U.S. gross national product (GNP) each year, "The dreaded word, rationing, now looks more likely than reform to stop the growth."[73]

Historically, rationing has referred to the process of denying goods, not only to those who cannot afford to pay but also to those who *can,* to serve some kind of national purpose. For example, during World War II commodities were rationed to allocate scarce resources to wartime purposes. Health care rationing is different. It is done not to conserve scarce resources, but because we recognize that if masses of people use them, the result will be health care cost inflation. Thus, we ration not because of a shortage but to control costs. This rationing presents an ideological problem in nations where health services are sold as commodities rather than delivered on the basis of the patients' medical conditions. Corporate America never intended to withhold services from those who can afford to pay; nor does it wish to restrict the development of the predominantly publicly funded medical knowledge upon which those services are based. The trick is to manipulate the public into continuing to pay for the social construction of medical knowledge while accepting that rationing will prevent the masses of people from reaping its benefits.

In reality, of course, health care rationing has been going on for certain categories of people for a very long time, as William B. Schwartz, physician, author, and professor of medicine at Tufts University, has pointed out. Schwartz distinguishes between overt or covert rationing. First, he says, we can ration explicitly, by "putting people on a waiting list for a hip replacement." Or, payers can use "silent rationing."[74] Quietly and behind the scenes they can pick and choose the care they will pay for and, thus, the care that can be delivered. It is this second, silent kind of rationing that has been going on for many years. The *Wall Street Journal* reports, "Insurers, employers and other third-party payers—through devices such as technology evaluation programs, medical review plans and even protocol at health maintenance organizations—are quietly but actively rationing more medical care in the U.S."[75]

Schwartz and his co-author, Henry J. Aaron, director of economic studies at the Brookings Institute, believe that we must, indeed, ration health care—not on the basis of patients' medical conditions, however, but according to mechanistic, bureaucratic processes. They believe that "the key to effective limits . . . will be hospital budget ceilings that allow annual increases only for inflation and a modest growth in real expenditures."[76] Thus the "free-market" system can remain intact while government regulations attempt to curb its abuses.

In late 1989, Congress approved a new rationing mechanism, the Medicare volume performance standards (VPS) system, in an attempt to reduce the payments that are made to physicians "by curbing the growth in the volume of physicians services."[77] The Physician Payment Review Commission (PPRC), which advises Congress, will make recommendations each year about how to set the volume target and will attempt to identify issues and problems as they emerge. In 1990, rationing was the first issue to be raised.

Commission members are, of course, aware that some form of

health care rationing exists everywhere, although it varies enormously from one nation to another. Uwe Reinhardt, commission member and professor of political economy at Princeton University, points out that, while European countries ration care by limiting technological developments and the supply of hospital beds, in the United States physicians must control patient demand. Reinhardt says, "They are put in the position of telling patients, There's an empty bed. There's a machine. There's an idle surgeon. But the budget is limited; therefore, go away."[78] The patient is not turned away, of course, if he or she has an elite insurance "product" or enough cold cash to buy the care. But services would be far less available under supply-side rationing, which limits the development of medical technology itself. Thus, supply-side rationing would affect elites as well as the larger public.

Reinhardt stresses that the VPS is a budgetary tool, not a quality control measure, and should not be identified as such. He says, "Let us not pretend that somehow with this instrument . . . we are going to drive American physicians to practice the right kind of medicine."[79] Reinhardt himself does not recommend that we continue to ration services in this particular way. Rather, he believes that the German system, which ties increases in physicians' fees to the overall increase in workers' wages, would be a better approach.

In December 1990 the American Hospital Association made its own rationing proposal for any basic benefits package that would cover all Americans. The policy suggested that the following procedures should not be covered by a national plan: life-sustaining medical interventions for extremely premature infants, liver transplants for individuals older than eighty, and ventilators and ventilator-related services for terminally ill patients.[80] Of course, such things as organ transplants are already "rationed by the wallet," as the *Wall Street Journal* has pointed out.[81] Organ transplants are delivered to the richest Americans, but not to those whose medical conditions make them the most likely candidates to benefit from the treatments.

When the state of Oregon attempted to pass a basic health services act in 1992, the Bush administration refused to allow it because it exercised overt rationing by setting some maximum standards. The Clinton administration has reversed that decision. The standards Oregon proposes to set vary for different categories of patients. Thus, "accountability" becomes increasingly more complex and particularistic. As a result, evaluating the "quality" of care becomes increasingly problematic, since it is based frankly on payment formulas that are specific to patients' demographic characteristics rather than their medical conditions. *Health Affairs* reports:

> Oregon is trying to ration health care through an accountable political process rather than by decisions of individual providers or state government. The Oregon plan involves three related pieces of legislation, each dealing with a different population: 1. those on public assistance, 2. uninsured workers, and 3. the medically uninsurable population.[82]

By 1991, many health care analysts were beginning to say aloud that overt rationing would be a better solution to our cost problems than the covert variety that has occurred in the past.

> If all else fails, some suggest that the next step in cost containment might be triage. Also known as rationing, triage was originally a battlefield practice, a procedure for stretching overtaxed resources by treating only the most severely wounded first. Translated into civilian life, this means deciding which patients, medical conditions and forms of treatment will be covered by health insurance and which won't.[83]

Of course, here it is not the most severely wounded but the most affluent that would be guaranteed treatment. Under "triage," the important questions are these: On what basis will we decide what services will be rationed? How will we choose the categories of patients to exclude? And, most important, who will get to answer those questions?

The American people are not opposed to rationing, in principle. In the early 1990s Northwestern National Life in Minneapolis did a survey to learn what Americans think of it. Based on Northwestern's definition of rationing—"denying health care services on the basis of predetermined criteria such as age of the patient or cost"—the survey indicated that "85 percent of Americans believed that some form of rationing would work better at containing costs than the current health insurance system." However, just who should be denied services was not clear. Only 26 percent of Northwestern's respondents believed that treating children should be given priority over delivering services to the elderly.[84] Americans are not yet willing to "throw their parents overboard" because their relatively severe health problems are "too expensive" to treat. Perhaps they are unwilling to accept the "Sophie's Choice" embedded in this argument, that a trade-off between their parents and their children is their only possible alternative. Thus they do not yet accept the principles underlying cost-benefit analysis as the way to solve our health care problems.

The question about who should make the rationing decision is also important. Northwestern's survey indicated that "50 percent of Americans preferred a panel of medical professionals to determine who should get care and who shouldn't. Eighteen percent wanted consumers to make the decisions, and only 3 percent trusted elected officials with that power."[85]

It is interesting that the health care journalist who reported these findings did not say if respondents had been asked whether they would trust insurance carriers or management experts to make rationing decisions, although this is the group that does so under managed competition. Nevertheless, Northwestern's survey results indicate that people still seem to trust physicians, as a group, more than they trust the alternatives they have been offered.

One interpretation of these results might be that Americans do not want to write off whole groups, such as everyone over sixty-five, to receive certain services. Instead, they would like the decision to be made on the basis of severity of illness. That would eliminate the possibility of treating patients on the basis of demographic categories, however. It would also make it impossible to use assembly-line, scientific management techniques to control providers; instead, it would necessitate allowing medical professionals to make treatment decisions rather than professional managers. The same objection would hold if the decision were made by family members and medical professionals working together. Although these might be the most intelligent and humane solutions for all concerned, they contradict the argument that our decisions must be made on the basis of universal principles, not "personal" assessments of medical situations. Given that a new "particularism" has emerged in modern societies—one based on membership in some demographic category rather than in a family unit—it is clear that this is an ideological argument.

Managing Indemnity Insurance

For twenty years, insurance carriers have been industriously creating new products. Their competitive strategies have led them to try to eliminate as much of their own risk as possible by "experience-rating" their customers. This system, which charges lower insurance rates to people who are the least likely to become ill, has created another market, a population of rather desperate people without insurance. As a result, yet another insurance product has now been invented, not to protect the public but to protect the managed care provider against loss. *Modern Healthcare* reports:

> A new stop-loss insurance product may help protect managed care providers from excessive medical expenses. The product, Riskcare, is a joint venture involving two insurers and a health maintenance organization underwriter. The stop-loss coverage was designed at the request of managed care providers and insurers who wanted to be shielded from catastrophic losses.[86]

This new product, bought by people with high-risk medical problems, was designed to allow managed care providers to exclude these high-risk people from buying their other "products" in order to reduce the cost of experience-rated premiums. Now, very sick people can buy a product customized to fit their needs, at a much higher rate of course, one that is probably prohibitive to all but the richest Americans. Thus the new product makes it possible to make a profit from people who previously would have been an economic liability. Simultaneously, it ensures that those who can afford it get every service that our socially constructed, largely publicly subsidized modern health care system has to offer.

Expert Provider Organizations

Many business leaders continue to believe that administrative techniques have actually begun to solve our cost problems. They see a new managerial form—expert provider organizations—as a *public* rather than a private sector initiative, one that is similar to the Canadian system of socialized medicine. For example, according to Steven M. Schecter, many business leaders "are proposing that we replace private sector attempts to control health care costs—attempts that are beginning to work—in favor of a public sector solution. An increasing number of CEOs appear willing to embrace a Canadian-style national health care system."[87] Pointing to the successes of a number of companies, Schecter says they "have succeeded in limiting their health care cost increases to just one third of the national average increases."[88] However, from the description he provides of the expert provider organization, it is difficult to understand why he describes it as a "public sector" initiative.

> A new model is emerging, one that will improve control of health care costs and improve quality. This model will in time supersede today's managed care entities: health maintenance organizations (HMOs) and preferred provider organizations (PPOs). I call the new model the expert provider organization. . . . The model calls for continued use of market power by employers and insurers, coupled with more widespread use of available information technology, to assist physicians and their patients in making better health care decisions. Because the model is technology based, its benefits can be distributed to medium and small companies as well as large.[89]

Exactly what have these companies done to contain their costs?

> First, most of the success profiles have exerted market power to obtain greater control of the health care delivery system. . . . Second, these programs have relied on the primary care physician. . . . Third, these programs have worked to influence employee decisions . . . creating incentives for employees to use "network" providers.[90]

These actions are certainly nothing new. However, their last initiative is intriguing.

> Finally, most of these companies profited by managing disability. Since 20 percent of employees generally account for 80 percent of health care costs, providing cost-effective health care to this subset of the population is fundamental to cost control. . . . Total quality demands that we pay attention to process in addition to results. Further, total quality demands that, instead of spending more and more time and money reviewing the care of physicians, we emphasize development of appropriate incentives and tools to enable physicians to deliver high quality, cost effective care *the first time around.*[91]

Presumably, Schecter believes we can weed out this "subset" of patients, identifying in advance the group that eventually will become seriously ill and, thus, will cost the most to treat. By giving physicians

certain "tools" we can enable them to practice really high-quality medicine, the kind that, presumably, will enable the provider to identify
and treat those patients *before* their illnesses become acute.

This view involves two fundamental and related problems. First, it
assumes that the sickest patients actually had contact with a physician
in the early stages of illness, but that is not the case for millions of poor
Americans. Second, in this country, we ration not only medical treatments but screening services as well, precisely because they have *not*
proven to be cost efficient; that is, the programs cost more to run than
they save in medical treatments. Of course, if we *could* tell in advance
which people are actually going to get very sick, without having to
deliver services to poor people or screen large populations, screening
would undoubtedly save money. But we do not know how to do that.

Like other managers, Schecter seems to believe that our problems
exist only because physicians are not "accountable." For reasons
known only to themselves, they steadfastly refuse to practice "good"
medicine, preferring "art" to "science."

In reality, the managers themselves have not been able even to
define high-quality health care, except in the terms of statistical, actuarial tables that say nothing about the status of any individual patients,
including those who eventually will become the sickest and, therefore,
the most expensive to treat. Thus no mechanistic managerial techniques for enforcing accountability can possibly force physicians to
deliver "good" care. They can only enforce conformance with statistical averages that are increasingly retrograde. This unpleasant reality
has not deterred the new experts from trying, however.

Summary

Although proponents of managed care claim that it cuts costs by eliminating unnecessary services and improving provider efficiency, it actually is little more than a complex, expensive, and stunningly ineffectual
rationing mechanism. It is based on the premise that we can control
health care costs by controlling the utilization of services.

However, rather than reducing utilization at the supply side—by
limiting facilities and equipment, as do countries with socialized
systems—managed care is a technique for "having it both ways."
Using this mechanism, our country can, simultaneously, maintain a
very sophisticated, high-tech health care system that is freely available

to health care elites while we systematically exclude less affluent Americans from the same kinds of services.

The heart of managed care is manipulation. When the legitimating facade of administrative "science" is stripped away, it is clear that, primarily, managed care is a political structure. Through the exercise of a variety of surveillance mechanisms and the use of a calculated combination of rewards and punishments, its most important objective is to coerce beneficiaries, patients, and providers into changing both their behavior and their expectations.

As an important part of that process, managed care helps to maintain the illusion that people actually are exercising "choice," to persuade the public that the same care is available to anyone who is "willing" to pay the price for it. This is obviously a bad faith claim, since, as the National Governors' Association report made clear, a conscious part of managerial strategy is to calculate exactly how much each "product" must cost to ensure that the masses of people will "choose" the one that rations care the most stringently. Thus, "market mechanisms" are exploited in a shamelessly Machiavellian way, as a strategy to control people. This is a far cry from the "free-market mechanisms" of economic theory, according to which it is people, through their purchasing decisions, who control the market.

It is clear that these manipulative techniques have not succeeded in cutting health care costs during the past twenty years. They have, however, played an important role in undermining the quality of health care that many Americans receive. The next chapter will discuss the ways that managed care proponents deal with this important issue.

5
Managing "Quality" through Outcomes Research

Sure, healthcare is different. It can't be sold like used cars or kitchen appliances. But it can be sold like hamburgers. . . . McDonald's provides what people want. It does so quickly, efficiently and with an almost obsessive focus on quality in all meanings of the word. . . . Hospital executives who reject the McDonald's comparison today will be the dinosaurs of tomorrow.
—*Dan Duda, Tal, Inc.*[1]

Beginning in the late 1980s, our national anxiety about health care costs began to give way to a new concern; the *quality* of health care being delivered had become increasingly problematic. Copious data made it clear that the United States spends more on health care services than any other industrialized country, only to achieve some of the worst morbidity and mortality statistics.

In quick succession, management experts responded by shifting their focus, at least verbally, from cost cutting to quality improvement. This new focus raised a major problem, however. Just as they had not been able to define "good medical practice" except in the form of statistical and actuarial tables, neither could they define "quality" in health care delivery systems.

In this case, an even more important problem muddied the water. Although all the new management experts talked about quality, they did not attach the same meaning to the term. The discrepancies arose from the fact that they worked for the entire spectrum of interested groups, including government, corporate employers, the new "quality management" industry, health care providers, and sometimes even the actual consumers of health care services. As a result, they rarely adopted the same focus. Instead, they defined "quality" as it related to four very different areas of concern: clinical effectiveness, medical accountability, managerial excellence, and cost efficiency. Some management experts bundle this multiple focus into the term "total quality management" and claim to address them all at once. This multiple focus has caused serious problems in defining goals, since improving quality in one area often reduces it in another.

Usually, although management experts agree in principle that these are all important areas of concern, they assign different priorities to them. Then, depending on which is their primary focus, they approach quality issues not only with different definitions of health care reality but with different goals and strategies as well. These different points of view result in enormous confusion, which is reflected in the media. Health care journalists continuously ask questions like these.

> What is quality medical care? Is it a minimum or maximum of acceptable medical performance? Can it be measured by examining how well providers meet a set of performance standards, or should it be defined in terms of measurable improvements in the health status of patients? What is the relationship between the utilization of healthcare resources and services and the quality of care?[2]

In response to this growing concern with quality, management experts launched a mammoth new enterprise during the 1980s, one that has now become a very important new component of the U.S. health care system—politically, organizationally, and economically. The enterprise is called by several names, including "quality assurance," "total quality management," and "outcomes research." These are distinctly different concepts, of course. Outcomes research, which actually may involve attempts to learn something about the clinical impact of treatments, is the most basic of the three. Information derived from outcomes research is supposed to be the basis for defining quality in order to assure that recalcitrant providers will deliver it, prodded to do so by ever-vigilant managers of course.

The fact that participants use the three terms almost interchangeably reflects not only their different practical interests but a lack of any accepted definition of quality. At the same time, it also serves an important function in attempts to create such a definition; it glosses over the difference between clinical outcomes and managerial processes, allowing participants to talk about cost containment and clinical results as if administrative efficiency and desirable clinical outcomes were one and the same. The most sophisticated of the health care managers are aware of this process, as a comment by Daniel Berwick of the Harvard Community Health Plan makes clear: "I'm afraid there will be an unconscious conspiracy of wishful thinking that low utilization and high quality are closely connected. . . . Sometimes that's true, but sometimes it's not."[3] Of course, this particular "unconscious conspiracy" has actually been in operation since the early 1970s, when industry first launched its utilization control initiatives.

From the beginning, then, the basic purpose of quality management has been elusive. Depending on the interest group that touts it, it should either shave costs or improve clinical outcomes. Usually, however, proponents of quality management simply claim it will do both. For example, government representatives began to support quality management in the mid-1980s for the same reasons that, throughout the 1970s, they supported the rationing mechanisms that were described in chapter 2. *Modern Healthcare* explained, "Although the research initiatives have been billed primarily as efforts to improve the quality of healthcare, budget-conscious lawmakers clearly were attracted to the idea by its potential for containing skyrocketing healthcare costs by identifying unnecessary procedures."[4]

The federal government sometimes does emphasize real clinical outcomes to some extent, perhaps because that is what the average citizen understands by the term "quality" in health care. For example, when Congress allocated funds for outcomes research in 1989, it specified that about two-thirds must be allocated to *clinical* outcomes research. According to J. Jarrett Clinton, M.D., acting director of the National Center for Health Services Research, that means the funds were intended for research that is actually designed to tell us something about "the effectiveness and appropriateness of treatments." The other one-third was to be used for more purely managerial purposes, "to develop research data bases, disseminate findings and, eventually, produce practice guidelines based on the research results."[5]

Unlike the federal government, corporate America has no need to be sensitive to voter reactions; it is concerned only with the bottom line. Consequently, any health care management unit that works for this interest group must stay firmly focused on costs and on satisfying the demands of its corporate customers. Such experts must focus on hospital services that are similar to those provided by hotels, restaurants, and accounting firms, not on clinical quality. For example, A. Blanton Godfrey, chair and chief executive officer of the Juran Institute in Wilton, Connecticut, says that total quality management in hospitals is not focused on direct patient care but on services that include "ways to improve billing procedures, pharmacy operations, operating room scheduling and communication among ancillary service departments." [6]

The Juran Institute, which was founded in 1970, is very influential in the quality management business. It "provides educational programming and services on managing quality" to corporate clients, including many *Fortune* 500 companies. Although he declined to give their names, Godfrey said in 1988 that the institute was working with five major health care companies.[7] One of them, it turns out, was the Harvard Community Health Plan, which will be discussed in detail below.

Another health care consultant, Michael Sachs, who heads the Sachs Group in Evanston, Illinois, gives lip service to the idea that improving clinical outcomes is a desirable goal, not for any softheaded reasons but because it will reduce health care costs and, thus, increase profits. *Modern Healthcare* reports: " 'By providing poor-quality care to patients, hospitals incur additional costs,' Mr. Sachs said. Poor-quality care results in clinical complications, which lead to longer stays, return trips to operating rooms and readmissions."[8] Of course, although this theory sounds perfectly obvious, it is unproven. It is similar to the commonsense assertion industry made in the 1970s, that preventive services would lower health care costs. Unfortunately, because the kinds of preventive services that were acceptable to industry turned out not to be "cost effective," they were soon abandoned. In any event, since standards for clinical quality have not yet been established, they could not have been implemented; therefore, we cannot possibly know what their impact would have been.

The theory is also questionable on other grounds. For years management experts have succeeded in reducing hospital utilization and shortening hospital stays, claiming all the while that they were also improving the quality of health care. Now the new experts tell us that those claims were untrue, that the quality of health care has deteriorated. That is an important reason why their services are needed now.

Sachs himself acknowledges that he does not know how to get from clinical research to better clinical outcomes. As a result, like other quality managers, he is content to focus on patient satisfaction and on other aspects of hospital services, just as business corporations do. Health care providers and their organizations seem to be somewhat more likely to stress the importance of clinical outcomes research than are other interested groups. In fact, hospitals began complaining years ago about a decline in clinical quality, even before quality management emerged as a new business operation. Such complaints were the basis for their opposition to the cost-cutting imperatives forced on them through DRGs and PROs.

When government, the media, and corporate employers themselves began to emphasize quality of care, hospitals were given a new challenge. The Joint Commission on the Accreditation of Healthcare Organizations (JCAHO) and the American Hospital Association (AHA) have responded to this new challenge with outcomes research projects of their own.

Despite its inability to define quality in health care, quality management has been a smashing success as a business enterprise. It provides a sophisticated, up-to-date version of the rational organizational process that Max Weber described, in which the accounting procedure simultaneously tells the manager what his profits are and how productive his accountant (or physician or hospital) is. However, in addition to focusing on individual workers or businesses, outcomes research also works at a broader, more systemic level.

First, outcomes research collects data that describe a wide range of very different phenomena, including the efficiency with which administrative tasks such as management and accounting practices are carried out, whether hospitals and professional workers follow acceptable medical practices, and, sometimes, even whether clinical procedures had any impact. The analytical distinction between medical accountability and clinical outcomes is important. Medical accountability data are collected to describe two things: first, how often each specific disease category is encountered, diagnosed, and treated; second, what specific services or treatments are delivered. This information is listed both by patient and by disease. The data give providers a "scientific-legal" legitimacy to justify their rationing of treatments of procedures in the name of cost efficiency while simultaneously telling them what categories of customers are the most profitable. For example, such data tell medical managers that "coronary bypasses" are more profitable than "strokes," while they simultaneously describe a statistical norm of practice and highlight physicians and hospitals that fall outside its range.

Clinical outcomes data, on the other hand, describe the impact that the treatment or service had, on the disease, on the patient's health, and on our national morbidity and mortality statistics. Although these are very different kinds of concerns, in discussions of outcomes research the lines between them are often ignored or crossed. Both health care analysts and management experts tend either to use them interchangeably or to claim that manipulating medical services through statistical processes will result in desirable clinical outcomes, an ideological leap that is not always supported by the data.

Next, on the basis of these data, outcomes research shows the effectiveness of managerial techniques that are designed to change the health care utilization practices of everyone involved, including practitioners, secondary personnel, managers, clerical workers, and patients. Logically, this is the same kind of process as using utilization review simultaneously to define and produce "good medical practice." In the very best Foucaultian style, outcomes research creates definitions of quality in health care delivery while it creates managerial techniques that force providers to deliver services based on those definitions of quality. Thus this exercise of power results in the construction of a new kind of expert knowledge.

In theory, at least, the purpose of any kind of research is to discover some truth, or at least to describe processes that actually exist in the world. Outcomes research does not achieve that goal. Rather, it creates definitions of quality in health care under the guise of studying it. At the same time, it contributes importantly to the emergence of a new kind of health care delivery.

Outcomes research also results in the creation of some degree of consensus. "Consensus," of course, refers to a convergence of opinion, usually around some social value; in today's world, however, to gain legitimacy consensus must also appear to be grounded in information. Since the informational basis for consensus varies enormously, depending on the institutional, occupational, economic, political, and ideological locations of the expert players involved, the very topics being discussed shift constantly and uncontrollably, like a gestalt image.

That inconvenient reality is reflected in the fact that three very different approaches currently characterize outcomes research. The first approach is already quite familiar. It defines quality as a convergence to a statistical mean, glossing over the reality that we do not know what the mean should be. Workers throughout the system, including physicians, administrators, peer reviewers, and clerical staff, must conform to these statistical norms, just as factory workers must accommodate to the speed of the assembly line, and for the same reason: to increase profits by maximizing worker productivity while minimizing customer services.

A second approach to outcomes research is to ask patients what they think of the treatments they have received. This approach uses patient satisfaction surveys in an attempt to learn what patients want and what they think are the quality problems within the system. To earn high patient satisfaction ratings on such surveys, these are some of the things hospitals are doing to improve the quality of their health care services, as reported by *Modern Healthcare:*

> calling patients after discharge to inquire of their well-being; providing parking and appropriate lighting of the institution at night; retraining cafeteria employees; conducting rallies; offering candlelight bedside dinners for new parents; and distributing membership cards in senior citizen clubs, which provide discounts on prescriptions and assistance with medical paperwork.[9]

Presumably, such attentions could increase some patients' satisfaction whether or not their medical conditions improved. However, patients may not equate hospital facilities, services, and clerical efficiency with clinical care to the same extent as do administrators. As Paul Ellwood, M.D., chair of InterStudy, has observed, "Patients don't go to a hospital to get satisfied. They go to get well."[10]

The question is: Do patients really distinguish between clinical and other services? More important, even if they do, are they in any position—socially, politically or economically—to compel the hospital to provide them with effective clinical services rather than simply with marketing perks?

The third approach to defining and identifying quality is more complex. It includes the two techniques just described—creating and enforcing provider compliance with statistical practice patterns and improving patient services—but it also attempts to determine what kinds of clinical effects the treatments have had. The aim of this kind of research is to learn whether a treatment or hospital confinement actually had the desired impact on a patient's health status. The various interested groups can be distinguished by the extent to which they actually attempt to learn something about the clinical quality of care and to create a health care delivery system that reflects that knowledge. Who actually does this research, and what did they learn from it?

In general, the groups engaged in doing outcomes research fall into five broad but analytically distinct categories. The first category consists of the many different kinds of organizations that make up the entire hospital industry. It includes huge hospitals, like Rush-Presbyterian-St. Luke's Medical Center in Chicago; for-profit and not-for-profit hospital chains; national and state hospital associations, including the powerful American Hospital Association; and the agency that provides accreditation to hospitals, the Joint Commission on the Accreditation of Healthcare Organizations. This organization has the potential to exercise great power, since hospitals must have its stamp of approval to receive reimbursement from most third-party payers.

The second category is composed of corporate groups of employers who participate in a variety of "total quality management" projects. Many corporations have been engaged in similar projects for almost two decades. Originally, their objectives were to avoid socialized medicine and to cut or shift the costs of health care for their own employees. Today they also are creating management systems that are commodities themselves, available for sale on the open market.

The third category consists of consulting, managerial, and accounting firms. This is an extremely diverse group of organizations that sells its services to many different kinds of customers. Some firms have worked in the health care industry for almost a decade, while others are relative newcomers to the market. This category also includes some providers, usually hospitals or health maintenance organizations that have developed a management product in the process of running their own health care service. Rush-Presbyterian is one example; the Harvard Community Health Plan (HCHP) is another. The HCHP is a health maintenance organization that worked closely with industrial control experts to develop a sophisticated management plan to contain its own costs. The plan has become a model for other providers that are now part of the HCHP "network."[11]

The fourth category consists of federal and state governments and their agencies. The Health Care Financing Administration (HCFA) has had a particularly powerful impact on health care delivery, although state governments have done so as well. In addition to doing its own research, government also stimulates other kinds of outcomes research projects, both by providing direct funding for them and by using certain kinds of sanctions designed to enforce compliance with standards that can only be set or justified on the basis of some kind of data. For example, it was because Medicare put pressure on the Joint Commission on the Accreditation of Healthcare Organizations that JCAHO began to take an adversarial position toward hospitals for the first time; then, when hospitals were unwilling or unable to provide the data that would be required to police them, JCAHO launched its own outcomes research project.

The fifth category consists of various kinds of clinical researchers, working in both academic and hospital settings. Their focus is primarily on clinical outcomes rather than managerial processes. Interestingly, these are the most prestigious kinds of research units. That is why the American Hospital Association put its own research subdivision, the Hospital Research and Educational Trust (HRET) in charge of its own outcomes research initiative, the Quality Measurement and Management Project (QMMP). The AHA could have chosen one of its participating hospital chains, one that was already doing research and had some data in place. Instead, it chose HRET because it believed that the research unit's academic ties would ensure that its research findings would not be suspected of reflecting the interests of the hospital industry. It is interesting that academic research continues to enjoy such high esteem, given that it has not yet been an important source of information for quality management in practical terms.

Most of the research groups described here actively avoid a focus on clinical outcomes, for a variety of reasons. First there is the very real threat that improving clinical quality will mean increasing costs. Then there are the technical and methodological problems connected with creating, collecting, and analyzing clinical data.

Even among themselves, management experts working in these diverse organizations have many different, competing, even conflicting, goals. They compete with each other for funding from other interested parties and organizations. They may also compete to create and use the best, most-profit-producing, total management product. On the other hand, they may also work together, endorse, or even fund each other, in a mass of research schemes that, increasingly, are characterized by wasteful, duplicated efforts.

This is an interesting development. Management experts know very well that an effective way to cut health care costs is to prevent providers from duplicating services; that was the major objective of the old health systems agency certificate-of-need program. In fact, limiting the number of facilities that are available to certain groups, especially eliminating duplicated services, is a time-honored mechanism for rationing health care services, one that preceded the total quality management movement by twenty years.[12] Thus, while their own relatively new industry is characterized by costly, inefficient duplication, quality managers use data to eliminate duplication among health care providers. Ironically, in the process they also eliminate the competition they say they aim to stimulate.

For example, according to Ernest Sessa, executive director of the Pennsylvania Health Care Cost Containment Council, employers are using cost control data to identify "high-ranking providers" in order to contract with them, exclusively, to do specific procedures.[13] Thus they are constructing a health care system characterized by increased market concentration and reduced competition, in direct opposition to their own stated goals.

In areas where there are few providers in the marketplace, corporate consumers are developing other strategies for controlling providers. For example, ALCOA, a large aluminum-processing company located in Pittsburgh, has worked actively with health care providers in its area for many years. ALCOA does business with a group of six hospitals in its area, following Walter McClure's "buy right" strategy. Buying right means picking only some providers in a geographic area, but not all of them, to deliver services. Supposedly, this motivates all providers to compete for the business. However, in areas where there are very few providers, employers do not have this opportunity. Richard Wardrop, retired director of health cost management at ALCOA who is now a health benefits consultant, believes that in such cases, employers will have to develop special relationships with their local hospitals. According to Wardrop:

> The strategy changes a bit in those communities. "Buy Right" in such a situation may mean changing providers. Or it may mean using your

company's position as a major health care purchaser, and a major community employer, to motivate the hospital to make some quality improvements. You say to that hospital ... "we want you to make a commitment to continuous improvement of quality, in return for which we will do some things for you."[14]

Since ALCOA has been "buying right" for several years, with no clinical quality data, the "quality" being discussed is presumably lower charges. However, Wardrop clearly sees how this process is congruent with a corporate purchasing strategy that has been implemented in other areas. For example, some American corporations are attempting to avoid paying the higher prices that often result from excessive competition among their suppliers of non-health-care-related products. Wardrop describes the strategy like this: "More and more companies are using fewer and fewer vendors, and they are picking them on their ability to satisfy the customers' requirements." The report continues: "For example, Ford Motor Company certifies certain vendors after it has determined their commitment to quality. Ford gives them a Q-1 flag to fly and stops inspections of the vendors' manufacturing processes. ALCOA is a Q-1 vendor to Ford for wiring harnesses. Ford used to have 20 vendors for that particular part; but no longer."[15]

Wardrop believes the same strategy will work in health care delivery. Once a provider organization has persuaded the employer that it does not do unnecessary surgeries, that it only practices effective medicine, then companies would be able to eliminate utilization review, the expensive " 'inspection' process in health care."[16] This strategy, which simultaneously eliminates competition and does away with the necessity of creating and maintaining expensive surveillance and control mechanisms, simply reinvents old-fashioned market monopolies.

A program that was implemented in the late 1980s by the Prudential Insurance Company of America provides a recent, working example of how this strategy has been used in the health care sector. The Prudential Insurance Company, reports *Modern Healthcare,* "is consolidating its heart transplant business and a few other selected tertiary services into 17 U.S. hospitals," thus creating a kind of national preferred provider organization. This highly specialized organization will simultaneously offer what Prudential calls "outstanding quality" and exclude competition from local providers. Prudential will provide "the patient and a significant other" with transportation to the closest facility as part of the price of the medical care. Thus Prudential has "introduced hospitals to what has become a 'global' market for healthcare."[17]

In reporting this "startling announcement" by Prudential, Arthur C. Strum, Jr., president of the Strum Communications Group in Chicago, points out that the consequences of this decision could be far reaching. If other payers imitate Prudential's actions, Strum says, it will become impossible to define primary services areas. Of course, this development would represent a major shift in policy. For twenty years, health care planners have attempted to wean patients away from the expensive services of physician specialists and to promote their reliance on primary care physicians. Now not only physicians but hospitals as well may become increasingly specialized in response to these new strategies implemented by corporate employers and insurance carriers. Once their competitors have been driven from the marketplace, economic theory suggests that the new hospitals will be able to set their own rates, so that new strategies will have to be devised to control them.

For the moment, however, another practice is emerging that may force American hospitals to compete on a more global level. In 1993, some insurance carriers began to ship their cardiac surgeries to private hospitals in London to take advantage of the cheaper services they offer.[18] A heart bypass operation in London costs $10,000, compared with $25,000 in the United States, for services that the insurance carrier says are of comparable quality. This assessment undermines the notion that in countries where sizable populations are serviced by socialized health care both quality of care and medical technology are inferior to ours.

Of course, regardless of where their patients go, *any* major reductions in cardiology practices would have a powerful impact on American hospitals, since cardiac surgery represents one of the industry's most profitable products. According to the Health Care Advisory Board in Washington, the net marginal profit of cardiac surgery, per patient, is $4,049. This profit has already shrunk in some places as a result of the fact that a "developing trend" in cardiology is to "discharge heart attack patients after only three days of hospitalization." Although the patients have done well in these cases, hospitals have not. Using this "aggressive treatment" has reduced their revenues by 30 percent.[19] Not only new utilization control strategies by managers and payers, but technological developments as well, are making bypass surgery less profitable. Advances in pharmacology and the advent of noninvasive lasers have been particularly effective.

Hospitals intent on protecting their bottom lines can use data not only to make their services more efficient or more clinically effective but also to discover the most "rational" ways to protect their profits. John Dankosky, executive director of the Pennsylvania Business Roundtable, a coalition of forty-two businesses in the state, has pointed out that fact in discussing the Pennsylvania Cost Control Committee data. Hospitals, he said, are "going to take a very close look at their operations and try to determine why they're doing better with respect to some DRGs and not so well with others. . . . We can't minimize the value of these data as an internal management tool [for hospitals]." [20]

Dankosky is, of course, correct. Providers are well aware that, in the past, about four heart catheterizations were required to yield one by-pass surgery. After increasing its use of noninvasive techniques, one hospital in Montana discovered that it must now do ten catheterizations "to achieve one surgery." [21]

Based on such data, Strum has told providers that, to protect their bottom lines, hospitals must develop a consistent way to ensure that they will continue to have adequate numbers of customers for their product. This is what he advises them to do:

> There are direct ratios between individuals seen for diagnostic services and those who eventually require inpatient care. Begin by calculating your ratios of catheterizations to surgeries and then establish positive means for filling the top of the funnel through *higher use of diagnostic procedures.* One major tertiary hospital in the South was able to increase its catheterizations by 10 percent in six months through the use of simple screening tests administered by referring physicians in conjunction with their heart specialists. . . . *The new rules of the game will require that you focus on volume* to justify your existence and to secure a reasonable return on your bottom line." [22]

To the extent that providers follow this advice, it will have an enormous impact on utilization patterns. Not only will the utilization rates of diagnostic procedures increase, so will those of surgical procedures and hospital inpatient services. More ominously, these practices target unsuspecting and asymptomatic people visiting their family practitioners. Both diagnostic and surgical services to this group are likely to increase.

Numerous studies indicate that coronary bypass surgeries are already overutilized.[23] One of them, conducted by the Rand Corporation and the University of California, indicates that, on average, 44 percent of open heart surgeries are "either inappropriate or 'of questionable necessity.' "[24] The cases that researchers ranked as inappropriate ranged from 37 percent to 78 percent, depending on which hospital was involved. The Rand researchers were particularly concerned by the fact that the hospitals "did not have any standards for determining when bypass surgery is necessary."[25]

If hospitals begin to "focus on volume," the situation could grow even worse. Given that we have not been able to eliminate the overutilization that a great deal of research tells us actually exists right now, increasing the number of asymptomatic people that receive diagnostic tests must subject that group to the same kind of overutilization. Thus overutilization of both diagnostic and surgical procedures can be increased and institutionalized as part of the process of implementing rational statistical and administrative processes in a system in which health care services are marketed as consumer products rather than delivered in response to symptoms. At the same time, diagnostic tests on really high-risk populations—those who are poor, who live in badly polluted environments, or who work in hazardous industries—are discouraged through a variety of rationing mechanisms, including utilization review and deductibles. Still others are simply denied access to treatment completely because they have no health care insurance. In contrast to this mindless, market-driven mechanism, testing high-risk populations is a central part of health care policy in Sweden and is a major component of Sweden's preventive medicine program.

Clearly, many factors determine how high-quality health care services are defined. The following section will describe some of the specific quality management and outcomes research projects that a variety of interested groups have put into place during the last decade.

Studies Sponsored by Hospital
Industry Organizations

Hospitals are particularly interested in doing outcomes research, for three specific reasons. First, they are the targets of the research; it is to control them that private industry and government want outcomes information. Second, they have possession of the requisite database, information that could give them an edge over other interested groups. And, third, they have highly trained medical professionals on staff who are better equipped than administrative managers to interpret the clinical information that is collected.

Although providers place more emphasis on clinical outcomes than do other research groups, even among providers this issue is problematic. Descriptions of JCAHO and AHA outcomes research will help to clarify why that is so.

The Joint Commission on the Accreditation of Healthcare Organizations (JCAHO)

Under its initiative, Agenda for Change, which was unveiled in 1986, the Joint Commission on the Accreditation of Healthcare Organizations collects clinical data for its own model information system. Thus clinical quality outcomes is the core of JCAHO's research.[26] To get the necessary data, JCAHO has begun to require hospitals to monitor their clinical outcomes.

As a result of this new requirement, JCAHO has come into conflict with the American Hospital Association (AHA), whose research experts claim that the Agenda for Change demands data that hospitals cannot supply. One critic of the system, W. Allen Schafler, M.D., associate medical director at the Humana Corporation, charges that "JCAHO has an application in search of a data base."[27] Nevertheless, the system is being tested at seventeen hospitals.

The fact that JCAHO has begun to do this kind of research for the first time requires some explanation. Because it is an accreditation organization, it seems that JCAHO *should* have been enforcing quality controls all along. However, critics have charged for years that JCAHO has been too friendly with the hospital industry to serve as an effective watchdog. For example, Clark W. Bell, editor of *Modern Healthcare*, says that JCAHO and the AHA "have maintained chummy relations over the years, and the AHA still controls seven of the JCAHO's 24 board positions."[28]

During the 1980s, various structural forces began to put pressure on JCAHO to do its job more stringently. For example, in January 1988, the New York state health commissioner, David Axelrod, M.D., wrote a letter to JCAHO's president, Dennis O'Leary, M.D., stating that "the services currently offered through the [JCAHO] accreditation process do not warrant the existing additional expenditures of public funds unless there is a clear demonstration of the impact of the constructive advice and direction provided by the JCAHO."[29] Almost immediately, the health care provider media began to report that JCAHO would give the names of conditionally accredited hospitals to the Health Care Financing Administration (HCFA), the federal government agency that oversees Medicare, thus reversing JCAHO's policy of keeping such information secret. The media at large also began to put pressure on JCAHO. For example, in October 1988 the *Wall Street Journal* published an article describing the care delivered at six JCAHO-accredited hospitals as "egregiously bad."[30]

In April 1989, JCAHO made a major policy change, yielding to demands that it make its accreditation data public,[31] just as Medicare and some PROs had begun to go public with mortality statistics. In addition, JCAHO began to find increasing numbers of hospitals that failed to comply with its standards. In 1990, JCAHO released a report stating that, "In 12 of 19 key performance areas, more than 25 percent of 5,202 hospitals surveyed weren't in significant compliance with standards related to quality of care." JCAHO stated that it would release updated compliance reports every year, acknowledging that it was opening up its accreditation process to public scrutiny in "an attempt to respond to calls from the public, government officials, and the media."[32]

Thus it was politics, not scientific knowledge or ethics, that finally moved JCAHO to address quality issues. Has quality actually improved, as a by-product of these political events? So far, that question remains unanswered. JCAHO's experience with the nation's 172 Veterans Administration (VA) hospitals suggests at least one reason why.

According to JCAHO's data, VA hospitals fell short of the quality levels met by community hospitals during the years 1987 to 1989. However, JCAHO's data are suspect in this case, according to competing experts, who claim that JCAHO monitored only how well hospitals *documented* their operations rather than studying clinical outcomes. Thus higher error rates in VA hospitals could "have as much to do with the inconsistency of JCAHO's survey process as a hospital's quality of care," as John Fears, director of a VA hospital in Hines, Illinois, has pointed out. To support his argument, Fears said, "We are now doing more than [JCAHO] requires and are finding that we have a high level of quality."[33] This confusion between the document and the "reality" it is supposed to describe is similar to a situation discussed in chapter 3. In that case, the courts recognized the difference between the act and the record by giving hospitals time to collect the appropriate information. Thus the PROs could not refuse to reimburse hospitals for services simply because the hospitals' record-keeping systems were inadequate.

The American Hospital Association

The American Hospital Association responded to JCAHO's newly adversarial behavior by launching its own outcomes research project in September 1988. An AHA subdivision, the Hospital Research and Educational Trust (HRET), was charged with carrying out the research project called the Quality Measurement and Management Project (QMMP). The three-year study was sponsored by a coalition that originally consisted of sixteen hospital systems, alliances, and associations; together, they represented more than twenty-five hundred hospitals.[34] Many of these organizations were already doing some kind of outcomes research, but, as noted above, the AHA chose HRET to coordinate the project because of its academic ties.

Although JCAHO has expressed support for the project, some of its officials believe that the kinds of tasks it took on were designed to upstage their own organization's Agenda for Change.[35] Thus experts in the two organizations duplicate each others efforts, to some extent, attempting to refute in advance their opponent's research claims.

The QMMP was designed to simultaneously define quality and establish a model for a quality management system that could standardize practice all over the country. Its goal was ambitious. "The initial QMMP scope of work included plans to develop a model information system to collect clinical outcomes data and clinical indicators to measure a patient's functional status after hospital discharge."[36] However, after Daniel Longo was installed as the new president of HRET in 1989, most of these plans were dropped. The QMMP moved away from clinical outcomes research, toward more managerial, organizational concerns.

This development is interesting given Longo's work history in "quality assurance." Between 1987 and 1989, he was vice president for quality assurance at the New York State Hospital Association; from 1986 to 1987 he was assistant executive director for quality management at Ancilla Systems in Chicago; and from 1984 to 1986 he was research director of JCAHO. In fact, while he was at JCAHO, Longo did research for the project that eventually became the Agenda for Change.[37]

An internal "scuffle" resulted when clinical research was dropped as a QMMP goal, since some of the project's sponsors wanted to continue building a clinical outcomes database. Longo acknowledged this fact but said the goal "wasn't realistic. We needed to address more fundamental issues."[38] Even so, the QMMP continued to focus on clinical outcomes to a greater extent than some other participants wished it to do. For example, in 1990 Brent James, M.D., director of medical research at Intermountain Health Care in Salt Lake City, said he had "almost recommended that we drop out of the QMMP. The project got off track. Dan [Longo] played a central role in getting us back in the right direction."[39]

The fact that hospitals participating in the QMMP have diverse and competing interests continues to be a problem. One important hospital management firm, the Hospital Corporation of America (HCA), actually did drop participation. In that case, HCA preferred to conduct its own outcomes research because it did not wish to emphasize severity of illness. Paul Batalden, M.D., head of HCA's quality initiative, believes that "the most direct pathway to quality improvement is through a total quality management strategy, not evaluating severity-of-illness systems." The initiative that HCA is launching "is a management system that incorporates industrial quality-control concepts in the daily operations of the system's hospitals."[40]

Severity of illness raises an important conflict among even those few quality managers who really are interested in clinical outcomes. Many analysts say it is impossible to study the quality of care without taking severity of illness into account.[41] In fact, many claim that the failure to consider this factor is the major flaw in the DRG system, which actually forces hospitals to withhold care from the sickest patients, who require more than the "mean" amount of care that the formula allows. In addition, the failure to take severity of illness into account confounds attempts to do clinical outcomes research even when the data are otherwise relatively comparable.

Competition among participating hospitals also makes the sharing of data problematic. It is true that the aura of "pure" research associated with the academic world requires these hospitals to agree to share the information the study produces. As William Read, HRET's former president, has said, "Any research generated by HRET is public information. We can't develop products that selectively position one hospital over another."[42]

In theory, hospitals participating in the research do not believe that this kind of cooperation will eliminate competition. For example, Brent James says the idea is to cooperate in order to compete; hospitals can compete over how well they use the methods.[43]

In the early stages of research development, there does appear to have been a great deal of cooperation. According to Dianne Seeman, who is vice-president of quality and risk management at HealthOne Corporation in Minneapolis, "Initially, people were reluctant to share information. They weren't sure the project was going anywhere. . . . Now that the project has taken off, there's a tremendous amount of sharing."[44]

Participating systems will not share everything, however. For example, Debbie Novak, vice-president for systems development at Voluntary Hospitals of America (VHA), says her organization will not share its cost quality management system, in which it has invested "tens of millions of dollars."[45] Thus the hospital systems participating in the HRET research project are in conflict over many issues in addition to questions about what to study. They also compete for the "products" the research generates, in the form of specific management techniques and systems.

At this point, competition, as well as the fact that a wide range of different research units with many different goals are engaged in the process, has led to a great deal of duplication, both of research and of systems development. This duplication occurs not only among the hospital systems participating in the HRET study but among other organizations conducting research as well.

Industrial Quality Control Research

Quality control experts from nonmedical industries have joined ranks with some hospitals to conduct outcomes research. This is a natural marriage. To do outcomes research, an organization must have access to some kind of specific patient treatment data. Hospitals have that data, but their experience with scientific management is limited. Their inexperience motivates them to collaborate with other, non-health-care industries to get expertise in "quality" management.

An example of this arrangement is provided by the partnership between the Rush-Presbyterian-St. Luke's Medical Center in Chicago and the Minnesota Mining and Manufacturing Company. First 3M created the management program; then it piloted the program at Rush. The two organizations signed a licensing agreement in March 1989 that gives 3M the right to market the management product to other hospitals.[46]

Rush also markets the product through its for-profit subsidiary, ArcVentures. According to Marie Sinioris, president of ArcVentures, the hospital does not charge for the consulting services that it dispenses to the three hospital clients that were brought in by 3M. It does charge its non-3M client hospitals, although Sinioris would not say how many such clients ArcVentures has or how much money the consulting business has earned for the hospital.[47]

Another example of such an approach is provided by the research project created by the Harvard Community Health Plan (HCHP).[48] The project, which is called the National Demonstration Project on Quality Improvement in Health Care, has received two grants from the Hartford Foundation. The first, for $220,000, ran from January 1987 through June 1988. The second, for $600,000, ran from January 1989 through December 1991.[49]

Daniel Berwick is the author of the project. He points out that managers must have quality information that is as good as their financial information if they are to ensure the delivery of quality care at an affordable price. Berwick concedes, however, that collecting quality information involves special methodological problems because no standard unit exists for measuring quality; financial reporting systems, of course, can use dollars as a standard of measurement. To solve this problem, Berwick devised his own relative value scale to measure quality. It ranges from zero, the lowest quality ranking, to 100, the highest ranking. Berwick does not wish to simply establish minimum performance standards; he wants managers to embark on a "search for excellence."[50] But this emphasis presents a problem even more serious than the methodological one; to achieve this excellence, what *facets* of quality should managers evaluate? Like other experts, Berwick has resorted to the use of statistical standards. *Modern Healthcare* reports:

> Dr. Berwick decided not to rely heavily on measuring patient outcomes because reliable outcome measures require large sample sizes and are

difficult to obtain. Instead, he decided to define criteria for the technical processes of care, or how physicians manage particular conditions. The computerized system works by issuing regular reports on patients' status, then issuing reminders if physicians fail to follow certain criteria of care. HCHP has completed or is in the process of completing standards for 13 specific conditions.[51]

Interestingly, even a plan as large as the HCHP is unable to find a "large" enough sample size to do clinical outcomes research. The "technical processes" that Berwick describes sound like those that were used to create the statistically derived and standardized DRG system and to develop methods for creating "scientific-legal" rationality. However, these techniques do not provide the only source of data for the HCHP project; it also does outcomes research that is designed to learn whether the system is efficient in managerial terms.

> In addition to tracking the clinical components of care, the system also reports on access, interpersonal care, integration (communicating and coordinating care), staff morale and satisfaction, the interaction of internal business systems and the condition of facilities. There are a number of measures for each area; for instance, the interpersonal category includes scores for patients' overall satisfaction with various medical departments and with staff, laboratory and pharmacy services. It also evaluates patients' intent to return to providers in various medical departments.[52]

Thus, as Berwick says, data for HCHP's quality reports come from both computerized medical scores and "a tremendous amount of patient interviewing."[53] Neither method captures clinical effectiveness.

Once the HCHP management project had been constructed, it was tested on twenty-one health care providers, who were paired with experts in quality control from a variety of other industries. For example, the Massachusetts Respiratory Hospital was paired with a public utility, the Florida Power and Light Company. Massachusetts Respiratory Hospital had a very specific problem to solve: it was paying out $24,000 a week to a temporary nursing agency because of a shortage of permanent nurses. After learning some quality management techniques from the Florida Power and Light Company, the hospital adopted an "innovative" program. It began to pay its nurses higher salaries and to offer them flexible work schedules; these were the two benefits nurses gained when they quit the hospital and went to work as nursing "temps," which many of them were doing. As a result of its innovations, the hospital reduced its dependence on temporary nurses and cut its agency fees from $24,000 to $8,000 weekly.[54]

In reporting this event, David Burda observed that the hospital had "recognized a valuable tenet of business: The key to high profits is high quality." It is no reflection on Burda to point out that this account provides an excellent example of shifting focal points. Even if we grant the questionable premise that the key to high profits is high quality, then what is the "quality" being discussed here? According to Burda, it is "the quality of one of [the hospitals] key products, nursing care." Thus, the administrative innovation "produced" a higher quality of nursing care, which could conceivably improve the patients' clinical conditions.

But these were the same nurses! Previously, they were employed by the temporary agency; now they are employed by the hospital. Although the data certainly demonstrate that the hospital saved money by hiring nurses on a permanent basis, they do not demonstrate that nurses are clinically better when they work for one employer than when they work for another.

It should be pointed out that many resources were used to achieve this "innovation." Before the hospital joined the project, the nursing director had demonstrated her awareness of the problem by offering nurses flexible schedules, in an attempt to retain them on a permanent basis. That strategy failed, according to Maureen Bisognano, the hospital's administrator.

When the hospital joined the national demonstration project and was paired with the Florida Power and Light Company, according to Bisognano, the hospital learned that it was necessary to use a team of people, not simply one nursing director, to find a solution to its problem. This team included "the administrator, the medical director, the chief financial officer, the director of employee relations, the nurse manager, the director of nursing and the nursing staff coordinator."[55] This high-powered team, using the utility company's "cause-and-effect diagrams," was finally able to confirm for itself that the hospital had to hire temporary nurses because it could neither retain those it already had nor recruit new ones.

In an attempt to learn why this was so, the hospital devised a scientific study; first, it surveyed nurses who quit their hospital jobs and went to work for an agency; then it analyzed the results, using the utility company's "Pareto charts" to distinguish between "dominant" and "trivial" causes. Using this technology, administrators learned that nurses preferred agency work "for two reasons, not one. Those reasons were higher salaries and, as the nursing director suspected, flexible hours."[56] Thus, it was the pay schedule, not inflexible scheduling, that was the truly "dominant cause" of the hospital's problem.

Nowhere in this account does anyone point out that the reason nurses were dissatisfied with their pay was because of cost-cutting mechanisms that another group of scientific management experts had put into place throughout the 1970s and early 1980s. During that time, managers attempted to cut some of their hospitals' costs by increasing nurses' "productivity," scientific management's euphemism for "work loads," while simultaneously ensuring that nurses would continue to receive the same, low wages they had been paid historically. Thus managerial techniques, combined with social developments such as the fact that both the pay levels and employment opportunities available to professional women had increased as a result of the women's movement, led to a severe nursing shortage within a decade. By the late 1980s, hospitals needed a new batch of expensive management experts to tell them that they must raise their wages both to attract people to nursing and to retain nurses on a permanent basis.

This media account may have been biased, of course, since it was taken from the administrators involved. For example, Bisognano seems to have believed that the problem was that the nursing director was able to identify only one factor, flexible scheduling, as the attraction that temporary service had for the nurses. However, both Bisognano and the nursing director must have known, as did everyone else who was interested in the health care system at the time, that low wages also played an important role. The probability is that the director was empowered only to change scheduling patterns, not to make changes in the hospital's nursing pay policy. Only highly trained, managerial experts can do that.

Government Research

Both the federal and state governments have become directly involved in doing outcomes research. Although the federal government sometimes emphasizes clinical quality, state governments have become increasingly intent on trying to contain costs as the federal government requires states to deliver certain Medicare and Medicaid services, even though it does not pay for them.

Throughout the 1980s and 1990s, the Health Care Financing Administration (HCFA) has become increasingly involved in assessing the quality of health care services. Using Medicare's peer review organizations, HCFA has launched several research initiatives, including the Medicare mortality studies.

Although their proponents claimed that these studies would reveal whether or not patients got well as a result of having received medical treatments, they also were used to put competitive pressure on providers, on the assumption that increased competition among them would automatically improve the quality of health care they delivered. Throughout the late 1980s HCFA released raw, unanalyzed mortality data that contained no provisions for taking severity of illness into account. HCFA's release of the data caused hospitals to complain bitterly, both about the quality of the data and because HCFA did not give them an opportunity to respond to the data in advance. Carol McCarthy, Ph.D., president of the American Hospital Association, questioned the validity of the data. "We need to make sure that the kind of information being released is, in fact, information about the quality of care. If we are content . . . to make our determinations on quality based on statistical manipulations, we're shortchanging ourselves. Misinformation about quality is not what the public needs."[57]

HCFA's administrator, William Roper, M.D., acknowledged that the mortality statistics did not measure quality. He also conceded that "it makes sense to have a phased release to providers and then to the general public."[58] In spite of that assessment, HCFA *did* release the data.

Why could not HCFA produce meaningful information? The agency has access to an extremely large, nationwide database, something Berwick says is hard to come by. On the surface, it appears to be a valuable asset. In actuality, it presents a complex set of real and methodological problems.

To begin with, the data are neither uniform nor consistently organized.[59] But, providers say, an even more important problem is the fact that the data contain no mechanisms for taking severity of illness into account. Without that capability, no study is likely to yield significant clinical outcomes information.[60]

Given that a lack of severity of illness measures confounds every research project, why has no one constructed an effective measure to take it into account? For one thing, to do so would interfere with the process of mechanistic standardization that is going on throughout the health care delivery system, as it is in other areas of work and social organization in the modern, Western world. To take severity of illness into account would mean health care workers would deliver a product that is "customized" to fit the patients' medical reality rather than one that is "standardized" to fit the principles of scientific management.

This development is interesting. As a *marketing* feature, customization is integral to all the economic and administrative aspects of health care organization. Insurance "products" are customized in many ways—to fit the public's demographic characteristics, or to enable patients or their corporate employers to exercise "choice," for example. At the same time, customized service is being managed *out* of the only place where it actually has the potential to improve clinical outcomes, that is, in the clinical services that are delivered to patients. The severity of their pathologies would have to be a crucial consideration if the goal really were to deliver high quality care.

Clinical Outcomes Research by
Medical Professionals

Some medical researchers actually seem to be doing real clinical impact studies. In addition to demonstrating the overutilization of coronary artery surgeries, they have pinpointed other kinds of overutilization as well.

Robert H. Brook, M.D., Sc.D., of the Rand Corporation, and Kathleen N. Lohr, Ph.D., of the Institute of Medicine in Washington, cite the findings of these medical researchers to support their argument that the financial incentives being used to cut costs are exacerbating problems with clinical quality. They see the connection as particularly relevant during the period when hospitals' profits dropped, under the DRG system, from about 14 percent in 1984–85 to below zero in 1988. They predict that clinical quality problems will grow worse unless a "clinical monitoring system" is developed "that could detect areas most threatened by such change and . . . intervene before levels of quality of care provided to the Medicare population were significantly undermined."[61] Problems with clinical quality also stem from a desire by providers to become better marketplace vendors. According to the health care media, that had already begun to happen by 1987:

> Many healthcare providers are trying to take advantage of consumers' interest in quality healthcare by touting the superiority of their products. Specifically, these providers are gathering data that illustrate the clinical quality of their services, then using the statistics to show buyers of healthcare services that their quality care is a good value.[62]

Some of these attempts seem to be focused on clinical outcomes, although that focus continues to be problematic because of the lack of tangible quality measures. Jacque Sokolov, M.D., and vice president and medical director at Southern California Edison in Burbank, the second largest utility in the country, says, "I think hospitals will have to spend significant time and resources to truly develop quality measures that will be demonstrated within these sophisticated systems."[63] Scott and White Medical Center in Temple, Texas, does attempt to track the outcomes of treatments that are delivered in both inpatient and outpatient settings, but its goal is to "promote uniform clinical practices," according to Kermit Knudsen, M.D., chief of staff at the center and president of the Scott and White Clinic. In that system, high quality in managed care means that "all patients are handled in essentially the same fashion. . . . We have more data on resource consumption relating to our HMO patients, but we have basically a single standard of practice."[64] In this description, "quality" is assumed to be assured through uniform, standardized treatment decisions. Although that is not certain to happen, the policy would meet at least some standards of basic fairness, if the same standards were used for patients across the various demographic categories who had the same diagnoses and severity of illness is taken into account.

Other providers actually do attempt to track the clinical outcomes of care. For example, administrators at the Cleveland Clinic selected some common diagnosis-related groups of illnesses, such as cardiac care or hip replacements. For those illnesses, the clinic gathers data to show the patients' morbidity, mortality, discharge status, and whether or not they were able to return to a productive lifestyle. Although the clinic will use all these results as a selling tool, payers are particularly anxious to learn "whether an employee can be expected to return to a productive lifestyle"[65]—probably the ultimate test of a treatment's "outcome."

For whatever their reasons, medical professionals have been somewhat more likely than other interested groups to do outcomes studies that focus on clinical effects. Some observers, however, have suggested that outcomes may not continue to be their major focus "as the health care environment changes." Bob Coburn, a managing consultant with A. Foster Higgins and Company in Washington, D.C., has pointed out that in the past, the "short supply items were physicians and hospital beds. Now they are patients and dollars."[66]

As part of the process of shifting the focus of physicians from clinical quality to cost control, the old mechanisms that were originally created to contain costs are being renamed to make them more palatable. For example, the Florida-based American College of Utilization Review Physicians, which was established to promote utilization review education in 1973, has changed its name to the American College of Medical Quality.[67] This manipulation of language is both a strategy and an outcome in the ongoing, social construction of health care reality.

The Social Control
Functions of Quality Data

Whatever else all this research accomplishes, one of its most important functions will be to find a way to ration health care services that the public will accept as legitimate. Rationing services requires patients, as well as providers, to change their behavior. A major purpose of outcomes research is to obtain information to legitimate a certain kind of "education" of patients, to train them to approach the purchase of health care in the same way they would any other consumer product.

Although this objective may sound reasonable to American listeners, it also may be unrealistic in practice. More knowledge, sophistication, and tolerance for complexity is required to interpret outcomes data than any patient is ever likely to possess, particularly the sickest ones, who cost the most to treat. Even confident, healthy, high-powered corporate executives with vast economic resources have been unable to decipher the quality data that have already been released. *Modern Healthcare* reports:

> Flagship corporations say they are willing to pay a premium for quality
> healthcare, if only they could determine how to tell which services truly
> are high quality. . . . So far, providers have made little effort to define
> quality in ways that sophisticated buyers or even average customers can
> understand. Quality hasn't been translated into an agreed-upon set of
> standards and benchmarks that can be applied throughout the industry.[68]

The fact that employers have not been able to figure out the data does
not deter them from attempting to translate the data for their workers.
Alan Greer, employee benefits manager for a chemical manufacturer in
Allentown, Pennsylvania, says that the reports are so complex that the
average person will not be able to base decisions upon them. Therefore,
employers will play a critical role: "Companies will have to analyze the
information, summarize it further and then share it with employees."[69]

Of course getting consumers to change their behavior through education or persuasion is a slow and often unreliable way to impose
change upon a populace. Thus the most sophisticated consumers of all,
corporate employers, continue to rely on muscle, on the old, tried and
true structural control mechanisms they have always used. And their
major focus continues to be on cutting and shifting health care costs.

The automotive industry provides an illustrative example. For
twenty years its representatives have pressured insurance companies to
adopt policies designed to control the utilization of health care services. Although the media today usually date these kinds of corporate
activities from the mid-1980s,[70] they began at least a decade earlier. In
the 1970s, in response to pressure from the automotive industry, Blue
Cross and Blue Shield of Michigan became the first insurance company in the country to reimburse providers for second opinions before
surgery. At that time, the objective was to reduce the utilization of
surgical procedures. The automotive industry also attempted to influence health care policy making at the national level. Its initiatives,
which had already been in place for several years, were described in
the letter the Washington Business Group on Health sent to HEW
Secretary Joseph Califano in 1977.[71]

During the 1980s, the automotive industry encouraged the Michigan Blues to pressure hospitals to comply with statistical, DRG-like
standards for private patients. Then, when the quality management
movement came to vogue, Blue Cross and Blue Shield of Michigan
became one of the first insurance companies to tie its hospital reim-

bursement policy to compliance with quality, as well as with productivity, standards.

In January 1990, again as a result of pressure from the automotive
industry, the Michigan Blues put a new, five-year contract into effect
that changed its payment method. In the past, payment had been
"based on a percentage of each hospital's operating budget." Under the
new contract, it is based on a prospective pricing system,[72] which is,
essentially, like the Medicare DRG system. And, like the DRG system,
its primary function is to control provider decision making and health
care services utilization; simultaneously, it will create and enforce
compliance with statistical norms, using statistical processes. For example, after the new system has been implemented, explains *Modern
Healthcare,*

> hospitals' inpatient days can't exceed 4 percent of what the Blues
> determine is necessary. . . . Hospitals with rates of less than 4 per-
> cent will earn a bonus payment that equals 4 percent of their reim-
> bursement. Those that fail to meet the target will be penalized with at
> least a 2 percent cut in reimbursements.[73]

Thus, the quality management system the Blues have constructed
simply controls providers mechanistically, through the old, familiar,
statistics-based reward-and-punishment process.

The important point is that the Blues took this step in response to
cost-cutting demands by the Michigan automotive industry. More than
660,000 auto company workers and their families are insured by the
Michigan Blues, making the automotive industry, as opposed to its
employees, an extremely powerful consumer of health care insurance.
Thus, as media reports point out, "the willingness of the Blues to
tackle such elusive topics as quality control and productivity comes in
response to the business community."[74]

Of course, Blue Cross and Blue Shield also has enormous consumer power, as a major purchaser of hospital services. The Michigan
Hospital Association reports that about "35 percent of all Michigan
hospital revenues come from the Blues."[75] Thus the automotive industry and Blue Cross and Blue Shield of Michigan, in tandem, have the
economic and political power to do health care "planning" directly for
the state of Michigan and, indirectly, for the entire country.

Today almost everyone in the United States, including government representatives, providers, private citizens, and corporate employers, has accused insurance companies of being responsible for the mess our health care system is in. That charge is justified in many ways, yet few observers seem either to realize or to acknowledge the role that corporate America has played in determining the policies and actions that health insurance companies take.

The new Michigan Blues program is no more designed to get at clinical quality than are those of most of the other interested groups that are doing quality management. Like other groups, representatives of the Blues, working with representatives from the Michigan Hospital Association, had to develop a system for defining quality before they could measure it. In the earliest stages, the committee had only the vaguest idea what a quality program would look like. Its goal was ambitious: to track "everything that happens to a patient from admission to discharge." In the long run, representatives of the Blues said, they hoped their monitoring program would describe clinical outcomes, that it would evaluate patients' conditions after they were discharged.[76] In the meantime, until the system actually can capture clinical data, what will the Blues evaluate? Quality reviewers will "focus on such issues as whether a patient fell or developed an infection" while in hospital.[77] Here, high quality means simply that the patient escaped actual harm during the hospitalization period. This quality management program will not attempt to learn whether patients received the correct treatment. Rather, "a separate utilization review program evaluates care."[78] Presumably, this statement refers to the utilization review that ensures compliance with statistically derived standards. Thus neither the new quality management system nor the old utilization review is designed to learn what clinical impact specific treatments have.

Insider Assessments of the
Quality Management Business

Whatever its failings may be, total quality management has become both a very big business and an important new component of the American health care system. As such, it contributes substantially to our nation's health care costs—precisely the ailment it is supposed to cure. And as the new industry becomes more entrenched, the infighting among competing experts has also intensified. Some managers insist that their expertise is of a higher quality than that of their competitors. *Modern Healthcare* reports, "total quality management purists . . . disciples of such quality giants as W. Edward Deming and Joseph Juran . . . say the healthcare market is becoming saturated with poorly trained total quality management consultants who are selling programs that have little chance of working."[79]

George Labovitz, who recognized the market relatively early, considers himself to be a "high-quality" quality expert. He founded Organizational Dynamics Incorporated in 1970, although he began to do health care consulting only in 1987. Labovitz says, "The market is becoming flooded by people calling themselves quality consultants. These people are one chapter ahead of their clients."[80]

Curt Lindberg, president of Voluntary Hospitals of America, agrees. He says, "I'm concerned that hospitals are making the wrong decisions on consultants and wasting hundreds of thousands of dollars. . . . Some consultants are real gems; some are semi-precious; and some are rocks."[81]

Matthew Kelliher, corporate director of quality management at Harvard Community Health Plan, charges that the accountancy firms that have flooded into outcomes research have no real understanding of the health care industry; they are simply selling old management products under new names. He says, "Consultants that used to sell productivity are selling quality improvement systems. Consultants that used to sell team building are selling total quality management. Consultants that used to sell cost accounting are selling cost-of-quality systems."[82]

Brent James, M.D., director of medical research at Intermountain Health Care, is also critical of the new consultants: "The big accounting firms are just following the market by selling total quality management. . . . These firms are learning at the expense of their customers. As an academic, that bothers me. You shouldn't charge for research."[83]

Total quality management purists also criticize the new interlopers entering the field on other grounds; they claim the new movement is without substance. It consists of "sloganisms" and directs most of its efforts toward achieving administrative, rather than clinical goals. James believes that, says *Modern Healthcare,* "hospitals are spending most of their money on programs that are designed to improve an organization's corporate culture or administrative services, not patient outcomes [although he also] believes total quality management can work equally well on clinical practices." He states, "Hospitals want to show their purchasers that they're on the band wagon, but most of the programs have no substance."[84]

If this trend continues, the purists fear that these new total quality management firms will transform their profitable new industry into "a passing fad." According to Paul Batalden, M.D., corporate vice-president and head of the total quality management program at the Hospital Corporation of America (HCA), "Everyone is running around trying to do 'it,' but they don't know what 'it' is. . . . Predictably, a number of people will never find it and say total quality management was a failure."[85] Batalden is considered to be one of the fathers of the total quality management movement in health care.

Members of the new firms brush aside such criticisms, however. George Whetsell, regional director of the Healthcare Operations Improvement Division of KPMG Peat Marwick, says, "The vast majority of total quality management is not new. Anybody that went through an industrial engineering program has been trained in total quality management."[86]

The Cost of Quality Management

Regardless of how participants define the goals of quality management, the costs of such programs now contribute significantly to our nation's health care bill. The U.S. Congress has funded the programs and will continue to do so in the foreseeable future. *Modern Healthcare* reports:

> After months of debate on financing for outcomes research, Congress finally approved a budget last month [June 1985] that allocates $32 million for such projects in fiscal 1990. . . . That is more than a fourfold increase in the $7.5 million spent in fiscal 1989 for such research. The law also authorizes the government to spend $75 million in fiscal 1991, $110 million in fiscal 1992, $148 million in fiscal 1993 and $185 million in fiscal 1994.[87]

These expenditures will put an additional strain on the Medicare trust funds, which will pay for 60 percent of the program. The rest will be financed from general revenues.[88] In the past, congressional grants for these purposes went almost entirely to university-based research; it is likely that schools will receive most of the newly authorized money as well.[89] However, because of the close ties among quality managers working in very diverse areas, it is hard to determine the true beneficiaries of grant money.

For example, the Harvard Community Health Plan (HCHP), which has close ties to Harvard Medical School, has also worked continuously with industrial quality control consultants in private industry, both to create its quality management program and to continue conducting outcomes research. Daniel Berwick, M.D., who originated the project, works closely with A. Blanton Godfrey of the Juran Institute, who is a principal investigator with the HCHP national demonstration project.[90]

Thus private industries and consultants of all sorts combine their expertise to create the total quality plans being put into place even though government funding may go mainly to academic research entities. In addition, private corporations fund much of the research themselves. For example, the national demonstration project has, as already noted, received two grants from the Hartford Foundation.[91] Foundations, of course, receive subsidies in the form of tax exemptions to further their particular political agendas, subsidies that are unavailable to the average citizen.

According to the General Accounting Office (GAO), quality assurance programs in the United States are currently "a disjointed mix of provider and payer initiatives that has done very little to improve the overall performance of the majority of providers."[92] Thus these new control mechanisms have failed to achieve their goals at the same time that they have become an additional, and expensive, component of our increasingly complex health care system.

To impose order on this "disjointed mix," the GAO recommends that we create a comprehensive national quality assurance strategy aimed at achieving several goals. First, the strategy would create techniques for collecting more effective data upon which to base quality assurance activities. Second, on the basis of those data, the strategy would create uniform standards of care, which would be enforced through national treatment guidelines for providers. Third, the strategy would improve techniques for assessing the quality of care and assuring that quality standards are met at the local level. And, fourth, the strategy would create "*a national organization to develop, implement and monitor the national strategy*."[93] Thus the GAO recommends that we create another mammoth apparatus for collecting more data and exercising more surveillance over providers. Then it recommends that we construct yet another national organization to keep the surveillance mechanism itself under surveillance. The slogan of management experts everywhere appears to be: "If it doesn't work, do more of it."

Summary

Proponents of outcomes research claim that the process will provide information that can be used simultaneously to cut costs and to assure that our system provides high-quality health care. So far, it has been unable to achieve either of those goals. Because the quality sought is always defined by the social, political, and economic position of the expert searching it out, we have not yet begun to do the real work of reorganizing health care delivery in the United States.

However, in their competition to control the power and economic resources that inhere in the health care marketplace, new management experts in a wide range of institutional settings are collaborating with their powerful employers to construct a new kind of "knowledge" in the form of various definitions of health care quality and reality. Thus both "quality" and the managerial techniques required to achieve it have become powerful new commodities being produced and sold in the health care marketplace. Both the knowledge and those who possess or buy it are legitimated and institutionalized as part of the process.

The American public is forced to buy this new commodity, and to participate in the legitimation and institutionalization process, whether it is willing or not. But the commodity is largely smoke and mirrors, in this very expensive late nineteenth-century version of the great American medicine show.

6
Conclusions

I don't think that's a realistic problem—that somehow
the rich people are going to get something a whole lot
better. However, if they do, in America, that kind of—
that's the way we are, you know. That's the way our
society works.
—*Alain C. Enthoven professor,*
Graduate School of Business, Stanford University[1]

The end of this story remains to be written, of course. Today, as in
the early 1970s, restructuring American health care is a topic that
figures prominently in the news. If this revived political interest
reflects a growing consensus that the existing system has reached its
upper limit of complexity and costliness, at the same time that it
excludes so many people as to make the situation politically risky,
something actually may change. This may be the culmination of the
political and ideological struggle to define our national health care
values and goals that has been raging for more than twenty years.
Or, if all the hoopla is simply the "sound and fury" that typically
accompanies a political upset such as our last presidential election,
it may signify nothing.

Only one thing is certain. Although some corporate employers now
favor a single payer, socialized system such as the Canadians have,
they are still in the minority. Robert Evans, a Canadian health economist, has literally equated the American free-market health care policy
with religion, stating that "the free market is not preferred because it
achieves other objectives, whether of cost, quality or access; it is *itself*
the objective."[2]

Partly for that reason, failure to achieve those cost, quality, and access objectives has not deterred free-market ideologues from intensifying their political and economic initiatives to ensure that we will continue to do what we have been doing for the past twenty years. Thus the same conflicting ideological interests that canceled each other out in the early 1970s were still reflected in the proposals being put forward in late 1993.[3]

At the most conservative end of the political continuum is a plan that would move us back fifty years in time; it would pass the cost of health care back to each individual American. We would each buy a basic health insurance plan for about $1,500 a year. In addition, individual consumers could choose to save money by paying for health care in a tax-deferred health investment plan, for a total cost to each individual of about $4,500 a year. After a time, however, unused funds in the investment plan could be rolled over into a retirement account.

President Bill Clinton, attempting to stand in a political middle ground that may not be as safe as it once was, favors managed competition. In that system, government would continue its attempts to "manage" health care costs while leaving the private sector free to compete for profits; our national response to medical reality would remain safely commodified. This plan is unpopular with a large segment of the business sector, since it would require American employers to pay a large part of the price, in an arrangement very similar to the Partnership for Health that President Richard Nixon proposed more than twenty years ago.

The most politically "radical" proposal put forward in late 1993 was the least likely to be adopted, even though polls indicated that it was the one most favored by the American public. It called for a single payer, government-operated system similar to the Canadian one.

If these conflicting proposals succeed in stalemating each other today, as they did twenty years ago, the strategy for change that industry implemented in the 1970s will continue to win by default. We will witness the further "evolution" of the initiatives corporate strategists launched, which have now been thoroughly institutionalized in ways described throughout this book.

Despite the self-serving claims that corporate leaders make—that only they, in the private sector, have either the ability or the motivation to achieve organizational "efficiencies"—industry's initiatives have accomplished no positive goals. Instead, they have succeeded only in increasing the complexity of our bloated and wasteful health insurance and administrative surveillance industries. All the political and economic manipulation has resulted in the social construction of a system that excludes millions of people from either health care services or insurance. The first victims of that process were the working poor. Today, many formerly middle-class people have been priced out of the insurance market as well.[4]

Industry's initiatives have not reduced our health care costs, which have continued to skyrocket. Instead, Americans simply pay more for much less, as our health care dollars are rechanneled into a massive administrative apparatus. The major purpose of that apparatus is not to ensure organizational efficiency but to carry out surveillance and control functions that subvert democratic processes, redefine professional knowledge, and manipulate providers and patients, all at the same time. We have not yet begun even to recognize the extensiveness or the political nature of these developments, let alone to calculate their economic and social costs.

The distinction between the value assumptions underlying managed competition and those underlying socialized medicine cannot be overstated. Victor Fuchs, a respected, longtime advocate of national health insurance, has argued that a national health insurance plan that covers virtually all Americans would serve an integrative function, that it would "forge a link between classes, regions, races, and age groups."[5] Thus Fuchs argues in favor of a national health care system that links us together because it is based on genuinely universalistic principles. This system is the antithesis of managed competition, which simultaneously helps to create and legitimate the ever-increasing levels of inequality, fragmentation, and separation that are occurring throughout our society.

When they are presented with this argument, advocates of managed competition speak from both sides of their mouths. First, they claim that managed competition will *not* lead to greater inequality; rather, it will ensure that everyone gets access to health care. On the other hand, they argue that inequality in health care delivery is acceptable, that it is the American way. The economist Alain Enthoven, who is credited with originating the concept of managed competition, states that perspective clearly.

> From the point of view of equalitarianism, managed competition would be a significant step in the direction of equalitarianism. . . . So I don't

think that's a realistic problem—that somehow the rich people are going to get something a whole lot better. However, if they do, in America, that kind of—that's the way we are, you know. That's the way our society works. If rich people want something a whole lot better and they're gonna do it with their own money, we let them do it. The whole purpose is to get everybody to have good, quality health care; it's not to make sure nobody gets anything better than anybody else.[6]

There are two logical problems with this statement. First, it glosses over the fact that it is *society,* not rich individuals, that pays for the construction of scientific knowledge and technology. Medical science is a social product. Much of it is carried out in universities that are subsidized by public money. When private corporations do the research, they, too, are publicly subsidized; often they receive tax breaks to help them develop the products or "knowledge" that will yield them huge profits in return. In addition, they can charge inflated prices for some products in order to force the public to subsidize their research and development projects directly, without the inconvenience of having to use government as an intermediary. Not incidentally, all of these charges contribute enormously to further inflation in health care costs, which represents an additional tax on the general public. Clearly the development of new health care technology is paid for by the public in many ways, whether the process is carried out by government-subsidized institutions or by the corporations that develop, produce, and sell medical commodities.

In this process, the costs and risks of creating medical "science" are socialized, while the profits remain securely in private hands. Rich people do not "pay for it themselves." Just as a massive tax on their personal incomes would not yield enough cash to pay off our national debt, neither could the rich pay the *real* price of the social construction of medical science. That cost would be too high even for them to absorb.

Second, there is the question of exactly what Enthoven means by "better." On what bases do managers who develop customized health insurance products or providers, attempting to market their services to the most profitable consumers, decide that certain treatments are better? More often than not, better care means little more than the freedom to use every technology available in our national health care arsenal, even in cases where there is virtually no likelihood that doing so will result in any kind of gain, in either the patient's health or quality of life. The beneficiaries of this care usually are those with elite health insurance products, although some publicly funded patients sometimes receive such services as well. In August 1993, for example, public funds paid for the surgical separation of the Siamese twins Angela and Amy Lakeberg, in a case where one twin was certain to die and the other had only a 1 percent chance of survival. In such cases, it is clear, health care services are not rationed on the basis of any kind of cost-benefit analysis.

We do ration services in the United States, of course, but we are more likely to do so on the basis of social class and the ability to pay than on cost-benefit analysis or even on the health status of the patient. We attempt to achieve our ideological goals first, on the assumption that doing so will result in achieving our practical goals as well. Thus for the last twenty years our primary goal has been to keep health care delivery safely in the free-market sector. Logically, this is the same kind of process that allowed the automotive industry to undermine urban mass transit systems after World War II.[7] Rather than attempting to construct the most efficient transportation system, we exploited our own need for transportation as an opportunity to earn a profit and create jobs. As a result, the United States is notable among modern, Western democracies for its dirty, inefficient, and expensive transportation system.

This ideology-driven approach provides a mechanistic formula for making public policy that relieves us of the responsibility for making hard moral and intellectual decisions. The refusal to make those decisions consciously and instead allowing them to be made through mechanistic manipulation by those who control the social structural apparatus is part of a social process that fragments us as a people. By customizing medical services to fit individual pocketbooks, we are constructing a system that delivers services based on patients' membership in some demographic category rather than on their health status. Medical products are distributed not strictly on the bases of need or even the probability that they will be successful but according to social characteristics such as class, occupation, marital status, age, race, and gender. This distribution represents a new, modern form of the ancient, traditional practice of "particularism" that characterized feudal societies in the Western world. It is the antithesis of the modern ideology that promotes "universalism." Although we have developed statistical models that appear to mandate the delivery of standardized treatments on a universal basis to all patients, the standards vary enormously for the different categories of customers who buy different, customized health care and insurance products.

The competition to define health care reality that has occurred as various interest groups have exercised power in the health care arena has not been equal. Corporate America has had far greater access than ordinary citizens to the social institutions and mechanisms through which corporate strategists can act out their ideologies, simultaneously implementing very concrete social policies and legitimating them with the new "knowledge" this exercise of power constructs. This is true for corporate employers who attempt to cut their own operating costs by eliminating health care services and insurance for their employees. It is also true for corporations that produce health care services and products as commodities, such as pharmaceutical and insurance companies and for-profit hospital chains. Even not-for-profit hospitals must play the same game to survive economically. All these industries oppose socialized medicine, for both economic and ideological reasons.

It is clear, as Michel Foucault would say, that in the process of exercising power, corporate planners have succeeded in creating the new kinds of knowledge that are required to legitimate that power. But it also is important to acknowledge, as Max Weber would do, that they have done so not simply by establishing new ideas but also by creating new bureaucratic control structures. This administrative machinery simultaneously implements policy decisions that are about as "real" as anything gets in the social world at the same time that it enforces and perpetuates industry's new version of "reality." These developments go a long way toward explaining the social construction of consciousness that Karl Marx described, in which the ideas that dominate within societies, historically, are those that serve the interests of dominant groups.

Despite emphasis on scientific management and empirical, statistical processes, the new knowledge that is being constructed is "moral" rather than "scientific." In the process of redefining "good health care," by equating it with adherence to statistical norms, we have also legitimated the idea that it is acceptable to withhold services from our sickest citizens by establishing a formal policy that they will not receive more services than those who are less sick. We enforce that policy through the mechanistic DRG system.

On the surface this process appears to be "universal," one that ensures that services will at least be distributed democratically, if not on the basis of the patients' actual physical conditions. The fact that our sickest citizens fall disproportionately into specific demographic categories, however, makes it clear the process is not democratic at all. In the United States, as in other industrialized Western nations, the sickest people are most apt to be the poor, the very old, and the very young. In all these categories, either women or children or both are disproportionately represented. Thus our system of rationing falls most heavily on very sick people in specific demographic categories.

This process has helped to divide and exacerbate hostilities among various groups of ordinary Americans. For example, the Oregon plan, which guarantees basic health insurance to everyone, grounds many rationing decisions on age differences. Thus, while the general public is often distracted by side arguments about the relative fairness of delivering heroic treatments to elderly people at the same time that infants are denied basic inoculations, the social class basis for inequality in health care delivery is conveniently glossed over. This divide-and-conquer strategy causes young and old to compete for crumbs instead of working together to make a real transformation in our health care delivery system.

A truly rational health care system would be based on nonmechanistic, substantive, cause-and-effect reasoning. It would make treatment decisions in response to the severity of a patient's illness and the medical prospects for success. Instead, we continue to use mechanistic health care delivery policies that mandate statistically standardized treatments to socially constructed demographic populations.

Although this mechanistic approach is very effective as a method of social control, it is inherently flawed as a tool for making policy decisions since it can never tell us what our goals ought to be. It is the antithesis of intelligent, humane health care policy making, which would require us to identify and deal honestly with important moral questions such as these: What do we really want from our health care delivery system? Do we want it, primarily, to maximize the health of our citizens? to serve as a bastion of free enterprise? to provide business and professional interests with profit and work opportunities? If our objective really is to maximize health, do we want to do that for everyone? After all, as Talcott Parsons said, a rational health care system is one that keeps a nation's citizens healthy enough to perform their social roles. Do we care about the health of people whose social roles we do not value, or those who are socially or economically help-less? The American people clearly do care, since their desire for universal access to health care services was an important reason they elected Bill Clinton president.

The mechanistic, free-market approach is flawed for another reason as well. It will perpetuate the abuses that have characterized health care delivery for the past twenty years. It cannot prevent ever-increasing health care cost inflation, since it is based on the continuing production and commodification of health care services for elite consumers. Corporate and government managers will increasingly ration the services that are delivered to socially powerless people in a vain attempt to control health care cost inflation at their expense. But both the commodification of services and rationing them on the basis of ability to pay will require increasing levels of expensive surveillance and control mechanisms to ensure that people get access only to what they can pay for. In the meantime, providers will continue to invent, market, and deliver many medical commodities to health care elites because they are, by definition, profitable.

Our current system is not the result of an "evolutionary" process; it did not emerge and grow because it was the most efficient or effective, because it had the most survival value. Rather, it emerged because it was planned, nurtured, supported, and enforced by extremely powerful corporate interest groups.

The impact of industry's political and economic initiatives has become much broader in scope during the last few years; it now operates at a global level. By shipping cardiac surgery patients to cheaper private hospitals in England, American insurance companies are likely to facilitate the emergence of a more powerful private health care sector there. If the practice becomes prevalent enough actually to cut costs in the United States, health care cost inflation would probably increase in England, putting an additional strain on that country's already stressed socialized system. Some may argue that we would be doing the country a favor, helping it to improve its health care system. It should be noted, however, that American insurance companies claim that the British system already delivers care that is as good as any that can be had in this country. Furthermore, if cost inflation does increase in England, hospitals there will almost certainly lose the new business that caused the inflation in the first place, since U.S. insurance carriers will stop sending them patients. They may even follow the lead of other industries and begin looking for cheaper providers in more far-flung locales, perhaps in third world countries, if they can persuade Americans to go there.

Some U.S. corporations may be having an even more direct impact on the socialized systems of other countries. Ralph Nader has accused American pharmaceutical companies of conspiring to wreck the Canadian socialized health care system by raising the prices of the pharmaceutical supplies that they sell to Canadians.[8] Such a strategy of economic "destabilization" in order to discredit and defeat an ideological competitor is entirely consistent with the one that industry has been using against the American people for two decades.

In sum, social change has occurred in health care delivery during the last twenty years through two different but mutually supportive processes. Existing occupational and organizational structures have been revolutionized, and new ones have been created. At the same time, new definitions of reality and knowledge have been constructed. It follows that, to change the structures that now exist, the same strategy would have to be used by some competing group with a completely different agenda. To eliminate managed competition and implement a system of socialized medicine, it will be necessary to create and exercise social power, just as industry has done. That process might involve using industry's own strategy, using government legislation, exercising economic power against insurance carriers and providers, and redefining medical knowledge. Or it may require the invention of completely new tactics. However, any strategy would have to build upon existing structures to some extent or find a fast way to create new ones to "carry" the action. Power is not a gas floating in the nether. It can only be exercised, either democratically or in an authoritarian way, through organizational structures such as government, business or economic systems, professional organizations, or citizen groups, for example. To use social structures effectively, we must stop denying the "reality" of their existence and develop a clear understanding of how they work in modern, complex cultures. If we do not learn how our system works, powerful groups who understand it very well will use it against us. Corporate employers, in combination with government, the massive health care industry, and the new experts who sell their services to all three groups will continue to manipulate structural processes to achieve their own ideological, political, and economic goals.

Appendix

The Theoretical Frame: Surveillance, Power, and Knowledge

The transformation of health care delivery in the United States during the last twenty years is only one of the latest developments in the long historical process that Max Weber called the "rationalization" of the Western world. According to Weber, over a period of many centuries, traditional, patrimonial techniques for legitimating authority have given way to "rational," bureaucratic ones. As part of that process, the authority of old-style, "free" professionals such as private practice physicians is being replaced by the organizational authority of professional bureaucrats.

Both these categories of professional workers attempt to legitimate their authority with claims that they possess a superior kind of "knowledge." But such claims raise two important questions about the nature of knowledge itself. First, what are the differences between what Weber called "formal" and "substantive" rationality? More important, which kind is it that actually governs modern decision-making processes? Are these processes actually rational in the sense that they reflect some kind of "reality," some cause-and-effect relationship? Or, are they only more mechanistic, as many contemporary analysts have suggested.[1]

Second, what are the social mechanisms through which knowledge is generated and supported? Historical descriptions of the rationalization process itself provide evidence, as Michel Foucault has argued, that power and knowledge have emerged together, that the exercise of power is always, at the same time, the creation of the new definitions of reality that support and legitimate the power itself.

The exercise of power has always required techniques for finding and sanctioning those who violate the rules. As historical rationalization has proceeded, those techniques have become increasingly sophisticated and efficient. In modern organizations, they are carried out almost entirely by the "technologies" of bureaucratic administration, as both Weber and Foucault were aware.

These, then, are the major conceptual components that have served as the focal points of this book: the historical rationalization process; the association of knowledge and power; and bureaucratic surveillance as the dominant mechanism of control that characterizes modern societies. Together, they make up the theoretical framework for my analysis.

Christopher Dandeker, in his own synthesis of Weber and Foucault, has argued persuasively that bureaucratic rationalization and intricate surveillance systems began to emerge together in early modern Western Europe.[2] So did the relationship between nation-states and capitalist economic systems; that is, the bureaucratic military organization that formed the basis for the power of the modern nation-state emerged in symbiotic association with the capitalist economic system that funded it. These unities—bureaucratic organization and surveillance, and the state and a capitalist economy—make up the fabric of Western European power and authority, both the formal power of the state and the informal power inherent in our economic system.

As Dandeker points out, in developing his rationalization thesis Weber himself synthesized the three major theoretical traditions that have been used to analyze rational-legal organization in the Western world: first, Marxism; second, the "modernizing" or "industrial societies" perspectives; and, third, Machiavellianism. All these perspectives are embedded, at least implicitly, in my analysis of the transformation of American health care delivery.

Marxists argue that the bureaucratic organization that embodies rational-legal authority has proliferated in the past because it serves the interests of capitalists in many ways. Most important, it allows them to exercise surveillance and control over their own workers.

Modernization theorists believe that bureaucratic organization is a response to increasingly technological modes of industrial production. Not only is formal organization required for efficient industrial production in such societies; it also provides organizational substitutes for the shared values and beliefs that are destroyed by modernization. Thus rational bureaucratic organization may be a basis for social solidarity in large, diverse populations, where "community" has been obliterated as part of the rationalization process itself.

Machiavellian theorists believe that bureaucratic organization is widely employed because it works to achieve power objectives more effectively than do other organizational forms. They point out that, in political struggles between states, bureaucratic modes of surveillance are technically superior to pure force. But Machiavellian theorists do not limit themselves to analyzing state political activities. Some have created a "bureaucratic politics perspective" that focuses on the roles self-interested bureaucratic and professional experts have played in expanding the surveillance capabilities of the organizations in which they work. Their occupational power, based on their position in the organization and the power of the organization itself, support each other.[3]

This perspective is central to my analysis of the role "experts" have played in supporting industry's strategies to transform the American health care system. In that process, experts have played crucial roles by creating the new knowledge that legitimates the construction of new power positions while simultaneously undermining the legitimacy of traditional knowledge. Thus my analysis of developments in American health care delivery is heavily indebted to Foucault's dual emphasis on the social construction of knowledge and on the modern proliferation of surveillance activities. Both these social processes are simultaneously the means and the result of exercising power.

Weber agreed with Marx that capitalism has been the major historical force driving the rationalization process. Because of their central importance, Weber often focused on capitalist bureaucratic organizations, rather than on government bureaucracies, to analyze the ways in which surveillance techniques function. He pointed out, for example, that in capitalist organizations, the "rational accounting system" performs a dual function. It simultaneously shows the manager whether operations are profitable and provides a mode of surveillance over employees, whose written records serve as a measure of their own productivity.[4] Thus surveillance operates both as the mechanism for achieving economic goals and as an ongoing strategy for establishing and maintaining power over subordinates. These two functions of surveillance are inseparable. Although Weber makes this point, for Foucault it is of central importance. This difference in emphasis is related in part to the perception each theorist had of the nature of "knowledge."

For Foucault, since knowledge is simultaneously the means and the product of the exercise of power, it can never be "value free."

> We should admit rather that power produces knowledge ... that power and knowledge directly imply one another; and that there is no power relation without the correlative constitution of a field of knowledge, nor any knowledge that does not presuppose and constitute at the same time power relations.[5]

Weber conceived of the bureaucratic organization itself as a power tool, as, says Dandeker, a "component in a structure of domination, serving the interests of leaders involved in the struggle for power."[6] But knowledge was another matter. For Weber, the separation of action based on knowledge and action based on values is not only possible, it is a primary requisite of the historical rationalization process. More than Foucault, Weber accepted knowledge at face value— some kinds of knowledge at least. Weber distinguished between formal and substantive rationality.[7] Formal, or legal-scientific, rationality is defined in terms of two parameters: the extent to which it complies with formal rules, and the accuracy with which it carries out numerical calculations. Both rules and numerical knowledge are necessary to construct "rational action," action that achieves some predetermined goal. That much Weber had confidence in. He recognized, however, that the goals themselves cannot be set through formal, rational procedures. Rather, they are determined through substantive rationality.

Goals are set on the basis of value judgments that cannot be determined by truly rational procedures; they are set as "matters of faith."[8] The consequences of this dilemma, particularly the fact that we must inevitably make leaps of faith in setting societal goals, are not sufficiently accounted for in Weber's analysis of historical rationalization. No formal rational process would ever be implemented in the first place unless someone had already determined a goal to be achieved. Formal and substantive rationality can be separated only for analytical purposes, as examples of ideal types. In the real world in which we humans attempt to define and meet our needs, they are two sides of one coin.

Karl Mannheim's distinction between substantial and functional rationality is useful for my purposes. In his typology, substantial rationality is a cognitive process, the ability to perceive cause-and-effect relationships. Functional rationality is mechanical; it consists of coordinated actions among components of some system that are designed to achieve some previously defined goal. Every component in this system, including human beings, is assigned a functional position or role.

Randall Collins notes that in Mannheim's analysis functional rationality is an organizational, not an individual, phenomenon; in fact, it diminishes individual workers, reducing them to "cogs in a machine," forcing them to obey orders without questioning them.[9] Substantial rationality, the power really to think, belongs only to the person at the top of the organization, the only person who actually is able to set goals.

This person is Weber's "charismatic leader," the one whose authority derives from personal qualities, not from rational-legal processes. From his analysis, Mannheim concluded that in modern societies "we can have large-scale organizations, with all their dangers to individual freedom, without gaining intelligent direction of social policy."[10] I have argued, in my previous and current work, that this has been one outcome of the transformation in American health care delivery that has occurred so far.

The real problem is the conflict over how goals are set. The fact that this is a value consideration is conveniently glossed over by arguments about the nature or origins of rational knowledge or about which kinds of knowledge actually *are* more rational. An analysis of the transformation of American health care delivery makes this point very clearly. Since formal rationality can only be evaluated in terms of how effectively it meets its goals, arguments about methods and techniques can not be carried out in isolation. The important questions are these: What are our national health care goals? Who gets to set them? No rule system or statistical calculations can answer those questions. However, corporate America has implemented strategies that attempt to use statistical, mechanical, functional procedures to do just that, to set health care delivery policy. The underlying, value-laden assumption of all these corporate strategies is that achieving "cost efficiency" through competition is the goal of the system, not creating a health care system that serves the national interest by reducing our embarrassing morbidity and mortality statistics. The means have become the goal. The ideological nature of the enterprise is obviated by the fact that corporate strategies have not even achieved their overtly stated goal of lowering health care costs, even though they have helped to deprive millions of Americans of health care insurance.

That industry should attempt to set health care policy in this way is not surprising. In capitalist cultures, Weber would agree with Marx to some extent, capitalists set the nation's goals. But it is "expert" technicians who create and use the knowledge required to achieve those goals. Weber made much of the fact that technical expertise based on the possession of formal qualifications is an important basis for incumbency of high-status, authoritative positions in modern cultures; thus he argued that rank is not determined by economic wealth alone.[11]

Of course, this analysis begs the question: What happens when these experts are not "free," when they work within complex organizations as mere "employees," like any other? In that case, as Mannheim would say, the fact that they "have" knowledge may be used to legitimate the decisions their organizational superiors make, even though it is not necessarily the basis for the decisions themselves.

Dandeker turns to Foucault to complete his description of the historical roles experts play. In particular, Foucault focused on the ways experts, or "disciplinarians," have contributed to the historical emergence and expansion of surveillance within government and corporate bureaucracies.

Disciplinary Knowledge, the Service Ethic, and Accountability

By "disciplinary knowledge," Foucault meant the kind of knowledge that emerges and grows through the academic disciplines. It includes both techniques and outcomes, which Foucault describes as sets of "systematized normalizations." That is, disciplinarians establish professional norms that govern both their methods and their analytical processes. Creating and acting on these kinds of professional norms play an important role in bringing about massive social transformations. Disciplinarians themselves serve many different functions in this process; they provide technical practices, a knowledge base, and the legitimating ideology of expertise. All of these function in the service of government and corporate policy planning in modern societies. Dandeker elaborates:

> There are close parallels between the surveillance and disciplinary systems of the modern prison, the factory, the hospital and military organizations. Whilst having complex historical roots, each reflects a *general* social transformation. Forms of knowledge such as penology, criminology, medicine and military science are not simply useful adjuncts to power strategies but are the very social products of the technologies of power. In turn, these forms of knowledge are means for developing power relationships.[12]

In short, power is legitimated by the kinds of knowledge contained in disciplines. Disciplinarians collect data, or documentation, that function simultaneously to legitimate both their own authority and the creation of yet another kind of "discipline," a kind of universal acceptance of and compliance with "standards." It is not only the disciplinarians who must comply with those standards; subject populations must do so as well. Thus Foucault uses the term "discipline" in two different ways. The first usage reflects the sets of normalizations centered around the disciplines themselves: their tactics, knowledge bases, and institutionalized structures.[13] The second usage describes the behavior of the larger population; the public acts out its subjection to the disciplinary powers not only in the military but also in factories, universities, prisons, and hospitals, through its "disciplined" work habits, political behavior, and so on.

Historically, the power-creating disciplines have been crucial both as repositories of orienting and legitimating data and as organizational mechanisms for exercising control. As part of that process, surveillance has become increasingly important as a control mechanism, although the way it is exercised varies, depending on the social arena in which it operates. The process in medical practice is different from that in penology, for example.

In both premodern and modern authority systems, expert "knowledge" provides a powerful legitimation for authority. In premodern systems, however, the traditional disciplines were far more autonomous in their exercise of power than they are today; that is probably the most important part of what defines them as premodern. In the modern world, new categories of employed, supervised, and accountable experts are more useful to authority; they are also more easily controlled than were their predecessors.

In particularistic, premodern societies, rulers needed disciplinarians who were generally respected both for their knowledge and for the *human* qualities that are supposedly reflected in the service ethic. Not only their expertise but their ethics legitimated their authority. Thus the service ethic, a value, was a necessary part of the social definition of reality, controlling both professional workers and the populace, either in "reality" or ideologically. Since there was no way to keep traditional experts under continuous surveillance, internalized mechanisms such as the service ethic were the major tools that existed to control them. Experts had to be prevented from exercising unbridled self-interest in their decision making—at least they had to be perceived as doing so, to some extent; otherwise they would have threatened the capacity of expert knowledge to generate power, either for the expert or for the ruler. Thus a certain level of trust, both in expertise and in experts, is required to create new knowledge and to use it to generate power. Historically, breakdowns in trust and in authority systems have occurred together. For example, the Protestant Reformation and public disgust with the worldly practices of the sixteenth-century Catholic priesthood occurred at the same time.

In contemporary society, a systematic breakdown both in public trust and in community has been an important part of the rationalization process itself. As both a cause and consequence of that breakdown in trust, surveillance systems have enforced compliance with organizational goals. Logically, the institutionalization of bureaucratic surveillance and its ideological companion, accountability, eliminates the possibility of trust, both as a social value and as a human capacity, since its underlying assumption is that people will not do what they claim to be doing unless they are watched. American college students of the 1990s, in sharp contrast with those of the late 1960s, often express the belief that this is actually a characteristic of "human nature."

But it is not the rationalization process alone that has had this impact. Political developments throughout the 1980s suggest that public trust has also been diminished by authorities themselves, either as an unintended side effect or as a deliberate political strategy as part of the process of exercising power. Jurgen Habermas has argued that an "unintended" elimination of trust has occurred as a result of the manipulation of scientific facts to achieve political goals in modern societies, which has led to a "legitimation crisis."[14] In that case, the exercise of power has actually created a distrust of any kind of knowledge. This particular "social psychology" makes collective action virtually impossible, a reality that furthers the interests of those already in power. For example, in the United States, the routine use of deliberately divisive political strategies and of the practice we have named "stonewalling" has left citizens almost completely unwilling to trust anybody. An important result has been that the kind of public participation that characterized citizens of the 1960s has been virtually nonexistent for twenty years.

But these relatively short-term political manipulations do not explain long-term attitudinal changes in the United States. For example, people's confidence in their physicians' dedication to the service ethic was already breaking down before industry launched its attack on professional power in the 1970s. In the previous decade, many politically active groups, from feminists to environmentalists, had already become increasingly critical of physicians. They claimed that many professional decisions were not based on scientific knowledge or the service ethic but on patriarchal values, economic considerations, and a desire to practice heroic rather than preventive medicine.

In fact, it was this failure of trust that prevented the traditional medical profession from being able to fulfill its historical functions for the capitalist state, to keep health care delivery in the private enterprise sector and to mask the social causes of disease by practicing curative rather than preventive medicine. Clearly, the historical rationalization of health care delivery was already on its way. What corporate strategists did was to change the direction the rationalization process was taking in American health care delivery, away from a socialized system and toward an increasingly capitalistic, competitive one. As part of that process, they ensured that providers would be made "accountable," not to their patients, who might have preferred the service ethic with all its faults, but to corporate consumers and the capitalist state, who increasingly subordinated the knowledge of physicians to that of "cost accountants."

Historically, the rationalization process has included an increasing reliance on complex technology, but the term "technology" refers to very different kinds of things. It may mean sophisticated, precision equipment that extends the capacities of professional workers, such as laser surgery and kidney dialysis machines that perform lifesaving treatment procedures. Or it may refer to the surveillance and control techniques that bureaucratic administrators use to control workers, clients, and publics.

The "technology" of the new class of experts that has emerged in American health care delivery is of the latter type. It consists of techniques for collecting and analyzing statistical data and for constructing administrative mechanisms to manipulate providers, to shape the treatment decisions they make. The new experts neither set goals nor deliver services to clients. Since they do not concern themselves with these functions, with the "details" of everyday implementation, they embody few value conflicts; in any case, they have no occupational means for acting on any values they might have. Thus they have no way of reproducing such values as components of professional knowledge, which, as a result, becomes increasingly mechanistic and content free. Their location in the bureaucratic hierarchy allows them to create certain kinds of knowledge but not others. Thus the real power belongs to whoever controls the organization, not to the expert. Increasingly, the new experts themselves are subjected to bureaucratic surveillance and control; expert knowledge operates under a far more centralized authority system in the capitalist or government agencies characteristic of modern societies than it did in premodern ones.

American medical practice has been increasingly grounded on a new knowledge base, on "scientific-legal" principles. This was a radical concept in the 1970s, although it is commonplace today. These principles are being established by experts who are more apt to have academic degrees in business administration than to have medical training. The importance of training should not be overemphasized, however, since education is not what determines or creates knowledge in this analysis. Rather, knowledge emerges out of the actual work that the expert does. Even if they are physicians, experts function differently when they work as administrators than when they work as health care practitioners.[15] Administrators in modern health care systems, like those in other businesses, collect and create data describing how the physicians who must work in their organizations practice medicine. Then, these data legitimate the administrators' right to exercise surveillance and control over the physicians. Few of these administrators actually set the goals, however; instead they implement the goals that serve the interests of their own employers, the corporation or the capitalist state.

Even in ancient times the most important kind of power, the ability to set goals, was not necessarily in the hands of those who actually created and possessed the knowledge, the experts. But it becomes even less likely to be in their hands as the rationalization process continues. Although experts do create social goods and privileges for themselves, they actually lose real occupational power in modern bureaucratic societies. As the "iron cage" of the bureaucratic network tightens, the ability of experts to create either knowledge or power can take place only in organizational settings. To the extent that this is true, experts are free only to create the knowledge that serves the interests of the organization. Thus knowledge creates power for organizations, not for individuals, despite our contemporary ideological emphasis on individualism.

Clearly knowledge alone is not a sufficient basis for power. It requires a social structural apparatus to carry it. And it is not necessarily experts and their knowledge that create the organization; it is far more likely to be the organization that creates the experts, as an inherent feature of the process of legitimating itself.

Surveillance and the
Modern Capitalist State

Foucault incorporates Weber's rationalization thesis in his analysis of "disciplinary society." However, he focuses far more on the power aspects of the process than on the rational basis of the expert knowledge that legitimates it. For Foucault, the most important feature of modern capitalism is not technical superiority but totalitarian control.

Although that control is legitimated by expert authority, increasingly it is embodied in the discipline and bureaucratic surveillance activities that are both the means and the outcome of exercising power. Essentially, a modern ruler has two logical strategies for ensuring compliance among subject populations: either he can punish rule breakers for their violations, or he can attempt to eliminate opportunities for disobedience. As Dandeker points out, both methods require support from an administrative surveillance system.

In addition to controlling individual behavior through punishment or deterrence, surveillance also allows those who exercise it to shape social developments. It yields important information, which the ruler can use both to construct "knowledgeable courses of action" and to impose those actions on their subjects, even those who "are autonomous from supervisory control."[16]

Dandeker spells out the different goals these surveillance activities can achieve. They not only allow the ruler to exercise supervisory discipline and to "will the future"; they also facilitate the development of many different plans and techniques that can be used to exercise control in a variety of institutional settings.[17] In its earliest stages, the settings are formal organizational structures. Increasingly, surveillance is extended to informal settings as well. Finally, it becomes "a constitutive feature of modern capitalism, penetrating thoroughly the whole social structure."[18]

Foucault analyzes data from the sixteenth and seventeenth centuries to describe how these innovations in surveillance came about. It was during this period that authorities discovered how effective the human body could be as the "object and target of power."[19] As a result, the scale of control that could be exercised was greatly extended. No longer was it necessary to attempt to control entire populations; rather, it was individuals who were increasingly controlled, not through persuasion, which is notoriously unreliable, but through "a discipline of the body." Military organization provided the earliest example of this kind of discipline; later, the techniques of the military were used in other organizational arenas. Increasingly time, space, and bodily movements all came to be supervised and controlled together. At the same time, physical spaces were beginning to be partitioned in ways that classified civilian populations into "ranks and grades," organizing them into "systematic networks of lateral and vertical relations." As a result, power arrangements were internalized and made invisible. Thus, " 'visible coercion' was supplanted by detailed disciplinary practices and the sustained observation and monitoring of conduct." [20]

It was through such processes that, eventually, surveillance became "panoptic"; that is, it became both total and invisible, organized so that individuals are "totally seen without ever being seen." [21] Thus panopticism ensures that surveillance and power will be exercised automatically. Foucault thought the best example of panopticism could be seen in prisons. Modern factories and office layouts provide other familiar examples. Such organizations include not only moving assembly lines that shape and control the workers' movements but work spaces with partial walls and no doors that control workers' behavior by making their actions both visible and audible. As a result, in the contemporary United States floor-to-ceiling walls and an office with a door have become even more important status symbols than a window to the outside world.

Developments in the far-flung American health care system during the last twenty years also provide excellent examples of panoptic surveillance, of the process through which the exercise of power is diffused, disguised, and institutionalized. The early, obvious regulatory forms such as the National Health Planning and Resources Development Act of 1974 have been eliminated and replaced by panoptic processes, such as the government-mandated and funded diagnosis-related group billing and accounting system, which achieves the same goals as did the formal regulatory agency. In the process, surveillance has become embedded in many different kinds of mechanisms that work automatically throughout the health care delivery system. Thus surveillance has been extended to cover ever-increasing categories of people, including the experts who actually carry it out.

Foucault explains the historical emergence of the panopticism that characterizes modern societies through two historical developments. First, a new, rational, calculating bourgeois class overthrew traditional, charismatic, monarchical power. A new basis for ensuring compliance from subjects had to be part of that process. Second, urban populations grew to be very large, and size caused administrative tasks to become much more complex. The new panoptic techniques, which were both effective and substantively neutral, could exercise control over large masses of people. Furthermore, they could be used by very different kinds of political regimes or other institutions. Throughout the sixteenth and seventeenth centuries, rulers continued to make "technical and epistemological discoveries relating to the effective exercise of power." This is a never-ending process. When I first began to study industry's initiatives to transform health care delivery, I was fascinated to see reflected in the writings of corporate strategists a growing awareness of the new uses to which their expanding data could be put.[22]

These new surveillance and control techniques were extremely popular with the new rulers both because they were technically superior and because they reflected and perpetuated class advantages.[23] The historical emergence of prisons provides a good foundation for Foucault's argument that class considerations were important. In eighteenth-century Europe, crimes that were common, even popular, among the general populace were serious challenges to the class power of the emerging bourgeoisie. The looting and rioting in Los Angeles in 1992 provide a contemporary example of how political outrage among historically oppressed groups can motivate and, in the eyes of some citizens, legitimate crimes against both private property and the state.

During the eighteenth century, the idea developed for the first time that criminal behavior only occurs among the lower class. Thus Foucault argues that the real function of the modern prison system is to stabilize bourgeois class power by separating criminals from political opponents. Dandeker explains, quoting Foucault:

> With the assistance of other institutions of social control, a swarming mass of a population practicing occasional illegality, which is always likely to spread and to become a formidable *political* force of class struggle, is replaced by a "relatively small and enclosed group of individuals on whom a constant surveillance may be kept." [24]

However, once surveillance has been created and legitimated in the prison system, it can be expanded and exercised over the population at large.

> Meanwhile, the control and surveillance of manageable delinquency provides an opportunity for the policing and surveillance of the general population, through the search for dangerous groups or challenges to the existing order. The prison then, is the focus for the administrative production of a divided and more easily manipulated working class.[25]

This "division" of publics is itself an interesting by-product of surveillance processes and is a key factor in controlling subject populations. In the case described in the last quotation, imprisonment works to formally divide the working class into the free and the incarcerated; in this first stage, direct surveillance can be exercised over the incarcerated. Then, data collected as part of administering the prison can function to exercise social control even over unincarcerated populations, to divide some groups from the larger population, keeping them "imprisoned" in their social "places." For example, demographic data showing that blacks are disproportionately represented among prison populations constructs public perception that many blacks are dangerous. This can be used to stigmatize and control even the unincarcerated. In the United States, such data have legitimated fear of black males in ways that have almost certainly limited their social opportunities.

These events may have provided both models and techniques for any "Machiavellian" politicians who seek to exercise control over their constituencies, teaching them the most efficient ways to do so. One common strategy among contemporary American politicians is to make use of demographic and social data collected by experts to identify constituencies on the basis of class, gender, race, ethnicity, and age. These demographic data enable politicians not only to meet their constituents' needs but to tell them whatever they most want to hear, to play on their hopes and fears. In that case, inherent in this process is the pitting of group against group, following the ancient advice to divide and conquer; eventually, the heart of this strategy may come to be divisiveness itself. It facilitates the implementation of policies that could not survive a democratic vote.

This strategy can be extremely effective in modern societies, with their diverse populations and sophisticated surveillance and data collection techniques. But it may also contain the seeds of its own destruction. It may be that in the United States, for example, divisive strategies have become so commonplace that they are no longer effective. If so, they may be discontinued, for a time, and replaced with a new strategy of candor and openness. Foucault described this kind of action and reaction as part of the process through which groups trade places, historically, acting out the ongoing strategy that he defines as "power."

When divisive competition between groups can be created, however, it can be exploited to the rulers' advantage in many different ways. It can be used, for example, to legitimate a lack of action by a government that justifies either its ineffectuality or its unpopular policies by blaming the conflict itself. Thus in the early stages of the 1992 presidential campaign, President Bush said he could not construct a national health care policy because there was no consensus about what should be done. Since the polls indicated that a majority of Americans wanted some kind of universal health insurance system in 1992, just as they did twenty years ago, it appears that the lack of consensus is less among competing interest groups than between the general public on the one hand and, on the other, a conservative government, allied with corporate America, and insurance companies, the three most powerful interest groups in the country.

The fragmentation and manipulation of populations has also been an effective strategy in transforming health care delivery. At the most obvious level, legislative, economic, and administrative mechanisms that separate people into competing groups, such as young and old, affluent and poor, straight and gay, insured and uninsured, and privately and publicly funded, do result in competition among groups, thus minimizing the possibility that they might engage in any coordinated political action.

Increasing the distrust patients feel for providers is another effective divisive technique that has been used both by government and by industry. Distrust is increasingly institutionalized not only through accountability mechanisms but through such tactics as publishing unanalyzed mortality data from hospitals, ostensibly in an attempt to make health care providers more "competitive." Thus, although the institutionalization of distrust occurs through historical developments to some extent, as part of the rationalization process, it can also be used deliberately, as a manipulative control strategy that is increasingly conscious. This strategy has been used in the United States during the last twenty years, as industry and government have developed a more sophisticated understanding of the consequences of their own exercise of power.

Of course, at the broader societal level, the institutionalization of distrust that accompanies the emergence of the ideology of accountability makes any kind of real community, any social life based on shared values, almost impossible. Interestingly, in the United States, the conservative forces that are most associated with the manipulation of accountability to achieve political goals are those who complain most loudly that a lack of values is the root of all America's troubles, including the Los Angeles riots. In particular, they focus on a "failure" of American family values, blaming it for all of our national problems, from drug abuse to economic crises. This charge appears to be an attempt to change the subject, to divert attention away from criticisms of the way government and business interests have handled the American economy since 1980. Thus, although it is the historical rationalization process, including the exercise of surveillance and power both at home and abroad, that undermines both shared values and the ability to trust in the first place, authorities can conveniently blame the lack of values and public cynicism for all the nation's problems.

In analyzing government bureaucratic control systems, Dandeker differentiates between those that "rule over" and those that "rule on behalf of subject populations."[26] Like Weber, he believes that socialist societies tend to rule over their subjects, while capitalist ones are more likely to rule on their subjects' behalf. Because the government bureaucracy is not accountable to subject populations in socialist systems, there is no enforcement from below. Thus the bureaucracy becomes extremely powerful and, ironically, more personal and competitive. In such cases, it loses what is supposed to be the defining characteristic of modern bureaucratic organization, its ability to function rationally, like a dependable machine. Dandeker elaborates, "In bureaucratic dictatorships then, personalism and competition pervade the system; factionalism operates in such a way that the ruler cannot relate to the bureaucracy as it if were a dependable administrative machine."[27] In capitalist states, too, personalism and competition can come to pervade "rational" systems, which then function to further the power of dominant capitalist groups, not to achieve the best possible goal in the most efficient way. For example, because administrative mechanisms are designed to achieve the political and economic goals of so many different interest groups, American health care delivery is probably organized more inefficiently than any other health care system in the industrialized world.

Perhaps the belief that capitalist states rule for the people may be more realistic in Europe than in the United States. In the United States, we may conceptualize and organize "social programs" differently from Western Europeans. It is certainly true that, despite our wealth, we are the only industrial-ized country in the world except South Africa without either a publicly funded family leave policy or a universal health care program. In general, the United States does not guarantee rights to our citizens in the form of universal social services to the same extent or in the same way as do other capitalist, Western industrialized nations. Rather, we claim to guarantee universal, indi-vidual rights; in theory, we attempt to provide equal access to the economic resources that allow citizens to buy social services for themselves.

In reality, of course, we guarantee neither social rights nor individual access, as our economic indicators make clear. The point is that, in contrast to Western European capitalist counties, in the United States governmental poli-cies and goals reflect an ideology that leans further toward individualism than toward social justice. Interestingly, those Americans who are most likely to receive the limited welfare-type benefits that do exist are blacks, Native Americans, and women. At different historical moments, and to different degrees, these groups actually have been excluded, both by custom and by law, from participation in the supposedly universalistic rational-legal govern-mental and economic sectors of our society.

But historical rationalization was occurring in Western Europe even before the United States was a nation. In Europe, political authority systems moved from personal administration by monarchs to the bureaucratic administration of modern states. Dandeker uses historical data to describe a range of political authority systems in a model of "ideal types."[28]

This model underlines the historical reality that in both traditional and modern systems, rulers differ in terms of the extent to which they rule over or on behalf of their subjects. Thus in traditional personal administrative systems rulers tend either toward petty tyranny or toward facilitating democratic pro-cesses. In modern bureaucratic administrative systems, they tend either to-ward bureaucratic dictatorships or toward utilization of rational-legal procedures. Standing between these two types is a system of patronage.

It should be noted that the rational-legal procedures that characterize lib-eral bureaucratic states may or may not work to serve the interests of the public. Dandeker argues that they do so in Western Europe, as opposed to the bureaucratic dictatorships that are more characteristic in communist countries. But even in the Western world, rational-legal procedures are no more inher-ently universalistic than they are democratic. Rather, they are categorical and systematic. As an inherent feature of their creation, rational-legal organiza-tions put people into different economic, legal, and scientific categories, then treat the groups very differently. Thus rational organization contains an inher-ent contradiction. Although it is supposed to be based on universalistic princi-ples, it increasingly institutionalizes and encourages its own kind of particularism.

Systems in transitional stages, poised between personal and bureau-cratic organization, tend to base authority on "patronage," a term Dande-ker uses to describe both a "social relation" and a "social system."[29] In the ancient European-style patronage systems, patron-client relationships were

Systems of Rule

	Personal Administration		Bureaucratic Adminstration
Autocratic Interests	Petty tyranny		Bureaucratic dictatorship
		Patronage	
Liberal Interests	Direct democracy		Rational-legal

Source: Dandeker, p. 45

characterized by power inequality, reciprocity, intimate association, and a certain level of voluntarism by all parties. Thus patron-client relationships contrasted in important ways with the lord-serf, the master-slave, and even with the employer-employee relationships characteristic both of traditional and modern societies. Although social relationships in all these systems are unequal, higher levels of personal interaction, reciprocity, and autonomy on the part of both patron and client seem to characterize patronage systems. Dandeker explains:

> Patrons are dependent on maintaining a high level of client support in a situation where clients are neither owned nor totally controlled and where client choice is a significant resource and dynamic in the system. . . . At the same time, patrons as "entrepreneurs" can compete for clients and are neither members of a hereditary status group nor disciplined bureaucratic subordinates of a ruler.[30]

Of course, these patronage relationships are unequal; one role is considerably more autonomous than the other. Thus even in patronage systems surveillance and control are exercised, although they are legitimated and carried out differently. In patronage systems,

> surveillance activities are performed by specialist intermediaries who are autonomous from both the controls of the subject population and of the discipline normally imposed by modern bureaucratic systems. [The patronage system is] characterized by personalism as well as the anonymous or impersonal features more prevalent in modern societies.[31]

This description of patronage is also a fairly accurate description of the way physicians worked in the United States until the 1970s. They exercised control and surveillance over patients, collecting data to construct records to which they alone had access. That right was guaranteed by the government itself, which did not "impose discipline" over them once they were licensed. Although their exclusive access to data was guaranteed under laws that were said to protect patient confidentiality, they protected physician autonomy just as effectively. Thus the confidentiality of patient records was one of the first service ethic principles that industry attacked as a self-serving hypocrisy when it undertook the task of transforming American health care delivery in the early 1970s.[32]

Today, although individual patients are usually unable to get access to their own records, the information in them is reported in great detail to utilization review agencies, both public and private, that work for government and for corporate employers. Although providers continue to resist government and corporate demands for data, they do so because they have been forced to absorb the substantial cost of collecting it, not because they claim to be protecting patient confidentiality. Regardless of such squabbles, the reality is that, through collection of this data, both providers and patients are placed under surveillance by utilization review agencies. Most recently, these agencies themselves have been subjected to the ever-widening circle of bureaucratic surveillance and control. This expansion is at the heart of the explosion of paperwork and bureaucratic administration that have caused our health care costs to continue to rise even as we have decreased access to services and reduced utilization rates.

Given the historical force of the rationalization process, why do systems linger in transitional, patronage authority arrangements before they finally move on and modernize? This question is tantamount to asking why history does not move in a neatly progressive fashion. Dandeker explains it on the grounds that the new system is too modern for the old personal ties of kinship to be effective while, at the same time, weak market forces or an ineffectual central government make it impossible for modern, rational integrative and distributional effects to operate.[33]

This explanation makes sense in terms of developments in American health care delivery. Here, until the 1970s, government expenditures stimulated growth in the health care system in ways that were antithetical to "free-market" mechanisms. At the same time, our national antipathy toward socialism made government regulatory controls over health care delivery almost unthinkable until the social movements of the 1960s occurred.

In the United States another factor was important as well. A traditional, patronage-type health care system has been favored historically by corporate America as well as the capitalist state, both because it was a free-market alternative to socialized health care and because it focused on curative medicine rather than on the social causes of disease. However, it became clear during the 1970s that traditional authority arrangements in medicine could no longer be counted upon to achieve those goals. The old "disciplinary" knowledge did not adequately support or reflect the power interests of dominant groups. At that point, industry began to rethink its attitude toward government regulation, if not toward socialized medicine.

On a more practical level, in the United States, lingering in the "patronage" phase of doctor-patient relationships may have been more compatible with public expectations and beliefs. Here not all citizens believe that government bureaucratic organizations are obligated to work "for" the public in the sense that they should create social services; in fact, many believe government bureaucracies are among the worst ways to solve problems. Thus, depending on which political administration is in power and on the condition of our economy, services may proliferate or perish. But, more important, since the rationalization of health care delivery has been accomplished here not through national insurance programs but through a combination of capitalist and governmental bureaucratic strategies, questions about whether rational organization functions in the public interest are particularly salient.

Of course trying to decide whether corporate activism has benefited "the public" depends in part on how one defines "the public." Should industry be defined as "the public," as well as the major "consumer," where health care issues are concerned? It is true that both industry and its supporters have claimed that the business sector is the appropriate spokesperson for the larger public. Still, the question remains, has the rationalization of American medicine during the last twenty years worked for or against the American public? Government and corporate strategists, and the new experts they employ, have justified their activism in part on the grounds that the traditional disciplines make knowledge inaccessible to others, mystifying it to serve their own interests. The new experts claim that they can create knowledge without mystifying it, that eliminating the old disciplinary elite will democratize knowledge, making it rule for rather than over the public. Although this construction of knowledge would continue to create power, they claim the new power would work for the people rather than against them.

These claims have not described developments in the United States health care delivery system. Here, it was industry, not experts attempting to democratize knowledge, that first began to demand the collection of new kinds of data. From the beginning, data collection was a tactic for taking control of health care delivery out of the hands of physicians. It certainly was not designed to empower the public but, rather, to disempower those who favored a national health insurance system or even those who supported our existing but limited public health programs. It has done just that. Thus establishing the reality of new kinds of knowledge continues to serve its power-creating functions. It also continues to serve as the means of transforming social institutions today, just as it has in the past.

In short, an analysis of industry's role in health care delivery makes it clear that it is much more accurately described as a very powerful interest group whose goals conflict and compete with those of ordinary citizens than as a public benefactor. The strategies industry implemented have combined in many ways to exclude from the decision-making process not only the expert physician in the traditional patron's role but consumer groups and patients, those who actually *use* health care services.

Government has increasingly supported corporate initiatives to transform health care delivery. Not only were government legislation and regulation used as tools in industry's transformation strategies; they continue to support it today in ways that have been described throughout this book. This use of state power is not new. Historically, the state has functioned as "a rational structure of domination and surveillance" holding a monopoly over the use of physical force, both military and civil, which is the basis of its ability to enforce compliance with its legislative directives, should that become necessary.[34] Usually it does not, of course, at least not in the United States. But force is not the only weapon the state commands. Far more important is its legal and administrative structure, which includes both formal, legal norms and rational, bureaucratic organization.

Administrative procedures are much more efficient ways to gain compliance than engaging in head-on battles that risk provoking opposition from subject populations. "Monetary reward, convenience and habit" are also useful. In government organizations, this array of control mechanisms "parallels the power of the modern business enterprise to separate its workers from the means of production."[35]

In administering its "welfare functions," the state also has the capacity to separate citizens from services to which they are legally entitled. For example, the DRG billing system reduced the health care services that were guaranteed to Medicare and Medicaid patients, making it unnecessary to amend the Social Security law itself. Such a move would have been very unpopular among one group that has remained politically active since the 1960s, senior citizens. It is supposed to be the case that, in rational-legal systems, changing "legal norms," or laws, can be done only through formal mechanisms that have been defined by legislation and other constitutional procedures, as Dandeker says. However, those mechanisms do not have to include the risky political process of going through Congress and taking a vote. Changes enforced through bureaucratic procedures work far more smoothly; the fact that politicians use this tactic deliberately is a matter of public record. For example, some hospitals have sued both peer review organizations and the Department of Health and Human Services for using "transmittals," bureaucratic procedures, to pass unauthorized costs on to hospitals. Thus, the rational-legal administrative mechanisms that the state commands can be used either to achieve illegal goals or to relieve the state of its own legal obligations, as well as to circumvent political opposition. They may also be used to enforce the moral attitudes of rulers, in opposition both to legal guarantees and to public opinion. The abortion gag rule imposed by the Reagan administration and continued by President Bush provides a well-known example.

Of course, even though these tactics raise public controversy, subject populations are far more likely to believe that bureaucratic controls are legitimate than to accept physical force. The point is that public tolerance is not based on substantive values such as a belief in freedom and democracy or a woman's right to choose, but on the "formal logical character of legal norms." Thus, it is mechanistic processes, not values, that legitimate modern authority systems. Values are not simply irrelevant in rational systems; they actually make the systems "unstable" because groups with competing values can challenge them at any time.[36] Challenges occurred in the United States during the 1960s, for example, when coalitions of politically active citizen groups caused Congress to pass the social legislation that corporate leaders opposed.

Many of the rational, surveillance mechanisms put into place since that time function very effectively to discourage the recurrence of such unwelcome public participation in the future.

But rationalization has not actually removed value considerations from decision making; it only makes them invisible. For example, corporate health care activists have said that their major goal was to cut health care costs. The cost-reduction mechanisms they used have been characterized by the functional rationality of statistical, systematic, "value-free" processes such as the diagnosis-related group billing system. When a value does intrude, such as the one most Americans place on human life, for example, corporate planners immediately subject it to a rational cost-benefit analysis. Then the value they place on rational analysis and action overrides the value we place on human life. Even such incidents as the Ford Pinto scandal have not caused us to question the cost-benefit process itself, a key component of rational decision making. We treat it as just one case of accidental malfunctioning, not as an indication that the approach itself is irrational, in the sense that it reflects both personal interests and very self-serving values.

Recognizing this ideological bias makes the seeming irrationality of corporate strategies and tactics comprehensible. In health care delivery, corporate strategies have led to the implementation of mechanisms that require extremely expensive bureaucratic surveillance; they have increased administrative costs enormously. Rather than recognizing how much the surveillance and control mechanisms have contributed to health care costs, we continue to add them to our national health care bill. And corporate planners continue to argue that the remedy for the failure of their strategies is to implement more of them, to increase even further the competition that actually requires ever-increasing administrative controls and, inescapably, higher administrative costs. It seems that the major goal never has been to cut health care costs but to institutionalize the surveillance and control mechanisms themselves; *they*, at least, are "rational."

A classic criticism of formal organizations has been that bureaucracies transform their means into their goals. Developments in American health care delivery provide a first-rate contemporary example of that process. Today, to oppose control mechanisms that their proponents tell us will ensure accountability is equivalent to opposing the flag, apple pie, and God, to name a few of the things Americans continue to value. We gloss over the questions that can be addressed only with "substantive" rationality: What should be our goals? Who should be accountable to whom, and for what? Thus a giant leap of faith is hidden in corporate strategies, embedded in the assumption that the use of "rational" means will lead automatically to "desirable" ends—guided, no doubt, by the invisible hand of that most sacred human value, competition.

Historically, this kind of transformation of means into goals has not been achieved without a struggle. In fact, Foucault points out that the power created through discipline and surveillance is never fully achieved; rather, it is always in the process of becoming. Power is not a thing but a strategy, which is realized through "a network of relations and tactics." Those relations, including what is accepted as "knowledge," constantly change in response to resistance from subject populations; the network "is in a constant state of tension," so that creating power involves a constant struggle "reaching into the depths of the social structure."[37]

For those who understand this process, the social chaos that often accompanies these power struggles does not inspire either fear or embarrassment but, rather, a bold shamelessness. When conflicts occur, the appropriate tactic is simply to continue reasserting one's version of reality, even when it is obviously incorrect, a manipulative ploy, or a lie. In modern industrial societies everyone is intimately familiar with this tactic; we have named it "stonewalling." The very use of the term simultaneously identifies, normalizes, and legitimates the practice. Since all versions of reality are attempts to exercise and create power, the content of any particular one is irrelevant; only the process matters. Whatever perspective wins will turn out to have been "true," for all practical purposes.

Notes

Introduction: Managed Competition—
The Private Regulation of American Health Care

1. Quoted in Michael L. Millenson, "Managed Care: Will It Push Providers against the Wall?" *Hospitals,* October 5, 1986, p. 66.

2. Robin Marantz Henig, " 'Managed Competition' Stirs a Lot of Hope, Much Sharp Debate," *AARP Bulletin,* March 1993, pp. 1, 16.

3. For a longer list of the corporations involved and a description of the initiatives provided by the corporate participants themselves, see the nine volumes of the Springer Series on Industry and Health Care listed in the bibliography and the position paper presented by the Washington Business Group on Health to Joseph Califano, secretary of health, education and welfare, in April 1977. The paper is titled *A Private Sector Perspective on the Problems of Health Care Costs.*

4. Eliot Freidson, *Professional Dominance: The Social Structure of Medical Care* (New York: Atherton Press, 1970).

5. Betty Leyerle, *Moving and Shaking American Medicine: The Structure of a Socioeconomic Transformation* (Westport, CT: Greenwood Press, 1984).

6. Alain Enthoven has been an advocate of competition in health care delivery for many years. He has been active in policy making in a wide range of areas. He held "several positions with the defense department during the 1960s. . . . A Rhodes scholar, Mr. Enthoven . . . [is] . . . professor of public and private management and professor of health research in the graduate school of business, Stanford University. . . . [He] has been an economist for more than 30 years. He has been a consultant to Kaiser Foundation Health Plans . . . since 1973." "Enthoven's Proposal: Managed-Care Solution to Plight of Uninsured," *Modern Healthcare* (interview), August 4, 1989, pp. 28, 30, quotation on p. 28.

7. Charles D. Reuter, "Compensation Management in Practice: The Real Cost of Managing Managed Health Care," *Compensation and Benefits Review,* May/June 1990, pp. 14–17, quotation on p. 14.

8. Jay Greene, "Consultants Survey: Firms Confront Intense Competition and Ethical Questions," *Modern Healthcare,* September 23, 1988, pp. 26, 44, 54, 60, 66, quotation on p. 44.

9. David M. Horn, "Successful Managed Care: A Team Effort," *Broker World,* October 1991, pp. 96–102, 160–61.

10. M.R. Traska, "Managed Care: Hospitals to Feel the Heat as Plans Handle Change," *Hospitals,* January 20, 1987, p. 44.

11. Dave Lenckus, "Texas Sues to Force Coverage of Treatment," *Business Insurance,* vol. 27, ISS: 42, October 11, 1993, pp. 3, 17.

12. Quoted in "Health Industry Status Debated by Experts," *Modern Healthcare,* November 8, 1985, p. 64.

13. William E. Sheeline, "Taking On Public Enemy No. 1," *Fortune,* July 1, 1991, pp. 58–59, citation on p. 58.

14. Springer Series, 2:3.

Chapter 1: The Twenty-Year-Old-Crisis

1. Quoted in Matthew Schwartz, "Health Costs Hit $3,217 per Worker," *National Underwriter,* February 11, 1991, p. 3.

2. "Senator Kennedy, Backed by Fourteen Senators, Introduces Bill Creating Comprehensive National Health Insurance Program," *New York Times,* August 28, 1970, p. A1.

3. "Nixon Administration Unveils Proposal for Multibillion-dollar Health Care Package," *New York Times,* February 19, 1971, p. A1.

4. "The Revolution of Social Regulation," in *Congressional Quarterly's Federal Regulatory Directory* (Washington, DC: Congressional Quarterly, 1990), pp. 5–9.

5. *Private Sector Perspective on the Problems of Health Care Costs* makes clear the corporate goal of keeping health care "private." It describes the program of "employer/consumers" as "the advance guard of a new private sector health system which shows every bit as much promise of success as any contemplated government programs" (pt. 1, p. 14).

6. John Ehrenreich and Barbara Ehrenreich, *The American Health Care Empire* (New York: Vintage Books, 1971); Sylvia Law, *Blue Cross: What Went Wrong?* (New Haven and London: Yale University Press, 1976); Rosemary Stevens, *American Medicine and the Public Interest* (New Haven and London: Yale University Press, 1971); and many others.

7. Allen Dobson et al., "PSROs: Their Current Status and Their Impact to Date," *Inquiry,* June 1978, pp. 113–28.

8. "Warning: Doctors Can Damage Your Wealth," *Economist,* October 20, 1990, pp. 17–18.

9. *MacNeil/Lehrer Newshour,* WNET, September 24, 1992, transcript 4462, p. 5.

10. Goran Dahlgren and Finn Diderichsen, "Strategies for Equity in Health: Report from Sweden," in *Perspectives in Medical Sociology,* ed. Phil Brown (Belmont, CA: Wadsworth, 1989), pp. 346–414.

11. Harry Braverman, *Labor and Monopoly Capital: The Degradation of Work in the Twentieth Century* (New York: Monthly Review Press, 1974).

12. Robert Alford, *Health Care Politics: Ideological and Interest Group Barriers to Reform* (Chicago: University of Chicago Press, 1975).

13. For a comparison of these competing ideologies, see Leyerle, *Moving and Shaking American Medicine,* pp. 12–14.

14. Howard Waitzkin, *The Second Sickness: Contradictions of Capitalist Health Care* (New York: Free Press, 1983).

15. Ehrenreich and Ehrenreich, *American Health Care Empire.*

16. Howard Waitzkin, "Social Structures of Medical Oppression: A Marxist View," in *Perspectives in Medical Sociology,* pp. 166–78.

17. Uwe Reinhardt, "Health Care: Business Forgets It Created the Mess. Now It Must Own Up to Its Mistakes and Help Find a Cure," *Business Month,* October 1991, pp. 56–57.

18. "Cost Containment Initiatives by topic," in *Private Sector Perspective on the Problems of Health Care Costs,* pt. 1, p. 12.

19. Robert Reich, presidential candidate Bill Clinton's economic adviser, said on the *Nightly Business Report,* Public Broadcasting System, October 5, 1992, that the percentage of the work force that was unionized had been 17 percent during the "last recession" and was now 12 percent.

20. Sidney S. Lee, "Health Policy, A Social Contract: A Comparison of the United States and Canada," in *Perspectives in Medical Sociology,* pp. 388–95.

21. Ibid., p. 390.

22. Leyerle, *Moving and Shaking American Medicine,* p. 47.

23. *MacNeil/Lehrer Newshour,* WNET, November 9, 1992.

24. Rosemary Stevens, "The Politics of Prevention," in *Perspectives in Medical Sociology,* pp. 368–88.

25. Karen Wright, "Going by the Numbers," *New York Times Magazine,* December 15, 1991, pp. 58–79.

26. "Study Shows that Women with Highest Exposure to Pesticide DDT Had Four Times Breast Cancer Risk," *New York Times,* April 22, 1993, p. A16.

27. Edward R. Stasica, "A New Look at Wellness Plans," *Business Insurance,* February 18, 1991, pp. 53–54; William K. Coors, "Wellness Comes of Age," *Chief Executive,* November/December 1990, pp. 36–39.

28. Michael C. Fiore et al., "Methods Used to Quit Smoking in the United States: Do Cessation Programs Help?" *Journal of the American Medical Association,* May 23–30, 1990, pp. 2760–65.

29. Steven Sullivan, "Cost Containment: Is It Working?" *Life Association News,* February 15, 1991, pp. 28–34, quotation on p. 34.

30. Quoted in ibid., p. 34.

31. "CDC: Americans Kick the Smoking Habit in Record Numbers," *Durango Herald,* May 22, 1992, p. A3.

32. "Cigarettes, Other Habits, Can Cost Someone a Job," *Washington Post,* April 30, 1991, p. 1; Rhonda L. Rundle, "U-Haul Puts High Price on Vices of Its Workers," *Wall Street Journal,* February 14, 1990, p. B1.

33. " 'The Market' Is Beginning to Protest," editorial, *Modern Healthcare,* May 1979, p. 5.

34. "Managed Care: Will It Push Providers against the Wall?" p. 66.

35. Quoted in Schwartz, "Health Costs Hit $3,217 per Worker," pp. 3, 23, quotation on p. 3.

36. Ibid.

37. Sheeline, "Taking On Public Enemy No. 1," p. 58.

38. William Grieder, *Who Will tell the People: The Betrayal of American Democracy* (New York: Simon and Schuster, 1992).

39. Quoted in "Enthoven's Proposal: Managed-Care Solution to Plight of Uninsured," p. 28.

Chapter 2: The Basic Components of Private Regulation

1. David M. Kinzer, "Our Realistic Options in Health Regulation," *Frontiers of Health Services Management* 5, no. 1 (Fall 1988): 3–40, quotation on p. 4.

2. Stevens, *American Medicine and the Public Interest,* pp. 505–10; Alford, *Health Care Politics,* p. 228.

3. Friedson, *Professional Dominance.*

4. Leyerle, *Moving and Shaking American Medicine,* pp. 47–49.

5. Ibid.

6. Martin Tolchin and Susan J. Tolchin, "The Rush to Deregulate," *New York Times Magazine,* August 21, 1983, sec. 6, pp. 34–74. This section draws heavily from Tolchin and Tolchin.

7. "Revolution of Social Regulation," pp. 5–9.

8. Tolchin and Tolchin, "Rush to Deregulate," p. 34.

9. Ibid., p. 36.

10. Ibid., p. 34.

11. Mark Dowie, "Pinto Madness," in *Crisis in American Institutions,* ed. Jerome H. Skolnick and Elliot Currie (New York: Harper Collins, 1991), pp. 20–35.

12. Quoted in Tolchin and Tolchin, "Rush to Deregulate," p. 34.

13. Ibid., p. 72.

14. Ibid., p. 36.

15. Quoted in ibid.

16. Ibid., p. 38.

17. Ibid., p. 34.

18. Ibid.

19. Mark F. Baldwin, "Hospitals Face Tougher PRO Reviews," *Modern Healthcare,* January 31, 1986, p. 16.

20. "Reagan Administration Seeks Elimination of Hill-Burton Rule," *Modern Healthcare,* November 22, 1985, p. 47.

21. Leyerle, *Moving and Shaking American Medicine,* pp. 49–50, 125.

22. "Medicare Will Cover More Surgery Center Procedures," *Modern Healthcare,* December 6, 1986, p. 29.

23. Kinzer, "Our Realistic Options in Health Regulation," p. 4.

24. Tolchin and Tolchin, "Rush to Deregulate," p. 74.

25. Quoted in "State Regulation Bounces Back on Quality Issue," *Hospitals,* June 20, 1988, p. 66.

26. Quoted in ibid.

27. Cathy Tokarski, "Physician-Office Pilot Project Takes Off into the Unknown," *Modern Healthcare,* December 29, 1989, p. 23.

28. Tolchin and Tolchin, "Rush to Deregulate," p. 74.

29. Quoted in *Private Sector Perspective on the Problems of Health Care Costs,* pt. 1, p. 5.

30. For more detail, see Leyerle, *Moving and Shaking American Medicine,* chap. 5.

31. "Cost Containment Initiatives by Topic," pt. 1, pp. 5–6, emphasis mine.

32. Ibid., pp. 6–7.

33. Ibid., p. 6.

34. Ibid., p. 5.

35. "Humana Inc. Denied CON for Illinois Teaching Hospital," *Modern Healthcare,* January 31, 1986, p. 11.

36. U.S. Bureau of the Census, *Statistical Abstract of the United States: 1990* (110th ed.) and *1991* (11th ed.) (Washington, DC: Government Printing Office, 1990, 1991).

37. David Burda, "FTC Testimony Will Hit CON Laws in Mich., Pa.," *Modern Healthcare,* March 4, 1988, p. 6.

38. For a description of panopticism, see pp. 181 below.

39. Quoted in Mark F. Baldwin, "Legislation Would Allow Planning Program Options," *Modern Healthcare,* February 14, 1986, p. 40.

40. Kinzer, "Our Realistic Options in Health Regulation," p. 12. Kinzer lists six kinds of "controls" that regulation has created over health care service delivery: fiscal, utilization, facilities and services, health manpower, quality, and demand.

41. Ibid., p. 14, emphasis mine.

42. Donald F. Beck and Jack Dempsey, "Health Care Costs: The Other Point of View," *Health Care Supervisor* 9, no. 2 (1990): 1–11, quotation on p. 8.

43. Quoted in *Private Sector Perspective on the Problems of Health Care Costs,* pt. 1, p. 9.

44. For a detailed account of HMO development and the HMO strategy, see Leyerle, *Moving and Shaking American Medicine,* chap. 4.

45. "Health Maintenance Strategy," *Medical Care,* May/June 1971, p. 32.

46. U.S. Bureau of the Census, *Statistical Abstract of the United States: 1990* and *1991.*

47. Kinzer, "Our Realistic Options in Health Regulation," p. 4.

48. Quoted in Schwartz, "Health Costs Hit $3,217 per Worker," pp. 3, 23, quotation on p. 3.

49. Eric J. Savitz, "No Miracle Cure: HMOs Are Not the Rx for Spiraling Health-Care Costs," *Barron's,* August 5, 1991, pp. 8–9, 21–23, quotation on p. 22.

50. Sue Shellenbarger, "Health: As HMO Premiums Soar, Employers Sour on the Plans and Check Out Alternatives," *Wall Street Journal,* February 27, 1990, p. B1; "GM Ends Agreement with 6 HMO Groups, Citing Growing Costs," *Wall Street Journal,* November 14, 1990, p. 1.

51. Kathryn M. Langwell, "Structure and Performance of Health Maintenance Organizations: A Review," *Health Care Financing Review,* no. 1 (Fall 1990): 71–79.

52. Judith Names, "HCFA Report Rips Practices at Humana HMOs in Florida," *Modern Healthcare,* December 24 to 31, 1990, p. 2.

53. Paul J. Kenkel, "HMOs' Savings Have 'Spillover Effect'—Studies," *Modern Healthcare,* January 13, 1992, pp. 30–31.

54. Quoted in ibid., p. 30.

55. Ibid., p. 30.

56. Quoted in ibid., p. 31.

57. Quoted in ibid.

58. Danielle A. Dolene and Charles J. Dougherty, "DRGs: The Counterrevolution in Financing Health Care," *Hastings Center Report* 15, no. 3 (June 1985): 309.

59. Kinzer, "Our Realistic Options in Health Regulation," pp. 22–23.

60. Dolene and Dougherty, "DRGs: The Counterrevolution in Financing Health Care," pp. 19–29.

61. Leyerle, *Moving and Shaking American Medicine,* pp. 48–49.

62. An example is provided by Evan M. Melhado et al., *Money, Power and Health Care* (Ann Arbor, MI: Health Administration Press, 1988).

63. Lee, "Health Policy, A Social Contract: A Comparison of the United States and Canada," p. 394.

64. U.S. Bureau of the Census, *Statistical Abstract of the United States: 1991.*

65. Kinzer, "Our Realistic Options in Health Regulations," pp. 28–29.

66. Reported in ibid., p. 29.

67. Leyerle, *Moving and Shaking American Medicine,* chap. 3.

68. Quoted in Conference Board, *Industry Roles in Health Care* (New York: Conference Board, 1974), p. 59.

Chapter 3: The Evolution of Private Regulation

1. Quoted in Cathy Tokarski, "Health Care's Hidden Costs: Debating the Benefits of Regulation," *Modern Healthcare,* August 20, 1990, pp. 35–36.

2. Sidney Marchasin, "One Hospital Tells the Cost of Regulation," *Wall Street Journal,* June 26, 1990, p. A18, from the abstract.

3. Ivan Illich, *Medical Nemesis: The Expropriation of Health* (New York: Pantheon, 1976).

4. Boston Women's Health Book Collective, *Our Bodies, Ourselves* (New York: Simon and Schuster, 1971).

5. Daniel Berman, *Death on the Job: Occupational Health and Safety Struggles in the United States* (New York: Monthly Review Press, 1978), pp. 137–38.

6. Braverman, *Labor and Monopoly Capital.*

7. *American Medical News,* September 28, 1979, p. 2.

8. "Requiem for PSRO (1972–1982)," *New York State Journal of Medicine,* April 1983, p. 687.

9. Morgan Ford, "PROs Maintain Surveillance over Medicare Admissions," *Private Practice,* March 1985, pp. 26–27.

10. Cathy Tokarski, "Hospitals Coping with the Shadow of Peer Review," *Modern Healthcare,* December 29, 1989, pp. 22–34, quotation on p. 30.

11. Springer Series, 6:34.

12. Baldwin, "Hospitals Face Tougher PRO Reviews," p. 16, emphasis mine.

13. Tokarski, "Hospitals Coping with the Shadow of Peer Review," p. 35, emphasis mine.

14. "OMB Is Studying Proposal for Peer Review of HMOs," *Modern Healthcare,* September 13, 1985, p. 35, emphasis mine.

15. Mark F. Baldwin, "Task Force Backs PRO Reviews," *Modern Healthcare,* November 22, 1985, p. 27.

16. Quoted in ibid.

17. "OMB Is Studying Proposal for Peer Review of HMOs," p. 35.

18. "Firm Will Monitor Quality of Care Offered in Military," *Modern Healthcare,* February 28, 1986, p. 24.

19. Tokarski, "Physician-Office Pilot Project Takes Off into the Unknown," p. 23.

20. Ibid.

21. Ibid.

22. "Acting HCFA Head Defends Agency's PRO Stance," *Modern Healthcare,* January 3, 1986, p. 31.

23. Mark F. Baldwin, "Administration Seeks Replacement for Nation's Peer Review Organizations," *Modern Healthcare,* July 4, 1986, p. 44.

24. Mark F. Baldwin, "Memorandum: PROs Fall Short in Monitoring Quality," *Modern Healthcare,* January 3, 1986, p. 47, emphasis mine.

25. Mark F. Baldwin and Kathy A. Fackelmann, "Blizzard of Paperwork: New Rules Are Burying PROs and Hospitals," *Modern Healthcare,* January 3, 1986, pp. 46–54, quotation on p. 44.

26. Dolene and Dougherty, "DRGs: The Counterrevolution in Financing Health Care," pp. 19–29, quotation on p. 21.

27. Quoted in Terese Hudson, "Risk Managers See New Regulations as Boon and Burden," *Hospitals,* September 20, 1990, p. 44.

28. Ibid., p. 46, emphasis mine.

29. Ibid., p. 48.

30. Susan B. Keener, "Getting the Most Out of Utilization Review Programs," *Journal of Compensation and Benefits,* July/August 1991, pp. 5–9, from the abstract in the Pro-Quest database.

31. Ibid.

32. "Providers Vent Frustration with Utilization Review," *Modern Healthcare,* June 17, 1988, p. 24.

33. Glenn Ruffenach, "Denials of Medical Claims Provoke a Legal Backlash," *Wall Street Journal,* February 13, 1990, Ap. 1.

34. Joel Brinkley, "Disciplinary Cases Raise for Doctors," *New York Times,* January 20, 1986, sec. I, p. 1. Sanctioning power is considerable. According to the *Times,* "the review panels have the power to bar a doctor or hospital permanently or temporarily from treating beneficiaries of Medicare." The "Federal Government can also impose a fine." In either case, once sanctions actually are imposed, "the Federal Government takes out an advertisement in the hometown newspaper of the doctor or hospital announcing that the sanction is in effect." The government also "notifies the doctor's state medical board, which can choose to take action against his license."

35. Kinzer, "Our Realistic Options in Health Regulation," p. 7.

36. Leyerle, *Moving and Shaking American Medicine,* pp. 40–42.

37. "Public Gains Access to Peer Review Data," *Hospitals,* January 20, 1987, p. 57.

38. Cynthia Wallace, "California PRO Releases Death Rates by Diagnosis," *Modern Healthcare,* May 8, 1987, p. 11.

39. Tokarski, "Health Care's Hidden Costs: Debating the Benefits of Regulation," pp. 35–38, quotation on pp. 35–36.

40. Quoted in ibid., p. 36.

41. Quoted in ibid.

42. David Burda, "Liability Seen as Side Effect of Substandard-Care Rules," *Modern Healthcare,* March 3, 1989, p. 46.

43. Quoted in ibid.

44. Quoted in ibid., emphasis mine.

45. Cathy Tokarski, "PROs Can't Shake Chill of Physician-Sanction Provision," *Modern Healthcare,* December 29, 1989, p. 33.

46. Ibid.

47. Ibid.

48. Quoted in ibid.

49. "What the Mediplans' New Anti-Fraud Drive Will Look Like," *Medical Economics,* April 18, 1983, p. 47.

50. Tokarski, "Hospitals Coping with the Shadow of Peer Review," p. 34.

51. "Pennsylvania PRO May Lose Contract," *Modern Healthcare,* April 26, 1985, p. 16.

52. Ibid.

53. Quoted in Tokarski, "Hospitals Coping with the Shadow of Peer Review," p. 34.

54. Quoted in ibid.

55. Ibid., p. 24.

56. Baldwin, "Hospitals Face Tougher PRO Reviews," p. 16.

57. Tokarski, "Hospitals Coping with the Shadow of Peer Review," p. 34.

58. " 'Super PRO' to Scrutinize Performance of 54 Agencies," *Modern Healthcare,* July 5, 1985, p. 43.

59. Quoted in Baldwin and Fackelmann, "Blizzard of Paperwork," p. 50.

60. "GAO Cites Higher Level of Inappropriate Care," *Modern Healthcare,* January 22, 1990, p. 17, emphasis mine.

61. Tokarski, "Hospitals Coping with the Shadow of Peer Review," p. 23.

62. "Peer Review Requirements Cost $4.3 Million—HCFA," *Modern Healthcare,* February 28, 1986, p. 23.

63. Marchasin, "One Hospital Tells the Cost of Regulation," p. A18, from the abstract.

64. "Court Ruling Will Clarify Hospital, PRO Relationship, " *Hospitals,* November 20, 1986, pp. 28–30, quotation on p. 30.

65. Ibid.

66. Ibid.

67. Ibid.

68. Quoted in Mark F. Baldwin, "Jurisdiction in Hospital Case Disputed," *Modern Healthcare,* April 25, 1986, p. 30.

69. Quoted in ibid., p. 30.

70. "Court Ruling Will Clarify Hospital, PRO Relationship," p. 30.

71. Tokarski, "Hospitals Coping with the Shadow of Peer Review," p. 24.

72. "PRO Rulings Could Cost NY Hospitals $80 Million," *Modern Healthcare,* April 26, 1985, p. 16.

73. Ibid.

74. C. McKeen Cowles, "Review Effect on Cost Reports: Impact Smaller Than Anticipated," *Health Care Financing Review* 12, no. 3 (Spring 1991): 21–25, quotation on p. 25.

75. Cathy Tokarski, "Utilization Review Not Turning Up Much Long-Term Gain," *Modern Healthcare,* December 29, 1989, p. 30.

76. Cathy Tokarski, "Patient Outcomes Emphasized in Recommended PRO Reforms: Report Also Backs Doubling of Budget," *Modern Healthcare,* February 26, 1990, p. 18.

77. Stratford Jones and Nancy Coe Bailey, "Utilization Review: The Art of Polite Interference," *Business and Health,* February 2, 1991, pp. 30–43, from the Abstract in the Pro-Quest database.

78. Stephen M. Shortell and Edward F.Y. Hughes, "The Effects of Regulation, Competition and Ownership on Mortality Rates Among Hospital Inpatients," *New England Journal of Medicine,* April 28, 1988.

79. Howard Larkin, "Planning and Policy," *Hospitals,* June 20, 1988, p. 66.

80. Ibid.

81. Allen Dobson, et al., "PSROs: Their Current Status and Their Impact to Date," *Inquiry,* June 1978, pp. 113–28.

82. Richard J. Arnould, David H. Finifter, and Leonard G. Schifrin, "The Health Care Cost 'Problem,'" *Quarterly Review of Economics and Business* 30, no. 4 (Winter 1990): 5–11; William P. Hojnacki, "Health Care Costs in the U.S.: The Role of Special Interests," *Journal of Social, Political and Economic Studies,* 15 (Fall 1990) 337–55; Jonathan E. Levin, "What Health Care Cost Crisis?" *Benefits Quarterly* 7, no. 3 (Third Quarter 1991): 75–79; Mark Pauly, "Financing Health Care," *Quarterly Review of Economics and Business* 30, no. 4 (Winter 1990): 63–80.

83. Beck and Dempsey, "Health Care Costs: The Other Point of View," p. 8.

Chapter 4: Managing Health Care Costs

1. Quoted in Paul Kenkel, "Managed Care Will Dominate within a Decade—Experts," *Modern Healthcare,* July 29, 1988, p. 31.

2. "Corporate Managed Healthcare Will Dominate 1990s, Experts Say," *Modern Healthcare,* October 11, 1985, p. 84.

3. Paul Kenkel, "Managed Care in Transition: Weak Plans Merge, Strong Companies Evolve to Contain Costs," *Modern Healthcare,* June 2, 1989, pp. 18–19, 22, 26, 29, 32, 34, 35, 36, quotation on p. 19.

4. Quoted in Sheeline, "Taking on Public Enemy No. 1," p. 59.

5. Kenkel, "Managed Care Will Dominate within a Decade—Experts," p. 31.

6. National Governors' Association Staff, "Strategies for Controlling Health Care Costs," *Journal of State Government* 64, no. 3 (July/September 1991): 88–90, quotation on p. 89.

7. Greene, "Consultants Survey: Firms Confront Intense Competition and Ethical Questions," p. 44.

8. The largest prepaid plan in the country, the Kaiser Foundation Health Plan, had been federally subsidized almost thirty years earlier. The Kaiser Foundation was created after World War II to buy clinics and equipment paid for by govern-

ment as "war surplus"; the foundation paid 1 percent of cost. Leyerle, *Moving and Shaking American Medicine,* p. 85.

9. Ibid., p. 104.

10. Quoted in Kenkel, "Managed Care Will Dominate within a Decade—Experts," p. 31.

11. Traska, "Managed Care: Hospitals to Feel the Heat as Plans Handle Change," p. 44.

12. National Governors' Association Staff, "Strategies for Controlling Health Care Costs," p. 9.

13. Quoted in Traska, "Managed Care: Hospitals to Feel the Heat as Plans Handle Change," p. 44.

14. Paul Kenkel, "Insurance Regulators Recommend Requiring Larger Cash Reserves for Open-ended Plans," *Modern Healthcare,* February 11, 1991, p. 52.

15. Ibid.

16. Paul J. Kenkel and John Morrissey, "Managing to Survive: It May Come Down to Size or Entrenchment," *Modern Healthcare,* August 4, 1989, pp. 21–22, reported on p. 21.

17. Sheeline, "Taking On Public Enemy No. 1," p. 58.

18. Quoted in Kenkel, "Managed Care Will Dominate within a Decade—Experts," p. 31.

19. Joyce Frieden, "Employers Negotiate with Hospital Group," *Business and Health,* September 1992, pp. 57–59.

20. Quoted in Julie Johnsson, "Managed Care in the 1990s: Providers' New Role," *Trustee,* September 1992, pp. 14–15, 17, quotation on p. 14.

21. Quoted in ibid.

22. Ibid., p. 15.

23. Quoted in ibid.

24. Ibid., p. 14.

25. Quoted in ibid., p. 15.

26. Paul Kenkel, "Managed-Care Growth Continued in 1987 Despite Companies' Poor Operating Results," *Modern Healthcare,* June 3, 1988, pp. 20–22, 28–29, 32–34, 38, quotation on p. 20.

27. Ibid.

28. Quoted in Paul Kenkel, "Providers Wring Some Risk Out of HMO Pacts," *Modern Healthcare,* October 21, 1988, p. 47, emphasis mine.

29. Ibid.

30. Kenkel, "Managed Care in Transition: Weak Plans Merge, Strong Companies Evolve to Contain Costs," *Modern Healthcare,* p. 22.

31. Alison Kittrell, "Employers Turn to Managed Care, Utilization Review to Control Costs," *Modern Healthcare,* May 9, 1986, pp. 96–98.

32. Quoted in ibid., p. 96.

33. Ibid.

34. "Two Reports Identify High-Cost Patients," *New York Times,* May 6, 1980, p. C1.

35. Quoted in Kenkel, "Managed Care Will Dominate within a Decade—Experts," p. 31.

36. Christine Woolsey, "Managed Care Not a Cost Panacea: Expert," *Business Insurance,* June 11, 1990, p. 14.

37. Charles D. Reuter, "Compensation Management in Practice: The Real Cost of Managing Managed Healthcare," *Compensation and Benefits Review,* May/June, 1990, pp. 14–17.

38. Quoted in Woolsey, "Managed Care Not a Cost Panacea: Expert," p. 14.

39. Quoted in ibid.

40. Leyerle, *Moving and Shaking American Medicine.*

41. Quoted in Neil McLaughlin, ."Right Theory, Wrong Timing: Paul Ellwood, M.D., Says Ascent of 'Supermeds' Has Been Delayed," *Modern Healthcare,* February 13, 1987, p. 16.

42. Ibid.

43. "Ellwood Explains His Theory, Terminology on Outcomes Method of Managing Care," interview, *Modern Healthcare,* January 13, 1989, pp. 30–31, quotation on p. 31.

44. Paul Kenkel, "Managed Care Will Dominate within a Decade—Experts," p. 31.

45. Reuter, "Compensation Management in Practice: The Real Cost of Managing Managed Healthcare," p. 14.

46. Ibid.

47. Leyerle, *Moving and Shaking American Medicine,* p. 20.

48. Bill Atkinson, "Competition Turns the Promising Alliances of Physicians, HMOs into Courtroom Battles," *Modern Healthcare,* June 19, 1987, p. 68.

49. Phillip E. Hoggard, "Hospitals, Physicians Need to Be Allies, Not Adversaries," *Modern Healthcare,* October 22, 1990, p. 50.

50. Quoted in M.R. Traska, "HMOs: A Shake-up (and Shakeout) on the Horizon?" *Hospitals,* February 5, 1986, pp. 41–43, 45, quotation on p. 41.

51. Quoted in ibid., p. 42.

52. Quoted in ibid., p. 41.

53. Ibid.

54. Kenkel and Morrissey, "Managing to Survive: It May Come Down to Size or Entrenchment," p. 21.

55. Ibid.

56. Paul J. Kenkel and John Morrissey, "Merger Shows Way to Grow and Still Keep Independence," *Modern Healthcare,* August 4, 1989, p. 24.

57. Springer Series, 5: 28–29. See also Leyerle, *Moving and Shaking American Medicine,* pp. 96–97.

58. Mark Baldwin, "Boston HMOs Ready for Stepped-up Battle," *Modern Healthcare* May 10, 1985, pp. 42–46.

59. Ibid.

60. Quoted in ibid., p. 42.

61. Ibid.

62. Ibid.

63. Quoted in Traska, "HMOs: A Shake-up (and Shakeout) on the Horizon?" p. 42.

64. Sullivan, "Cost Containment: Is It Working?" p. 31.

65. Ibid.

66. Ibid.

67. Ibid.

68. "HMOs Weigh Medicare Gamble," *Modern Healthcare,* January 13, 1989, p. 47.

69. Quoted in Lynn Wagner, "HMO Payment Increase Proposal Meets Resistance," *Modern Healthcare,* May 14, 1990, p. 21.

70. Ibid.

71. Quoted in Paul J. Kenkel, "1991 Medicare Rates Have HMOs Eyeing Changes," *Modern Healthcare,* October 22, 1990, pp. 55–57, quotation on p. 55.

72. Paul J. Kenkel, "Medicaid HMOs Struggle for Viability: Federal Plan Aims to Ease the Burden," *Modern Healthcare,* April 23, 1990, p. 32.

73. "Health Care: Rational Choice," *Economist,* March 23, 1991, p. 32.

74. Henry Aaron and William B. Schwartz, "Rationing Health Care," *Across the Board,* July/August 1990, pp. 34–39.

75. Glenn Ruffenach, "Medicine: Debate Grows over Rationing Medical Care," *Wall Street Journal,* March 27, 1990, p. B1.

76. William B. Schwartz and Henry J. Aaron, "Must We Ration Health Care?" *Best's Review,* January 1991, pp. 39–41, quotation on p. 41.

77. Lynn Wagner, "Physician Payment Panel Debates Threat of Rationing Due to Spending Controls," *Modern Healthcare,* January 29, 1990, p. 27.

78. Quoted in ibid.

79. Quoted in ibid.

80. David Burda, "AHA's Latest Reform Plan Could Lead to Rationing," *Modern Healthcare,* December 3, 1990, p. 2.

81. Spender Rich, "Organ Transplants: Rationing by Wallet?" *Wall Street Journal,* September 1, 1991, p. 1.

82. Daniel M. Fox and Howard M. Leichter, "Rationing Care in Oregon: The New Accountability," *Health Affairs* 10, no. 2 (Summer 1991), pp. 7–27, quotation from the abstract in the Pro-Quest database.

83. Sullivan, "Cost Containment: Is It Working?" p. 32.

84. Reported in ibid.

85. Ibid., pp. 32–33.

86. Paul J. Kenkel, "New Stop-Loss Product May Protect Managed Care Providers from Catastrophic Care Losses," *Modern Healthcare,* November 20, 1987, p. 60.

87. Steven M. Schecter, "Health Care: The Expert Provider Organization," *Chief Executive,* November/December 1991, pp. 45–48, quotation on p. 45.

88. Ibid.

89. Ibid., p. 46.

90. Ibid. pp. 46–67.

91. Ibid., p. 48, emphasis mine.

Chapter 5: Managing "Quality" through Outcomes Research

1. Dan F. Duda, "Marketing Must Turn Savage," *Modern Healthcare,* April 16, 1990, p. 50.

2. Judith Graham, "Quality Gets a Closer Look," *Modern Healthcare,* February 27, 1987, pp. 20–31, quotation on pp. 20–21.

3. Quoted in ibid., p. 27.

4. Lynn Wagner, "Outcomes Research Gets Budgetary Blessing," *Modern Healthcare,* December 15, 1989, p. 45.

5. Quoted in ibid.

6. Quoted in David Burda, "Providers Look to Industry for Quality Models," *Modern Healthcare,* July 15, 1988, pp. 24–26, quotation on p. 25.

7. Ibid.

8. Ibid.

9. Robert B. Kimmel, "Agreeing on a Definition of Quality Care May Be Healthcare's Biggest Challenge," *Modern Healthcare,* March 24, 1989, p. 37.

10. David Burda, "Hospitals Not Sure How to Ensure Quality," *Modern Healthcare,* July 15, 1988, p. 26.

11. David Burda, "The Two (Quality) Faces of HCHP," *Modern Healthcare,* March 18, 1991, pp. 28–31.

12. David Mechanic, *The Growth of Bureaucratic Medicine* (New York: John Wiley and Sons, 1976).

13. Pamela Taulbee, "Measuring Hospitals by Outcomes," *Business and Health,* November 1990, pp. 20–26, quotation on p. 24.

14. Quoted in ibid.

15. Ibid., p. 26.

16. Ibid.

17. Arthur C. Strum, Jr., "Signs Show Major Changes Are in Store for Hospitals' Bypass Surgery Business," *Modern Healthcare,* September 23, 1988, p. 80.

18. *Marketplace,* National Public Radio, April 29, 1993.

19. Strum, "Signs Show Major Changes Are in Store for Hospitals' Bypass Surgery Business," p. 80.

20. Quoted in Taulbee, "Measuring Hospitals by Outcomes," pp. 24–25.

21. Strum, "Signs Show Major Changes Are in Store for Hospitals' Bypass Surgery Business," p. 80.

22. Ibid., emphasis mine.

23. Robert H. Brook, M.D., Sc.D., and Kathleen N. Lohr, Ph.D., letter to the editor, *Journal of the American Medical Association,* March 18, 1988, p. 1646: "The Collaborative Study of Coronary Artery Surgery showed that outcomes from coronary artery bypass surgery varied more than 20-fold across the academic hospitals in which the study was performed, even after controlling for numerous clinical factors." This letter is in response to another letter, questioning whether there really is a problem with the quality of care delivered under Medicare.

24. Strum, "Signs Show Major Changes Are in Store for Hospitals' Bypass Surgery Business," p. 80.

25. Ibid.

26. David Burda, "Prospects of Quality Measurement Project Excite the Participating Systems, Alliances," *Modern Healthcare,* January 6, 1989, pp. 40–45.

27. Quoted in ibid., p. 44.

28. "AHA's Public Criticism of JCAHO Surprising," editorial. Quoted in *Modern Healthcare,* October 27, 1989, p. 24.

29. "NY May Not Pay Hospitals for JCAHO's Inspections," *Modern Healthcare,* February 10, 1988, p. 9.

30. Quoted in David Burda, "JCAHO Plans to Identify Quality Offenders," *Modern Healthcare,* January 20, 1989, p. 3.

31. David Burda, "Hospitals Worried and Unhappy about Disclosure of JCAHO Data," *Modern Healthcare,* May 19, 1989, p. 60.

32. David Burda, "JCAHO Releases Survey on Hospital Compliance," *Modern Healthcare,* November 19, 1990, p. 2.

33. Quoted in Cathy Tokarski, "VA, Critics Differ on Meaning of JCAHO's Quality Scores," *Modern Healthcare,* July 2, 1990, p. 34.

34. David Burda, "HRET Chief Dons Many Hats as a Leader in Healthcare's Continuing Quality Quest," *Modern Healthcare,* December 3, 1990, p. 38.

35. Ibid.

36. Ibid.

37. Ibid.

38. Quoted in ibid.

39. Quoted in ibid.

40. Quoted in Burda, "Prospects of Quality Measurement Project Excite the Participating Systems, Alliances."

41. Jesse Green et al., "The Importance of Severity of Illness in Assessing Hospital Mortality," *Journal of the American Medical Association,* January 12, 1990, pp. 241–46.

42. Quoted in Burda, "Prospects of Quality Measurement Project Excite the Participating Systems, Alliances," p. 42.

43. Ibid.

44. Quoted in ibid., p. 44.

45. Quoted in ibid.

46. David Burda, "Total Quality Management Becomes Big Business," *Modern Healthcare,* January 28, 1991, pp. 25–29, reported on p. 26.

47. Ibid.

48. The project has been renamed. Originally, it was called the National Demonstration Project on Industrial Quality Control and Health Care Quality. Burda, "Two (Quality) Faces of HCHP," pp. 28–31.

49. Ibid.

50. Quoted in Graham, "Quality Gets a Closer Look," p. 27.

51. Ibid.

52. Ibid.

53. Ibid.

54. David Burda, "Providers Look to Industry for Quality Models," *Modern Healthcare,* July 15, 1988, pp. 24–26, reported on p. 24.

55. Ibid., p. 26.

56. Ibid.

57. Quoted in Graham, "Quality Gets a Closer Look," p. 22.

58. Quoted in ibid., p. 27.

59. Hugh Jones, "Quality in Health Care Can Be Demonstrated," *Business Forum* 15, no. 4 (Winter 1991): 18–20.

60. Green et al., "Importance of Severity of Illness in Assessing Hospital Mortality," pp. 241–46; Donald M. Berwick and David Wald, "Hospital Leaders' Opinions of the HCFA Mortality Data," *Journal of the American Medical Association,* January 12, 1990, pp. 247–49; Kim Carter, "Severity Plays Crucial Role," *Modern Healthcare,* February 27, 1987, p. 27.

61. Brook and Lohr, letter to the editor.

62. Kari E. Super, "Providers Tout Quality to Get Edge in Marketing," *Modern Healthcare*, February 27, 1987, p. 27.

63. Quoted in Julie Johnsson, "Managed Care in the 1990s: Providers' New Role," *Trustee*, September 1992, pp. 14–15, 17, quotation on p. 15.

64. Quoted in ibid.

65. Super, "Providers Tout Quality to Get Edge in Marketing," p. 27.

66. Quoted in Sara J. Harty, "Doctors Study Health Quality, Not Cost Control," *Business Insurance*, February 18, 1991, p. 80.

67. Ibid.

68. Peter Boland, "'Quality' Must Be Defined Before It Can Be Professed," *Modern Healthcare*, August 4, 1989, p. 37.

69. Taulbee, "Measuring Hospitals by Outcomes," p. 24.

70. Linda Perry, "Mich. Blues Plan Initiates Payment Bonuses, Penalties Tied to Standards of Quality," *Modern Healthcare*, October 6, 1989, p. 58.

71. *Private Sector Perspective on the Problems of Health Care Costs.*

72. Perry, "Mich. Blues Plan Initiates Payment Bonuses, Penalties Tied to Standards of Quality," p. 58.

73. Ibid.

74. Ibid.

75. Ibid.

76. Ibid.

77. Ibid.

78. Ibid.

79. Burda, "Total Quality Management Becomes Big Business," p. 25.

80. Quoted in ibid., p. 26.

81. Quoted in ibid., p. 27.

82. Quoted in ibid.

83. Quoted in ibid.

84. Quoted in ibid., p. 28.

85. Quoted in ibid.

86. Quoted in ibid., p. 27.

87. Wagner, "Outcomes Research Gets Budgetary Blessing," p. 45.

88. Ibid.

89. Ibid..

90. Burda, "Two (Quality) Faces of HCHP," pp. 28–31.

91. Ibid., pp. 28–29.

92. Quoted in "Quality Assurance Requires Comprehensive Plan—GAO," *Modern Healthcare*, May 7, 1990, p. 40.

93. Ibid., emphasis mine.

Chapter 6: Conclusions

1. Quoted in Patricia Neighmond, "Managed Competition Considered for Health-Care Reform," *Morning Edition*, National Public Radio, April 9, 1993, transcript, pp. 19–20.

2. Quoted in Linda A. Bergthold, *Purchasing Power in Health: Business, the State, and Health Care Politics* (New Brunswick, NJ: Rutgers University Press, 1990), p. 60.

3. Three such plans were described on *Morning Edition,* National Public Radio, August 18, 1993.

4. "Middle-Class Lacking Health Insurance up 1 Million, New Study Shows," *Public Citizen,* March/April 1993, p. 8.

5. Quoted in Melhado et al., *Money, Power and Health Care,* p. 80.

6. Quoted in Neighmond, "Managed Competition Considered for Health-Care Reform," pp. 19–20

7. Bradford Curie Snell, "American Ground Transport," in *Crisis in American Institutions,* pp. 327–41.

8. *Morning Edition,* National Public Radio, December 3, 1992.

Appendix. The Theoretical Frame: Surveillance, Power, and Knowledge

1. Roslyn W. Bologh, *Love or Greatness: Max Weber and Masculine Thinking—A Feminist Inquiry* (London: Unwin Hyman, 1990); Philip Morowski, *Against Mechanism: Protecting Economics from Science* (Totowa, NJ: Rowman and Littlefield, 1988); Leyerle, *Moving and Shaking American Medicine.*

2. Christopher Dandeker, *Surveillance, Power and Modernity: Bureaucracy and Discipline from 1700 to the Present Day* (New York: St. Martin's Press, 1990). This entire section is heavily indebted to Dandeker.

3. Ibid., pp. 5–6.

4. Ibid., pp. 163–64.

5. Michel Foucault, *Discipline and Punish: The Birth of the Prison* (New York: Penguin, 1979), p. 27, quoted in Dandeker, *Surveillance, Power and Modernity,* p. 23.

6. Dandeker, *Surveillance, Power and Modernity,* p. 22.

7. Henry Etzkowitz and Ronald Glassman, *The Renascence of Sociological Theory* (Itasca, IL: F.E. Peacock, 1991), p. 228.

8. Dandeker, *Surveillance, Power and Modernity,* p. 8.

9. Randall Collins and Michael Makowsky, *The Discovery of Society* (New York: Random House, 1989), p. 225.

10. Quoted in ibid.

11. Dandeker, *Surveillance, Power and Modernity,* p. 9.

12. Ibid., p. 23, emphasis in original.

13. Ibid., p. 24.

14. Jurgen Habermas, *Legitimation Crisis* (Boston: Beacon Press, 1973).

15. Betty Morrow (Leyerle), "Professionalism as the Accomplishment of Work Setting" (M.A. thesis, Brooklyn College, 1975).

16. Dandeker, *Surveillance, Power and Modernity,* p. 37.

17. Ibid., p. 8.

18. Ibid., p. 23.

19. Ibid., p. 24.

20. Ibid., pp. 24–25.

21. Ibid., p. 25.

22. Leyerle, *Moving and Shaking American Medicine,* pp. 39–40.

23. Dandeker, *Surveillance, Power and Modernity,* p. 26.
24. Ibid., p. 26, quoting Foucault, *Discipline and Punish,* p. 275.
25. Dandeker, *Surveillance, Power and Modernity,* p. 27.
26. Ibid., p. 43.
27. Ibid., p. 50.
28. Ibid., p. 45.
29. Ibid., p. 46.
30. Ibid., p. 47.
31. Ibid., p. 46.
32. Leyerle, *Moving and Shaking American Medicine,* p. 40.
33. Dandeker, *Surveillance, Power and Modernity,* pp. 47.
34. Ibid., p. 10.
35. Ibid., pp. 11–12.
36. Ibid., pp. 10–12.
37. Ibid., p. 23.

Bibliography

Books, Research Papers, and Position Statements

Aaron, Henry, and William B. Schwartz. "Rationing Health Care." *Across the Board,* July/August 1990, pp. 34–39.

Alford, Robert. *Health Care Politics: Ideological and Interest Group Barriers to Reform.* Chicago: University of Chicago Press, 1975.

Arnould, Richard J., David H. Finifter, and Leonard G. Schifrin. "The Health Care Cost 'Problem.'" *Quarterly Review of Economics and Business* 30, no. 4 (Winter 1990): 5–11.

Beck, Donald F., and Jack Dempsey. "Health Care Costs: The Other Point of View." *Health Care Supervisor* 9, no. 2 (1990): 1–11.

Bergthold, Linda A. *Purchasing Power in Health: Business, the State, and Health Care Politics.* New Brunswick, NJ: Rutgers University Press, 1990.

Berman, Daniel. *Death on the Job: Occupational Health and Safety Struggles in the United States.* New York: Monthly Review Press, 1978.

Bologh, Roslyn W. *Love or Greatness: Max Weber and Masculine Thinking—A Feminist Inquiry.* London: Unwin Hyman, 1990.

Boston Women's Health Collective. *Our Bodies, Ourselves.* New York: Simon and Schuster, 1971.

Braverman, Harry. *Labor and Monopoly Capital: The Degradation of Work in the Twentieth Century.* New York: Monthly Review Press, 1974.

Brown, Phil, ed. *Perspectives in Medical Sociology.* Belmont, CA: Wadsworth, 1989.

Collins, Randall, and Michael Makowsky. *The Discovery of Society.* New York: Random House, 1989.

Conference Board. *Industry Roles in Health Care.* New York: Conference Board, 1974.

Congressional Quarterly's Federal Regulatory Directory. Washington, DC: Congressional Quarterly, 1990.

Cowles, C. McKeen. "Review Effect on Cost Reports: Impact Smaller Than Anticipated." *Health Care Financing Review* 12, no. 3 (Spring 1991): 21–25.

Dandeker, Christopher. *Surveillance, Power and Modernity: Bureaucracy and Discipline from 1700 to the Present Day.* New York: St. Martin's Press, 1990.

Dolene, Danielle A., and Charles J. Dougherty. "DRGs: The Counterrevolution in Financing Health Care." *Hastings Center Report* 15, no. 3 (June 1985).

Ehrenreich, John, and Barbara Ehrenreich. *The American Health Care Empire.* New York: Vintage Books, 1971.

Etzkowitz, Henry, and Ronald Glassman. *The Renascence of Sociological Theory.* Itasca, IL: F.E. Peacock, 1991.

Fox, Daniel M., and Howard M. Leichter. "Rationing Care in Oregon: The New Accountability." *Health Affairs,* 10, no. 2 (Summer 1991): 7–27.

Foxman, B., et al. "The Effect of Cost Sharing on the Use of Antibiotics in Ambulatory Care: Results from a Population-Based Randomized Controlled Trial." *Journal of Chronic Diseases* 40 (1987): 429–37.

Freidson, Eliot. *Professional Dominance: The Social Structure of Medical Care.* New York: Atherton Press, 1970.

Green, Jesse, et al. "The Importance of Severity of Illness in Assessing Hospital Mortality." *Journal of the American Medical Association,* January 12, 1990, pp. 241–46.

Grieder, William. *Who Will Tell the People: The Betrayal of American Democracy.* New York: Simon and Schuster, 1992.

Habermas, Jurgen. *Legitimation Crisis.* Boston: Beacon Press, 1973.

Hojnacki, William P. "Health Care Costs in the U.S.: The Role of Special Interests." *Journal of Social, Political and Economic Studies* (Fall 1990): 337–55.

Illich, Ivan. *Medical Nemesis: The Expropriation of Health.* New York: Pantheon, 1976.

Jones, Hugh. "Quality in Health Care Can Be Demonstrated." *Business Forum,* Winter Special 1991, pp. 18–20.

Kinzer, David M. "Our Realistic Options In Health Regulation." *Frontiers of Health Services Management* 5, no. 1 (Fall 1988): 3–40.

Langwell, Kathryn M. "Structure and Performance of Health Maintenance Organizations: A Review." *Health Care Financing Review* 12, no. 1 (Fall 1990): 71–79.

Law, Sylvia. *Blue Cross: What Went Wrong?* New Haven and London: Yale University Press, 1976.

Levin, Jonathan E. "What Health Care Cost Crisis?" *Benefits Quarterly* (Third Quarter 1991): 75–79.

Leyerle, Betty. *Moving and Shaking American Medicine: The Structure of a Socioeconomic Transformation.* Westport, CT: Greenwood Press, 1984.

Mechanic, David. *The Growth of Bureaucratic Medicine.* New York: John Wiley and Sons, 1976.

Melhado, Evan M., et al. *Money, Power and Health Care.* Ann Arbor, MI: Health Administration Press, 1988.

Morowski, Philip. *Against Mechanism: Protecting Economics from Science.* Totowa, NJ: Rowman and Littlefield, 1988.

Morrow (Leyerle), Betty. "Professionalism as the Accomplishment of Work Setting." M.A. thesis, Brooklyn College, 1975.

National Governors' Association Staff. "Strategies for Controlling Health Care Costs." *Journal of State Government* 64 (July/September 1991).

Pauly, Mark. "Financing Health Care." *Quarterly Review of Economics and Business* 30, no. 4 (Winter 1990): 63–80.

A Private Sector Perspective on the Problems of Health Care Costs. Position paper presented to Joseph Califano, secretary of health, education and welfare, by the Washington Business Group on Health, April 1977.

"Requiem for PSRO (1972–1982)." *New York State Journal of Medicine,* April 1983, p. 687.

"The Revolution of Social Regulation." *Congressional Quarterly's Federal Regulatory Directory,* pp. 5–9. Washington, DC: Congressional Quarterly, 1990.

Skolnick, Jerome H., and Elliot Currie, eds. *Crisis in American Institutions.* New York: Harper Collins, 1991.

Springer Series on Industry and Health Care. Center for Industry and Health Care, Boston University Health Policy Institute. New York: Springer-Verlag.

Vol. 1, *Payer, Provider, Consumer,* ed. Diana Chapman Walsh and Richard H. Egdahl, 1977.

Vol. 2, *A Business Perspective on Industry and Health Care,* ed. Willis Goldbeck, 1978.

Vol. 3, *Background Papers on Industry's Changing Role in Health Care,* ed. Richard H. Egdahl, 1977.

Vol. 4, *Health Services and Health Hazards: The Employee's Need to Know,* ed. Richard H. Egdahl and Diana Chapman Walsh, 1978.

Vol. 5, *Industry and HMO's: A Natural Alliance,* ed. Richard H. Egdahl and Diana Chapman Walsh, 1978.

Vol. 6, *Containing Health Benefit Costs: The Self-Insurance Option,* ed. Richard H. Egdahl and Diana Chapman Walsh, 1979.

Vol. 7, *Industry's Voice in Health Policy,* Richard H. Egdahl and Diana Chapman Walsh, 1979.

Vol. 8, *Women, Work and Health: Challenges to Corporate Policy,* ed. Richard H. Egdahl and Diana Chapman Walsh, 1980.

Vol. 9, *Mental Wellness Programs for Employees,* ed. Richard H. Egdahl and Diana Chapman Walsh, 1980.

Stevens, Rosemary. *American Medicine and the Public Interest.* New Haven and London: Yale University Press, 1971.

Tolchin, Martin, and Susan J. Tolchin. "The Rush to Deregulate." *New York Times Magazine,* August 21, 1983, sec. 6, pp. 34–74.

U.S. Bureau of the Census. *Statistical Abstract of the United States: 1990* (110th ed.) and *1991* (111th ed.). Washington, DC: Government Printing Office, 1990, 1991.

Waitzkin, Howard. *The Second Sickness: Contradictions of Capitalist Health Care.* New York: Free Press, 1983.

Journals and Periodicals

AARP Bulletin
American Medical News
Barron's
Best's Review
Broker World

Business Forum
Business and Health
Business Insurance
Business Month
Chief Executive
Compensation and Benefits Review
Durango Herald
Economist
Fortune
Hospitals
Inquiry
Journal of the American Medical Association
Journal of Social, Political and Economic Studies
Journal of Compensation and Benefits
Journal of the National Cancer Institute
Life Association News
Medical Care
Modern Healthcare
National Underwriter
New York Times
New England Journal of Medicine
Private Practice
Public Citizen
Trustee
Wall Street Journal
Washington Post

Broadcast Reports

MacNeil/Lehrer Newshour, WNET
Marketplace, National Public Radio
Morning Edition, National Public Radio
Nightly Business Report, Public Broadcasting System

Index

About the Author

Betty Leyerle is Professor of Sociology and Human Services at Fort Lewis College, Durango, Colorado. She is the author of *Moving and Shaking American Medicine: The Structure of a Socioeconomic Transformation* (1984). Dr. Leyerle holds a Ph.D. in Sociology from the City University of New York.